Northern Ireland: Between War and Peace

The Political Future of Northern Ireland

PAUL BEW, HENRY PATTERSON
AND PAUL TEAGUE

Lawrence & Wishart
LONDON

Lawrence & Wishart Limited
99A Wallis Road
London E9 5LN

First published 1997

British Library Cataloguing in Publication Data.
A catalogue record for this book is available from the British Library.

ISBN 0-85315-771-5

Photoset in North Wales by
Derek Doyle & Associates, Mold, Clwyd.
Printed and bound in Great Britain by
Redwood Books, Trowbridge, Wiltshire.

CONTENTS

INTRODUCTION

This book is an attempt to outline the shape of a possible political settlement in Northern Ireland. It does so by means of an analysis which is partly historical and partly economic.

THE COMPLEXITY OF HISTORY

The four historical chapters (chapters one, two, three and eight) provide new material on the genesis of the crisis in the 1960s up to the opening of multi-party 'talks' on 10 June 1996; they contain new research on the apparent *rapprochement* that existed between the Belfast and Dublin regimes on the eve of the outbreak of 'the Troubles'; and on the attempts to reduce the intensity of the Nationalist-Unionist conflict, by means of a power-sharing executive in 1974, and the Anglo-Irish Agreement in 1985; in addition, we bring forward in our discussions new evidence, both of the 'talks process' of 1992, and of the peace process which ended with the bomb at Canary Wharf in early 1996.

The first two chapters are an attempt to provide an analysis of the history of Anglo-Irish relations from the period of the formation of two states in Ireland (1921-23) to the Anglo-Irish Agreement of 1985. Roy Foster has noted that 'views of history can be obscurantist as well as enlightening', and that,

> looking at Anglo-Irish relations over the last hundred years, it is striking how consistently 'history' is produced as an argument, or a witness, at junctures when discourse should – one might think – be concentrating upon affairs more immediately at hand.[1]

We would hope not to obscure the past nor to provide some pre-cooked historical recipe for present problems. Rather, our historical chapters hope to illustrate the complexity of the major forces in play in the triangular London-Dublin-Belfast set of relations, and the dangers of unilateral simplifications of either the Nationalist inevitabilist approach – of 'history is on our side' – or the Unionist

1

paranoid vision – of a British/Dublin conspiracy that has placed Northern Ireland on 'the window-ledge of the Union'.

Much of the Republican optimism that led to the IRA cease-fire of August 1994, and the associated Unionist fears of a 'sell-out', was based on radically over-simplified views of the nature of Britain's interest in Ireland. But Britain's interest has been a complex and layered one, as the chapters attempt to demonstrate. The partition settlement allowed the British ruling class, by and large and for most of the time, to turn its back on the 'Irish Question' and leave Britain's remaining territorial involvement in the hands of a Protestant power structure in Northern Ireland. However, Britain continued to have strategic interests in the island, which were catered for both by Northern Ireland, and the access to the Treaty ports provided in the settlement negotiated with the Republic in 1921. When these interests appeared to be threatened – as happened in the late 1930s and early stages of the Second World War – a clear propensity to look again at the settlement of 1921 and to re-open the question of a possible accommodation between Dublin and Belfast, in the broader 'imperial' interest, was manifest, to the chagrin of the Unionist elite.

These chapters also show that, apart from the calculations of what was demanded of relations with Belfast and Dublin by strategic interest, in the post 1945 period there were also political reverberations from the re-ordering of Anglo-Irish trading relations, as the Republic's government under Sean Lemass sought a reintegration into the UK economy system. In a European context, where the ideology of functional integration argued for the reductionist inevitability of economic integration leading to political unity, the destabilising effects of the Lemass project – in large part unintended – would soon be apparent.

Coincidentally, as Britain's imperial pretensions were undermined by decolonisation and its increasingly obvious demotion to second rank world power status under a US nuclear umbrella, the high political concerns of its political elite in relation to Ireland shifted from the strategic to the diplomatic: the concern was not to be embarrassed internationally, particularly in the US, by Britain's Northern Ireland involvement. It was in this context that a long-standing tendency became manifest, to post-evangelical guilt – about the negative and destructive aspects of the British state's long involvement in Ireland – a guilt to which key figures in the British political elite were prone. But it became manifest – as Freud argued was to be expected with repressed feelings – in a displaced form. It was the Ulster Unionists and their provincial rigidities who became the lightning conductor for those in the metropolis who felt disturbed and embarrassed by the British record in Ireland.

The process of convergence between the elites of Britain and the Irish Republic, which took place in the 1960s was, however, brutally disrupted by the onset of the 'Troubles', as the one element in the equation hitherto largely ignored by London and Dublin – Northern Ireland Catholics – became mobilised in an unprecedented fashion. This mobilisation destroyed the forms of elite convergence developing in the late 1950s and early 1960s, which had by-and-large assumed the continued existence of a Unionist dominated northern state.

Chapter two analyses the negotiation of the Anglo-Irish Agreement as a radical, if contradictory, policy departure from the approach that had been adopted at the onset of Direct Rule in 1972. This had sought to stabilise the north and salvage Anglo-Irish amity through a largely internal process of reform and power-sharing devolution. We argue that the Anglo Irish agreement, rather than representing a clear turn to disengagement on the part of Thatcher, as has recently been argued by Andrew Gamble, marks a return to the unfolding disposition of the 1950s and early 1960s – to minimise the international costs of what was seen as an unavoidable involvement, by strengthening and improving relations with Dublin.[2] In the last three decades, the decline of Unionist bargaining power, both economic and political, has meant that, whereas the elite convergence of the 1960s left the Unionist regime untouched, the process that has gone on since 1985 has involved radical institutional innovation in the governance structures in the north.

For the fetishised view of the Union, unfortunately still influential amongst the protestant political class in Northern Ireland, these changes are perceived as augurs of inevitable British extrication. This book argues instead that this view elides a crucial difference: between a state in the north based on the domination of one communal bloc, and one where the union with Britain would continue to exist but would be based on governance structures that reflect the conflicting national aspirations of its inhabitants. As Nationalist commentators as divergent as the Republican Anthony McIntyre and the SDLP deputy leader Seamus Mallon have noted, most Nationalists would settle for 'Sunningdale Mark 2', which would leave the north firmly within the

Union for the forseeable future. However, as chapter two shows, the shift in British policy was not without its contradictions and resultant ambiguities. This in itself has greatly hindered the process of political accommodation in Northern Ireland, by unintentionally contributing to Nationalist maximalism, and to the Unionist penchant for assuming that every political innovation propels them further down the slippery slope to a United Ireland.

Any political conflict has its economic context. Changes in policy, as can be seen, are affected by economic considerations, two obvious examples being the effects of trading relations between the UK and the Republic of Ireland, and relationships within the European Union. Equally, further economic cooperation between North and South (not just between London and Dublin) can be a source – though not to be overestimated – for some political progress. Other areas of the economy which connect to a political discussion of the future of Northern Ireland are the links beteen economic discrimination and sectarianism, and an estimation of the effects on the economy of the political crisis, or indeed of a political settlement. We now turn to the economy, as the second part of our examination of the situation on the ground in Northern Ireland.

THE ECONOMY

In Northern Ireland economics and politics are not separate spheres of social action, but are deeply enmeshed with each other. This interaction has several dimensions. First of all, the debate about the character and performance of the regional economy has got caught up in the political divisions between Nationalism and Unionism. Those of a Unionist persuasion argue that the economy is in a healthy state while Nationalists believe that it is a disaster area, propped up by subsidies from the British government. These sharply contrasting views are not easily reconciled and have led to much uncertainty about the functioning of the economy in the present, and its potential in the future. For example, during the ceasefires there was considerable debate about whether a permanent peace would bring an economic bonanza or whether it would leave economic performance untouched. Being ensnared in the political divide in such a way means that mixed, confusing, messages are being transmitted about the Northern Ireland economy.

The purpose of the first essay on the economy (chapter four) is to minister Proinsias de Rossa pointed out in a key Belfast speech in early 1996: 'A durable settlement is possible and necessary – and a settlement which is transitional to something else would not be durable'.[4]

Paul Bew
Henry Patterson
Paul Teague

NOTES

1. Roy Foster, 'Anglo-Irish Relations; and Northern Ireland: historical perspectives' in Dermot Keogh and Michael H. Haltzel (eds.) *Northern Ireland and the Politics of Reconciliation*, Cambridge, 1993, p13.
2. Andrew Gamble, 'The Crisis of Conservatism' in *New Left Review* 214, November/December 1995, p.15; 'Under both Thatcher and Major the Conservatives have pursued a strategy of disengaging Britain from Ireland ...' This is simply wrong as chapter two shows – it confuses a disposition on the part of one element in the political elite for state policy. It was long before the Downing Street Declaration that the Ulster Unionists had to realise that '... there was now no party at Westminster which was committed in principle and in all circumstances to the maintenance of the Union.' (p15)
3. Ronan Bennett, 'New Labour and Northern Ireland,' *New Left Review* 220, Nov/Dec 1996: 'Three years ago Tony Blair said he believed Ireland was "insoluble". He told me this on the only occasion we met.'
4. 'Why did the Peace Process Collapse?' *The Times*, 30.11.96.

PART I

BRITAIN AND IRELAND IN THE TWENTIETH CENTURY

1

BRITAIN'S IRISH INTEREST

In his Whitbread Speech of 9 November 1990, the recently appointed Secretary of State for Northern Ireland, Peter Brooke, portrayed the British government as both open-minded and disinterested on the question of the constitutional future of Ulster: 'The obstacle to the development of a new and more inclusive Irish identity if people want this for themselves is not to be found in Great Britain.' People in Britain 'would not bar the way' if the people of Northern Ireland decided to seek such a new identity.

One sentence would come under intense scrutiny: 'The British government has no selfish strategic or economic interest in Northern Ireland: our role is to help, enable and encourage.'[1] Brooke had recently sanctioned the reactivation of the secret line of communication which had existed between republicans and the British government for over 20 years. As part of this process an advance copy of the Whitbread Speech had been forwarded to Sinn Fein.[2] The declaration of Britain's lack of strategic or economic interest would be repeated in the Downing Street Declaration of December 1993 and was clearly an important factor in the IRA's decision to declare a 'complete cessation' of military operations on 31 August 1994. It lay behind the widespread feeling in the Unionist community that a 'secret deal' had been done by Britain and the IRA. Yet both Republican hopes and Unionist fears would seem to have been misplaced: it has become inceasingly clear that no deals were done.

Nevertheless, the Brooke speech had served to convince John Hume, the leader of Northern Ireland's predominant nationalist party, the Social Democratic and Labour Party (SDLP), that the Anglo-Irish Agreement of 1985 had indeed been a watershed in Anglo-Irish relations, indicating that the British state had shifted decisively from a pro-union to a neutral position. Hume and his colleagues had tried to convince Gerry Adams and his Sinn Fein colleagues of just this point in months of controversial dialogue in 1988. Although these talks had ended in fundamental disagreement, core Republican leaders would be encouraged by the Brooke speech to test the neutrality claim through a cease-fire. However, as this chapter and the next will attempt to demonstrate, the debate on neutrality is based on an historically impoverished view of Britain's relationship to the two Irish states since partition. The policies adopted in particular periods were often the result of a process riven by major internal debates, reflecting differing strategic approaches and departmental interests. Notions of some long-term interest in partition obscure the way that the shifting balance of forces between Unionism and Nationalism in Ireland has affected the calculation of British interest. Thus, even after the Government of Ireland Act, which established the northern state, Lloyd George asked Sir James Craig, Northern Ireland's Prime Minister, to enter a united Ireland on the basis of Sinn Fein accepting a settlement based on dominion status. The British objective at this time – November 1921 – was a settlement which would consolidate power in the hands of Sinn Fein 'moderates' and marginalise the 'extremists'. Such a settlement, it was thought, would best suit Britain's strategic concerns and Ulster Unionists were pressurised to make a grand sacrifice for the broader imperial interest. Notions that Unionist distrust of British intentions is a relatively recent phenomenon – based on developments like the abolition of the Stormont parliament in 1972 and the Anglo-Irish Agreement – are radically misconceived. While the outbreak of the Irish Civil War (1922-1923) and the victory of the 'moderates' would remove the need for pressurising the northern government, partition clearly reflected Ulster Unionist resistance to any all-Ireland framework rather than Britain's strategic interests, which could just as well have been served by unity within the Empire.

From the end of the Civil War to the modernisation attempts of Northern Ireland's Unionist Prime Minister, Terence O'Neill, in the 1960s, the predominant disposition on the part of the British political elite was to insulate this last vestige of the Irish problem from the rest of the British political system. Once it was assured of the triumph of what was seen as the more moderate section of Sinn Fein in the Civil War, a previous inclination to pressurise Ulster Unionism towards a more accommodating position on the issues of the conditions and rights of Northern Ireland's Catholic population and possible co-operative links with the south evaporated. The 1923 ruling by the Speaker of the House of Commons, which effectively banned the discussion of any matter which was the responsibility of a minister in

Northern Ireland, provided a significant protection of the Unionist regime from Westminster scrutiny.

It was a policy manifestation of a profound shift in the elite's attitude. In the nineteenth and early twentieth century the British political elite engaged with the Union of Britain and Ireland in the most profound and passionate way. It was an obsession, in different ways, for Gladstone, Salisbury, Balfour and Lloyd George. It was a core theme of the highest level of intellectual discourse in the country: J.S. Mill, Cardinal Newman and Matthew Arnold all devoted major energies to the subject. As late as 1914, passionate debate about Ireland engaged the mind of the British political class and intelligentsia.

All this changed with the settlement of 1921-2. After the 1920s the governing class in England gave up on Ireland, which it now saw as doing its own thing. The Irish Civil War; the flirtation of so many Nationalists with fascism both in the 1930s and the early 1940s; the partisan communalism of the Stormont regime – none of this engaged core policy-makers in London. It was really only the 'Troubles' in the north which brought Ireland back to reluctant attention. The predominant British concern with the island was to see that it stayed 'switched off'. However, at the margins of high politics lurked vague romantic fantasies stimulated by a combination of departmental obsessions and broader, if ill-founded, strategic calculations.

APPEASEMENT AND THE 'SWINGE OF GUILT'

From time to time in the inter-war period there would be a degree of departmental concern in Whitehall with what was perceived as an Ulster regime that was prone to sponge off the Exchequer while at the same time ruling in a partisan fashion. The Treasury was from the start a major critic of what it regarded as the penchant of the Ulster Prime Minister for making 'incredible' demands for funding.[3] A Whitehall concern about 'subsidisation' of Northern Ireland would recur at intervals throughout the history of the Northern Ireland state, and would interact with broader strategic and political concerns at times, to create major problems for Unionism.

This was apparent during the negotiations which led to the Anglo-Irish Agreement of 1938, bringing to an end a period of intensely conflictual Anglo-Irish relations which had begun with Fianna Fáil's electoral victory in 1932. The reluctance of Northern Ireland's Prime Minister, Sir James Craig, to support the proposed accord was ill-received in Whitehall, where it was regarded as an example of selfish provincial ingratitude. Whether Craig's opposition was motivated by genuine concern for the fate of northern trades damaged by southern tariffs or whether it was, as the Treasury claimed, 'really political and not economic',[4] the Ulster position was a real obstacle to Chamberlain's attempt to improve relations with Dublin as part of his appeasement strategy: 'He wished to demonstrate to the great powers of Europe that Britain was a country prepared to take matters on trust; that she was willing to negotiate, to make concessions and to live with promises rather than immediate tangible benefits in the belief that these would soften the belligerent nature of the Fascist powers.'[5]

Britain relinquished control of those Irish ports granted to her under the Treaty, and the Economic War was ended on terms favourable to the Irish and galling to Unionists. Moreover attention was also paid to De Valera's claim that Stormont's treatment of its minority made any tariff concessions to northern traders impossible.[6] The Home Office and the Dominions Office prepared minutes on the question of the treatment of Catholics: While the former took a generally defensive position the Dominions Office was critical, comparing De Valera's success in breaking with the IRA with the Craig regime's continued dependence on the Orange Order.[7]

Deidre McMahon has described Sir Henry Batterbee of the Dominions Office as 'a good example of Gladstonian atonement in action', and quotes Correlli Barnett's sardonic comment on elite attitudes to former colonies: 'The combination of a cheerfully rapacious colonial past and post-evangelical conscience gave the British a constant swinge of guilt.'[8] In this connection, she points to the anti-Unionist and pro-unity positions shared by Batterbee and Sir Warren Fisher of the Treasury. Certainly, Batterbee was rather uncritical of De Valera's regime: in a letter to Fisher he claimed that De Valera 'had succeeded in establishing a religious liberty and toleration.'[9] He was also convinced that geography, Catholic population growth and commercial considerations would operate towards unity and that, while Ulster could not be coerced, the British government would be 'foolish to try and impede the play of natural forces.'[10] While conditions for a 'final settlement' did not yet exist he favoured a pro-active programme: ministerial visits to Dublin, the appointment of a High Commissioner and the encouragement of cross-border enterprises.[11]

Fisher combined traditional Treasury disdain for Craig's 'sponging' – the Northern Ireland government 'comes to us when bankrupt', and the north 'would gain greatly from the termination of the present wholly uneconomic partition' – with what McMahon refers to as 'pronounced nationalist sympathies' and 'an emotional view of Irish history'.[12] He sent a note to Neville Chamberlain during the negotiations emphasising the need to remember justifiable Irish resentments: 'It is too readily forgotten by us English that our record over the larger part of the period has been outrageous ...'[13] Batterbee was also convinced of '... how bad our record has been in the past and to what extent it is the fault of bad government that the Irish are as trying and difficult as they are.'[14] As we shall see, in subsequent periods when the economic or strategic/political interests of the British state were seriously affected by developments on the island, there would be similar sentiments expressed by senior members of the political elite – although not until Sir Patrick Mayhew's Coleraine speech in 1992, where he expressed regret for Britain's contribution to the 'often tragic history' of Ireland, did a senior British minister publicly make reference to the seamy side of British rule in Ireland.

The expression of anti-Unionist and pro-unity sentiments by two senior officials is obviously not a sufficient basis for deciphering a broader current of elite opinion, let alone a strategic disposition. In his impressive account of Northern Ireland during the Second World War, Brian Barton refers to a report prepared by senior officials for Clement Attlee in 1949, as the British government considered its response to the Irish decision to leave the Commonwealth. Referring to the inter-war period, the report claimed that 'all political parties were then able to take the line over partition that there was nothing that they would like better than to see a united Ireland.'[15] That there was no positive embrace of partition was clear, but the bottom line for the British political elite remained – in 1938 as much as in 1921 – that Ulster could not be coerced. However, it could be (and certainly was) urged to 'take the broader view' and to recognise that the wider interests of the British state demanded potentially painful sacrifices. In 1938 this meant that the Agreement, as negotiated, was carried through with only minimal concessions to Craig's complaints.

In 1940, in the month of Dunkirk when there was an acute need felt in London to attempt to persuade De Valera to forsake neutrality, Craig was asked to participate in an inter-governmental discussions on how best to defend the island. When he refused point blank to consider any discussions involving de Valera, the British government moved directly to offer Dublin 'a solemn undertaking that a union of Ireland would become an accomplished fact at an early date.'[16] Irish suspicion of any British government's ability to deliver on such an undertaking, together with a strong feeling in the Department of External Affairs that Britain would be defeated, ensured a refusal. This would be the last occasion until the 1980s that the British political elite would be strongly disposed to make an agreement with an Irish government at the expense of Ulster Unionism.

However, it is necessary to register the limits of British concession. As Chamberlain put it, Northern Ireland government attitudes were not due 'solely to obstinancy and unreasonableness' and it would be pointless 'to increase goodwill between Britain and Eire ... (if they) forfeited the confidence and goodwill of Northern Ireland.'[17] A coming together of the two Irish states was clearly favoured, but this was in the context of a move by the Irish state towards closer relations with the other island. The elite consensus is well summed up in a vignette from the memoirs of Sir Richard Pim, an Ulsterman on Churchill's personal staff during the war. It is an account of a lunch in July 1942 attended by John Andrews, the Prime Minister of Northern Ireland, David Lloyd George and Churchill:

> The three Prime Ministers proceeded with the assistance of wine glasses, salt and pepper pots, to discuss in detail the Irish question since 1900. The discussion lasted over an hour and needless to say it was superbly interesting. Both Mr. Lloyd George and Mr.Churchill made it clear that they regretted no step which they had taken on the Irish Question, neither under any circumstances would they permit the coercion of Ulster in the future. At the same time, both made it very clear that they still entertained the hope that in the future some statesman would rise in Ulster who would feel justified in making a move towards closer harmony with the south. Similarly, it was their hope that Eire would produce a statesman who would make a reciprocal move towards close harmony with Northern Ireland. They believe that if such a change of heart was to be found in the North and in the South, then the North, because of the history of its ancestors, would automatically become the real controller of the new Ireland, which they would bring again fully within the folds of the British Empire.[18]

What is expressed here is the desire to promote a 'new Ireland' embodying a coming together of the two states within a broader process of drawing Ireland back into a closer relationship with the Empire. Though a touch whimsical, at the time it expressed the desire for better relations with the Irish state, which would ultimately have a real impact on British policy towards Northern Ireland.

UNIONISM'S FINEST HALF HOUR

The Second World War and Ireland's neutrality pushed such considerations into the background. Irish neutrality radically diminished Britain's willingness to listen to De Valera's complaints about partition, and considerably increased the warmth and sympathy with which the Unionist government's case was viewed in London. The strategic value of northern ports and airfields ensured much greater bargaining power for Unionists on a range of issues from the financing of the welfare state and post-war industrial strategy to the strengthening of the constitutional position in the 1949 Ireland Act.

This piece of legislation, which provoked the all-party Anti-Partition Campaign in the Irish Republic, was in fact less absolutist than the advice given to the cabinet by its officials: that the strategic implication of the South's neutrality·in the Second World War was that '... it will never be to Great Britain's advantage that Northern Ireland should form a territory outside his Majesty's jurisdiction. Indeed, it would seem unlikely that Great Britain would ever be able to agree to this even if the people of Northern Ireland desired it.'[19]

The Ireland Act was the Attlee administration's response to the decision of the Irish government to leave the Commonwealth, but even in these circumstances, the feeling in London was that it would be unwise to proceed as far as treating Irish citizens in the United Kingdom as 'foreigners'. The government's original view was that there was no alternative but to treat citizens of the Irish Republic in precisely that manner, since: 'It seemed that the continued discrimination in favour of the Irish Republic would lay the United Kingdom open to claims for similar treatment from foreign countries under most favoured nation provisions of commercial treaties. It was out of the question to give such treatment to the goods and nationals of foreign countries. It seemed therefore that Irish Republican citizens would have to come under the ordinary immigration control of aliens and that the preference system would have to disappear.'[20]

The final decision to maintain the 'special relationship' with Ireland by treating citizens of the Republic as 'non-foreign' reflected a number of pressures, including strong support for the Irish case from the Commonwealth governments of Canada, Australia and New Zealand. A central consideration was the recently concluded Trade Agreement which revised some of the provisions of the 1938 Agreement and centred on Ireland increasing its exports of live cattle and foodstuffs in return for more coal and industrial plant from Britain.[21]

The British state had an interest in maintaining the existing set of economic relations with the Irish Republic. Irish cattle were essential to the British livestock industry and down to the late 1950s British manufacturers enjoyed substantial tariff prefences in the Republic's market. As Peter Thorneycroft of the Board of Trade informed the Prime Minister in 1956: 'In 1955 our imports from the Irish Republic totalled about £98 million, of which a very large proportion consisted of cattle, food and agricultural products. Against this our exports to the Republic totalled some £114 million, of which the bulk was manufactured goods ... for some of these goods at least we should have difficulty in finding markets elsewhere.'[22] To have treated Irish citizens as foreigners, much though it would have pleased many Ulster Unionists, would have disrupted the undoubted benefits that the British economy derived from the existing set of Anglo-Irish trading relations.

Most fundamentally, as the Commonwealth Relations Office noted, the 'practical advantages' of the 'non-foreign' policy had lost none of their force: 'In particular it would be extremely difficult to treat citizens of the Irish Republic as aliens in the United Kingdom.'[23] 'Practicality' denoted the British desire not to do anything which would undermine the longer-term possiblities of an accommodation between north and south. The effect of the war on Unionism's position at Westminster would be a diminishing resource, while the interest of the British state in working out, maintaining and improving trade and political relations with the Republic would remain a substantial, if underrated, facet of Anglo-Irish relations for two decades after 1945.

THE BRITISH STATE AND 'TECHNOCRATIC ANTI-PARTITIONISM'

The importance of Britain's underlying disposition to draw what it perceived as an isolationist and Anglo-phobe state back towards more amicable and cooperative relations becomes clear only with the increasing availability of state archives in Dublin, London and Belfast. These demonstrate a clear increase of official and ministerial contacts between London and Dublin from the late 1950s onward, as the crisis-stricken Irish economy forced a radical reversal of the protectionist policies that had been followed with particular enthusiasm by Fianna Fáil governments since the 1930s. This intersected with a strong belief on the Irish side that the beneficial effects of the 1938 and 1948 trade agreements for Irish agriculture had been eroded.

This situation led to a prolonged process of negotiations between 1957 and 1965 which produced the disappointing – for the Irish – trade agreement of 1960, and subsequently the Anglo-Irish Free Trade Agreement of 1965. Both agreements resulted in an even closer set of economic relations between the two countries, which was particularly important for Irish agriculture. This *de facto* integrationism was, however, ideologically compensated for by Sean Lemass's strong belief that the world-wide trend towards trading blocs, and specifically developments like EFTA and the EEC, would make partition anachronistic. It has been argued that Lemass was one of the earliest proponents of 'technocratic anti-partitionism', i.e. he believed that the development of closer economic relations between north and south in the context of moves towards European economic integration would bring about political unity.[24] This only partially reflects the complexity of his position. For, while he was vigorously pursuing closer forms of cooperation with the north in a range of areas, he was also publicly making clear his desire for a political settlement in which London would play the role of catalyst by publicly declaring that it favoured an end to partition through the coming together of north and south.

The ending of the 'cold war' between north and south symbolised by the O'Neill/Lemass meeting at Stormont in 1965 needs to be re-evaluated. The important point is not so much Lemass's maintenance of a clear anti-partitionist agenda, albeit of a 'technocratic sort', but the perception of British interest and the intention that lay behind it. For it is clear that ministers and officials in Dublin really did believe that the British elite concerned with Ireland favoured disengagement. As his biographer points out, for Lemass 'The starting point was a fervent nationalism, rarely expressed, masked by the image of the calculating man of affairs.'[25] Yet this nationalism did not dictate an anti-partitionist rhetoric whatever the circumstances. In the difficult conditions after the Second World War, Lemass publicly stated the problems involved in ending partition and even admitted that his government had 'no plan as such' to achieve this objective – 'an abject confession of impotence' as a northern nationalist editor described it.[26] By the end of the 1950s, however, he began to believe that a combination of economic changes and the decolonisation process meant that a realistic, if gradualist, strategy for bringing about unity was now possible. He was convinced that in the context of decolonisation elsewhere, British politicians and officials were embarassed by Northern Ireland and would be glad to be rid of this 'colonial' encumbrance.[27] Central to this misconception of British intentions was a misreading of a genuine British concern to have a regime in Dublin less influenced by De Valerean fixations.

There was a visible sigh of relief in British government circles when Lemass succeeded De Valera as leader of Fianna Fáil and Taoiseach in 1959. Already experienced in the Anglo-Irish trade talks going on in the context of Britain and Ireland's possible membership of broader free trade arrangements, Lemass was pushing for a revision of the 1938 and 1948 agreements, which would have extended the system of price support provided by the British Ministry of Agriculture to Irish farmers in return for tariff advantages for United Kingdom exports to the Republic.[28] Although the British were not prepared to accept Lemass's proposals, they were anxious not to be seen to rebuff the Irish, and put forward a set of less far-reaching measures. Even these were roundly opposed by the Northern Ireland government on the grounds that the terms would adversely affect Northern Ireland producers – a complaint which the British officials regarded as 'overdrawn' – and, more fundamentally, because they resented the fact that '… a country which had cut itself off from the United Kingdom and Commonwealth should receive benefits at the particular expense of Northern Ireland …'. It was claimed that, given 'the state of tension caused by IRA activity [this would] tend to sharpen political criticisms in Northern Ireland when the concessions were announced …'[29]

The Northern Ireland government's concerns were taken seriously in London. By 1960 the IRA's assault on the northern state, which was launched in 1956, had clearly failed to develop into a serious threat or to elicit support from Nationalists in the north. However, it would not be called off until February 1962 and there was therefore some basis for Unionist concerns. But the British government still felt it was necessary to try and educate Belfast about the advantages of trying to deal with Lemass in a more positive way. A substantial memorandum on 'Economic Relations with the Irish Republic' was drawn up, under Treasury supervision, by officials in the departments involved and sent by the Home Office to Stormont.

This document provides interesting evidence on the British government's conception of where British interests lay in relation to the Irish state, and of the role that the Northern Ireland government should play in consolidating better inter-state relations. First there was an undoubted economic interest in attempting to accommodate Lemass. This was in part based on an overly-pessimistic view of the Republic's economy:

> The economic prospects of the Irish Republic are not good Their efforts to diversify their economy by the development of secondary industry have had only limited success. They depend, and are likely to continue to depend for as far ahead as can be seen, on selling their agricultural goods to the United Kingdom, but their prospects of expanding their market here are very poor. They are likely to be hit as the EFTA tariff reductions come into effect ... it is impossible to be optimistic about the Republic's economic future.[30]

Given that economic and social relations with the Republic 'are probably closer than with any other country, foreign or Common-wealth' and that the Republic was ranked eighth in terms of Britain's world markets, 'a depression there must to some extent affect our own prosperity. It would therefore be desirable to try, if we can, to find some way of helping their economy.'

The more specific interests of British and Northern Irish manufacturers also came into play. Since the 1938 Trade Agreement, the Republic had developed a range of industrial exports to Britain and the north, taking advantage of the duty-free entrance which was primarily intended to help their agricultural exports. At the same time, the southern market was protected by tariff barriers which, 'notwithstanding the preferential rate which they afford us, causes us considerable embarassment. The contrast in treatment – duty-free entry on one side and, in many cases, a highly protective rate on the other – is a source of constant irritation to United Kingdom manufacturers.' The British wanted to use Lemass's approach as an opportunity 'to recast the pattern of our trade with the Republic more to our advantage.' In fact, as the Belfast government and its manufacturers had been particularly vocal in their denunciation of the *status quo* in trade in manufactured goods, the British government wanted to know if, in the eventuality of them not being able to get an all-round settlement in this area, they should respond to Lemass's offer of a separate north–south deal on tariffs against northern goods? Lord Brookeborough's cabinet in Belfast brusquely dismissed any proposal to treat Northern Ireland differently from the rest of the United Kingdom – it was but the thin end of the traditional anti-partitionist wedge.[31]

From London's point of view, there were clear political reasons for not brushing off Lemass's overture:

> With the ending of Mr. De Valera's lengthy dominance of the Irish political scene and the emergence of Mr. Lemass, himself a business man at the head of a more business-like administration, the political atmosphere in the South is changing. This metamorphosis will be neither rapid nor dramatic. But already there have been signs that the Dublin government are anxious to move away from the negative attitudes of earlier administrations. The spirit of 1916 and 1922 is on the wane. While it is too much to expect that any political leader in the Republic would ever abandon the hope that Partition will one day cease, Mr Lemass has been realistic enough to admit that this must be a long term objective. Moreover unemployment and discontent in the Republic may encourage support for and recruitment to terrorist organisations. If Mr. Lemass who has publicly committed himself deeply to seeking an improvement in his country's prospects by negotiation with the United Kingdom, receives from us a completely negative response, his policy of greater flexibility towards the United Kingdom is unlikely to prosper.[32]

Although, due to the Unionist response, London did not pursue the possibility of a separate north–south deal, concessions to the Republic were made, and it is clear that this was in the hope of consolidating in power a more 'flexible' Taoiseach. Lemass's continued raising of the issue of 'practical' matters of north–south cooperation was not seen, in London at least, to be fatally damaged by the fact that he clearly hoped that increased linkages would eventually lead to a political payoff. It was believed that the anti-partitionist element was now safely relegated to a relatively distant objective.

In fact, anti-partitionism remained a part of Lemass's approach for two main reasons. First was the continuing presence of Frank Aiken as Minister of External Affairs. Aiken's instincts on the north were much more traditional than Lemass's, but his status as one of the historic founders of the Fianna Fáil party and his close relations with De Valera meant that Lemass was unable to remove him from this key department; as a result, the traditional tone was periodically sounded. A second factor was that anti-partitionism was an ideological resource to dampen down Fianna Fáil fears that Lemass had jettisoned the material base of the nationalist project – protectionism – in his overtures to England for a free trade agreement.

The desire to improve north–south relations and the adoption of an approach on partition which, whatever its ambiguities and contradictions, did emphasise that it could only be removed in the long term, showed the British that Lemass offered a real basis for eliminating at least some of the sources of friction in Anglo-Irish relations. In this context, Brookeborough's response to Lemass's overtures on north–south discussions on trade issues was not well received in London. The pre-requisite that Brookeborough laid down for talks was constitutional recognition of Northern Ireland. Even members of the Unionist establishment such as Sir Robert Gransden (Secretary to the Stormont cabinet, Private Secretary to the Prime Minister from 1939 to 1957, and Agent for Northern Ireland in London from 1957 to 1962), privately criticised this position when it continued to be publicly articulated by Brookeborough's successor, Terence O'Neill: 'This was a completely unrealistic attitude and could not be defended as O'Neill could not reasonably expect any government here formally to recognise the constitutional position of Northern Ireland.'[33]

In a letter to Jack Sayers, the liberal Unionist editor of the *Belfast Telegraph*, Gransden made it clear that he believed that the possiblities for north–south cooperation should be explored on a low-key basis by officials 'without the searchlight of publicity' and that if anything positive emerged ministers should be involved and a 'summit' between O'Neill and Lemass should then take place. He alluded to the perception in London that Belfast was increasingly an obstacle to improved relations with Dublin: '... there is no doubt of the feeling beyond our shores that we are inward-looking and that we should make an effort to 'shake hands' over some matters at any rate.'[34]

After his historic meeting with Lemass in January 1965, O'Neill told a meeting of Ulster Unionist Westminster MPs that, although Harold Wilson would have liked to claim credit for the meeting because of the Irish vote in his constituency, in fact it had been arranged solely on

O'Neill's initiative. This may have soothed the susceptibilities of those MPs prone to suspicions of Wilson because of the exaggerated hopes invested in his administration by some northern nationalists. However, it is unlikely that they were particularly happy to be told that former Prime Minister Harold MacMillan had on three occasions asked O'Neill if relations with the Republic could not be improved 'because of the embarrassment which the existing situation caused in America and elsewhere'[35]

Some indication of MacMillan's attitudes were given by the former Chancellor of the Exchequer, Lord Amory, who was British High Commissioner to Canada. Amory had visited London just after Lemass had been there to discuss trade issues and told the Irish Ambassador to Canada that he had been officially briefed on the visit:

> ... he understood that the Taoiseach had made a very good impression on all concerned; his approach was a very pragmatic one, and this was appreciated in London where 'practical' men are prized. He (Lord Amory) thought that the time had come where some practical steps should be taken to bring North and South somewhat nearer. He knew the new Northern premier, Terence O'Neill, and would consider him more open to such an approach than his predecessor though it would be well to bear in mind that he also was very much 'dyed in the wool'. (Lord Amory's phrase.) 'What we must try to do', he said, 'is to try to bring you together like that', arching his hands in a form like that of Rodin's 'Cathedral'.[36]

Echoing the sentiments of 'post-imperial guilt' expressed by Batterbee and Fisher in the 1930s, Lord Amory related the effect of reading a copy of Cecil Woodham-Smith's *The Great Hunger*, a powerful attack on the culpability of the landlord class and the British government for the Great Famine of the 1840s, given him as a Christmas present: 'he had read it with fascination, it was a "dreadful story" ... he had never before recognised the extent of the tragedy; it made him realise how we must feel about things'. The ambassador reported how, at his most recent meeting, Lord Amory had gone out of his way to emphasise the importance of Britain's 'special relationship' with the Republic: 'he intervened with some deliberation to tell the assembled guests that, looking around Europe and the world at the moment, Britain had problems of all kinds, and he thought it a remarkable thing that these problems touched nearly every country except their nearest neighbour, Ireland. With Ireland they had no problems at all, and indeed their thinking was on very similar lines to that of the Irish government'.[37]

Lemass was convinced that sentiments such as these expressed a general disposition on the part of the British political elite to review the whole partition issue, which was seen in the context of the broader process of decolonisation and MacMillan's 'Winds of Change' speech increasingly as an anachronism. What Lemass desired was not some declaration of intent to withdraw but, as he put it in speech to the National Press Club in Washington on 16 October 1963, '... a clear statement by British political leaders that there would be no British interest in maintaining partition when Irishmen wanted to get rid of it. That has not yet been said. If the belief which still prevails in some quarters – and which was probably well based at one time – that Britain wishes to maintain Partition irrespective of Irish interests or desires, should be demolished, it would be a factor of great significance and would produce an immediate and beneficial improvement in the whole situation'.[38] As he was also convinced that the post-1959 recovery in the Republic's economy, together with a major crisis of the staple industries of the north, removed the only substantial argument for partition from a Unionist viewpoint, such a British declaration was thought essential to strengthening those in the north who were in favour of change.[39]

However, although there was an undoubted sympathy for Lemass in London and a desire 'to do business' with what was seen as a more pragmatic and flexible government, there were strict limits on the degree to which British ministers and officials would pressurise the Unionist government. The Conservative government's position remained that set out in a reply to a question in the House of Commons on 14 March 1957, when it was stated that the British government would always be ready to 'consider sympathetically' any proposals which had the support of the Dublin and Belfast parliaments for an end to partition. As Cornelius Cremin, Irish Ambassador to London, explained to Duncan Sandys, Secretary of State for Commonwealth Relations, what Lemass was seeking was a statement that went beyond sympathetic consideration to positive approval. Sandys responded that 'our position is very delicate' and that it would be extremely difficult for British ministers to say anything which might give the impression that they were 'abandoning the people in the north'.[40]

The Permanent Under-Secretary of the Commonwealth Relations

Office, Sir Saville Garner, had already flagged up some of the problems with Lemass's request; he made two 'personal observations on the Partition issue'. The first was that any statement made by 'authoritative British statesmen should not exacerbate the situation and, in particular, should not create perturbation in the North'. Secondly, he remarked that 'any British government would probably find it quite impossible to assist in ending Partition in circumstances which would almost certainly involve opposition from pro-Partitionists in the north, without the resultant status cutting them off entirely from their existing relations with London and the Commonwealth'.[41]

The willingness to consider ending partition should Ireland re-join the Commonwealth certainly gave some indication of British flexibility: the Archbishop of Armagh, Cardinal D'Alton, had suggested the idea in 1957, it was subsequently taken up by the pro-Nationalist Labour peer, Lord Longford, and was rumoured to be an approach favoured by the Leader of the Opposition, Harold Wilson.[42] In a speech to the Oxford Union in 1959, Lemass referred to Cardinal Dalton's proposals in order to highlight what he saw as the 'confused' loyalties of Ulster Unionists: on the one hand they stressed their own commitment to the Commonwealth, on the other, they vigorously rejected the Cardinal's idea. This, Lemass claimed, was a result of their wrong-headed notion that it was in the interests of the British state to resist all efforts to widen internal Irish contacts.

Underlying this argument was Lemass's fundamental belief in the need for the British authorities to make a public statement of support for the coming together of the two states. As a precedent, he offered the example of King George V's address to the opening session of the Northern Ireland Parliament in 1921, when the king said: 'that they [Britain] would welcome the advent of the day when the Irish people, North and South, would work together in a common love of Ireland upon a foundation of mutual justice and respect'.[43] However, to put this remark into context, it should be pointed out that the undoubted pro-unity sentiment in the King's address reflected the desire of the British elite at the time to achieve a settlement with the more moderate wing of Sinn Fein, and their view that this would be possible if the deal had an integral all-Ireland dimension to it, albeit one which accepted a Unionist right to opt out. When the Republican movement split and the moderates won the Civil War, British interest in pushing an all-Ireland dimension evaporated. If Lemass hoped to revive it then he would have to offer more than trade concessions and a commitment to improving north–south relations, but, as Cremin explained to Garner, 'This [rejoining the Commonwealth] was a very delicate issue'.[44] British nervousness over the Unionist response was matched by Lemass's need not to antagonise important elements of traditionalism in his own cabinet and party.

Lemass continued to reiterate both his belief that the British political elite had shifted in its attitude to partition and his request that this be given public expression. But it was clear to him by the end of 1963 that the Conservatives would not provide the statement, and that neither Jack Kennedy's Irish Catholic roots nor Harold Wilson's large Irish Catholic electorate would induce a commitment to the Irish position.

An attempt had been made to enlist the assistance of President Kennedy who was due to visit Ireland in June 1963. An Irish request for pressure on Britain to make a public declaration in favour of unity was not enthusiastically received. The Irish Ambassador to Washington reported, 'He is, by his education, British-inclined. And in the present international conjuncture, he makes no secret of his firm attachment to Britain'. He recorded Kennedy's reaction: 'there is a long built-in history involved, which includes religious differences, and it has to be seen like that from the British point of view; he is convinced that no British minister would feel able to make a public statement of the kind suggested'.[45]

When Harold Wilson became leader of the Labour Party in 1963 he had been asked by the United Ireland Association, the successor organisation to the British section of the Anti-Partition League, to provide a statement on Labour Party policy on partition. In what the Irish Press referred to as an 'evasive answer' he suggested that partition was a matter for the Irish people themselves and neither the British government nor any political party had the right to interfere.[46] The Irish embassy in London decided to help a Mr Havekin, the secretary of the Association, to draft a response to Wilson's letter. At its core was a critique of Wilson's implied claim of British neutrality on the question of partition: '... to disclaim any power on the part of the British Government to intervene to end partition is in essence tantamount to endorsing the *status quo*. Such an attitude may perhaps appear, in the abstract, to be one of neutrality. But this is not, of course, the case. At best it would be a neutrality *vis-à-vis* a situation which in all important respects favours the Six-County Administration and its continuance. In support of this proposition, my Committee would adduce the fact that the Belfast Administration is subsidised each year by the British taxpayer to the tune of £91 million.'[47]

However, it was precisely the fact of the subvention that Sir Saville Garner had used to counter Irish pressure for a more pro-active role for Britain on ending partition: 'on the substance of the issue [Partition] Sir Saville's only comment was that the passage of time has changed the position in two important respects. Whereas, he said, in the 1920s we were all living in *laissez-faire* social and economic conditions, today the ordinary British taxpayer is subsidising the inhabitants of the Six Counties, like those of North Wales, through the heavy outlay on the social services; and through the agricultural policies adopted here, the Six County farmer is, likewise, greatly assisted by the Exchequer.'[48] Lemass would also have known of the effect of the disparity between levels of social service and benefit in north and south, and the fact that many northern Catholics were not. enthusiastic for any rapid move towards unity. He had received a letter on precisely this issue from a Strabane nationalist who demanded reassurance because '... there is a lot of Catholics in Strabane town against the unity of the country. They think that if Ireland was united that your government would not pay the same money that Britain is paying them ... I told them they would get the same money. Would you guarantee the Six Counties the same money?'[49]

It was the difficulties raised by such economic issues for traditional forms of anti-partitionism that had encouraged Lemass to shift to a much more gradualist approach. At his first meeting with Harold Wilson he had said that the sort of north–south coopertion he was advocating would be 'without prejudice to the political position of either side although he naturally hoped that in time it would lead to a better understanding which would bring about political reunification'.[50] A perspective on unification of this type, implicitly dependent on a period of cooperation and a hoped-for shift in Unionist attitudes, was far removed from his party's or the state's official ideology. He also made clear to Wilson that despite his public requests for a British statement in favour of unification he was happy enough with the position adopted by the government, instancing a recent visit by Sir Alec Douglas Home to Belfast where he had spoken in favour of north–south cooperation.

It was not surprising that such a custodian of De Valerean verities as Lord Longford became increasingly frustrated with Lemass's approach. Eamonn Andrews, Chairman of the Radio Éireann

Authority, wrote to the Taoiseach after lunching with Longford who had recently been appointed Lord Privy Seal in the new Labour administration. He was concerned that Longford was unhappy with Lemass's approach: '... he seemed to think our Government was not all that serious about tackling Partition in the immediate future, at least from the point of view of making a Parliamentary issue out of it in Britain. The interpretation seemed to be that it would be better to get on with the job and let the record speak for itself and have what impact it might on Partition.'[51] Lemass's reply brusquely dismissed the peer's critique: 'His impression about how serious we are about ending Partition may arise from the fact that we do not think his ideas as practical as he believes them to be.'[52]

It seems clear that once Lemass had bedded down the radical shift in economic policy he lost any serious interest in sounding more traditional anti-partitionist notes. By the time of his meeting with Terence O'Neill he had brought his party and government to a perspective on unity which was very clearly summed up in a civil service memorandum on a possible agenda for talks with Stormont on north–south links. The paper suggested two principles which should now govern the government's approach to unity: first that London should be disregarded as 'a factor in maintaining partition' and second that the Republic's government should 'Concentrate on the parliament and people in the Six Counties'.[53]

An intriguing aspect of the period of north–south *détente* is the lack of attention paid by any of the key players in Belfast, Dublin or London to the position of Northern Ireland's Catholics. Elsewhere we have highlighted the Home Office's role in ignoring attempts by the Northern Ireland Labour Party (NILP) and the Campaign for Social Justice to press the Wilson government into action on a range of issues like discrimination and the Special Powers Act.[54] The Dublin archives show an equal lack of concern over these matters. Partition had worked similar effects in Dublin and London in the sense that Lemass's technocratic anti-partitionism and London's olympian desire to promote better relations between the two states were equally contemptuous of what were perceived as the narrow-minded recessive passions of northern Nationalists and Unionists.

A *rapprochement* with the Irish Republic was made easier by Lemass's decision to try to encourage the Nationalist Party in the north to adopt a more positive attitude to engagement with the possibility of reforming the northern state rather than rely on the traditional staple of anti-partitionist propaganda. Thus when officials in the Irish Department of External Affairs considered the possibility of updating the material produced for the 1949 All Party Anti-Partition campaign, a proposed 'Discrimination' pamphlet drawn up by two northern Nationalists was seen as too traditional and 'political' in tone. As one official put it, the pamphlet did not tell Irish Nationalists anything new, while 'If the pamphlet is directed at a non-Irish audience I very much doubt if it will get further than their waste-paper baskets. I am afraid it is regrettable but true that very little, if any, interest in the problems of the Northern Ireland minority is taken outside Ireland.'[55] The traditional links between the Department of External Affairs and northern Nationalists were attenuated and Lemass did little to hide his view that part at least of the problem in the north was the 'narrow outlook' of the Nationalists there.'[56] By the time Lemass retired, to be succeeded by Jack Lynch, relations with Eddie McAteer, the leader of northern Nationalists, were frigid. As one official of the Department of External Affairs noted,

> A persistent feature of Nationalist speeches in the last few weeks has been the emphasis placed on the loss of contact, social and otherwise with us. While the fact that we are no longer conducting a sustained propaganda offensive mitigates against a revival of the pre-1960 informal relationship between officers of the department and Nationalist MPs and Senators, a general weakening of the link through neglect or over-cautiousness on our part might be detrimental to the long term interests of Irish unity... The Leader of the Nationalist Party has complained – with some justification – that Dáil deputies have more contact with parliamentarians abroad than with Nationalists at Stormont.[57]

These comments were provoked by a leader in the *Belfast Telegraph* on a speech by McAteer in which he hinted at the possiblity of the Nationalist Party becoming the Offical Opposition at Stormont and also called for more north–south economic cooperation within a European context. The *Telegraph* commented, 'But while the Nationalists look outward to Europe there must be a basic unreality and hence a limited function for a party dedicated to such a lost cause as a united Ireland. They have had little enough encouragement recently from Dublin and this should be a clear warning to them to seek their salvation elsewhere.'

The Dublin official quoted above went on to suggest that some attempts should be made to bring 'our friends' in from 'out in the cold' by at least strengthening social ties with invitations to departmental receptions. However, a more senior official, while agreeing that the Department of External Affairs needed a clearer policy *vis-à-vis* the Nationalists, rejected any initiative on a departmental basis: '... it seems to me that the primary need is for a clearer understanding between the political parties on this side of the Border and the Nationalists in the North. In the absence of contact at that level I do not think that we can engage in any activity at the official level with the Nationalists.' What was necessary, he thought, was the creation of 'a new indentity of purpose between the Nationalists in the North and the political parties here which would offer a platform which would have greater appeal for the younger electorate, would meet its present day concerns and offer the prospect of a better future'. However, such a platform was 'impracticable at the present time and unlikely in the future. It is not therefore clear whether any purpose would be served in suggesting at the present time that the political parties here should tackle this problem'. A policy of maintaining the status quo despite Nationalist complaints was defended in terms of the effects it would have on pushing the latter towards more realistic positions: 'The alternative to taking any action at the present time must inevitably be that the gap between the Nationalists in the North and the people here will grow wider in the future. This development will of course force the Nationalists to adopt policies which are fully in keeping with their status in the Six Counties itself and which will offer some hope of attracting support from those who are at present committed to the Unionist Party'.[58]

In Dublin, the strong desire to foster better links with the northern state had clearly come to mean a willingness to keep northern Nationalism at arm's length in the hope that this would force it to adopt a more 'realistic' and participationist approach to the Northern Ireland state. Little attempt was made to sooth Nationalist sensibilities. Thus, when McAteer contacted the Department to arrange a meeting with its permanent secretary, and was told that he would be absent with the Taoiseach in Denmark, McAteer was reported as saying that the absence of Lynch would not affect his visit '... as, in twelve months of office, he [Lynch] has never once invited him [McAteer] to meet him or to come to Dublin. He made a remark to the effect that he felt hurt or unhappy about relations with us'.[59] Jack Lynch

Lynch was a convinced adherent of Lemass's northern strategy and showed no inclination to make things difficult for the O'Neill administration in Belfast.

This was made clear in response to one of Harold Wilson's occasional indulgences in the rhetoric of Irish nationalism. Wilson seemed to combine a practical policy of non-intervention in Ulster with a penchant for destabilising speeches hinting at his own sympathies for unity. Thus, in a speech to the Council of Europe in Strasbourg in January 1967, he claimed that no one would be happier than Great Britain if the 'Irish Problem' were resolved by agreement on the island.[60] Although Wilson was hailed by Frank Aiken as going much further than any previous British minister, Jack Lynch rejected a subsequent request from a leading northern Nationalist that he respond by offering, in the light of the Government of Ireland Act, to 'lead your Cabinet to meet at any venue O'Neill and his Cabinet may choose, to discuss and do, what the boss P.M. of the United Kingdom asked'.[61] Lynch's reply made it clear that he would consider only those measures that achieved 'practical and positive' results. 'As to the question of what further steps might be appropriately taken by us now with a view to hastening the day when re-unification will be achieved, I am not fully convinced that the course you suggest would be the most fruitful. It would certainly add to the discomfort of the Six County Cabinet but I would like to be sure it would have positive aspects as well.'[62]

The crisis which would destroy the Unionist regime and mark the onset of two decades of violence, erupted at a time when Anglo-Irish relations had never been better. British governments had seen in Lemass's new anti-partitionist strategy a non-threatening opportunity to draw the Irish state closer, and within that context they pressurised Stormont for a positive response to Lemass's north–south cooperation proposals. However, this attempt at Anglo-Irish *détente* was basically at cross purposes. Lemass pursued cooperation with the north in the belief that it would contribute to an undermining of the border; London pursued better relations with Dublin as an end in itself. To this end, the British government was prepared to encourage a change in attitude at Stormont, but nothing more. Dublin mistook the British elite's irritation at Unionist inflexiblity as a sign of a more profound desire for movement on constitutional change. The British position in the 1960s, as in 1921, was to favour an accommodation with 'flexible' Irish Nationalists, to expect a contribution from Unionists to this process, but to baulk at any suggestion that would involve a frontal clash with Stormont.

Yet this whole approach was a reflection of the profound lack of knowledge of Irish conditions which the 1921 settlement had created. Drawing Ireland closer may have made sense in broader political and even strategic terms, but to expect the Unionist regime – even with a modernising leader – to be part of this process contributed sigificantly to its destablisation and thus to the frustration of a narrower if more immediate interest: that of preventing the British state from having to intervene directly in the Ulster conflict.

NOTES

1. O'Brien, B., *The Long War: The IRA and Sinn Fein from Armed Struggle to Peace Talks*, Dublin 1995, p211.
2. *Setting the Record Straight: A Record of Communication between Sinn Fein and the British Government October 1990–November 1993*, published by Sinn Fein in Belfast, January 1994, p17.
3. Bew, P., Gibbon, P., and Patterson, H., *Northern Ireland 1921-1995: Political Forces and Social Classes*, new and revised edition, London 1996, p31.
4. Sir Warren Fisher of the Treasury commented, 'Are we never to be allowed by Ulster to come to terms with the South? Is the tail always going to wag the dog?' quoted in Deidre McMahon, *Republicans and Imperialists: Anglo-Irish Relations in the 1930s*, New Haven & London 1986, p276.
5. Boyce, D.G., *The Irish Question and British Politics 1868-1986*, London 1988, p84.
6. McMahon, *op.cit.* p271.
7. Bew *et.al.*, *op.cit.* p74.
8. McMahon, *op.cit.*, p235. Barnett's portrayal of the inter-war governing class as one which had succumbed to the late-Victorian secular religosity inculcated by public schools and Oxbridge and saw international relations in terms of romantic ideals and moral purposes instead of power and strategic calculations has very clear resonances for Anglo Irish relations where it would manifest itself in the notion of drawing the Irish state back into more harmonious relations with the United Kingdom. In this case the influence of this mentality extended well beyond the end of the Second World War. See Correlli Barnett, *The Lost Victory: British Dreams, British Realities 1945-1950*, London 1995, pp123-125.
9. McMahon, *op.cit.* p235.
10. *Ibid.*, p235.
11. *Ibid.*, p235.
12. *Ibid.*, pp236 & 241.
13. *Ibid.*, p236.

14. *Ibid.*, p235.
15. Barton, B., *Northern Ireland in the Second World War*, Belfast 1995, p3.
16. *Ibid.*, p39.
17. McMahon, *op.cit.*, p274.
18. Sir Richard Pim's *Memoirs*, 21 July 1942, quoted in Andrew Gailey, *Crying in the Wilderness, Jack Sayers: a liberal editor in Ulster 1939-69*, Belfast 1995, p17. Churchill, after the war, gave the impression in private conversation with Basil Brooke , the Unionist prime-minister, that he was in favour of Irish unity though 'not by force and only with our consent.' Quoted in Brian Barton, 'The Impact of World War II on Northern Ireland and on Belfast-London Relations', in P. Catterall and Sean McDougall, *The Northern Ireland Question in British Politics*, London 1996, p67.
19. Bew *et. al.*, p107.
20. 'The 1948 Political Settlement with the Irish Republic', paper prepared by the Commonwealth Relations Office for those participating in the Anglo-Irish trade talks in 1957, PRO, MAF40/471, 9 February 1956.
21. Bew, P., and Patterson, H., *Sean Lemass and the Making of Modern Ireland*, Dublin 1982, p41.
22. Memo to Prime-Minister, PRO, MAF 40/471, 9 February 1956.
23. 'The 1948 Political Settlement with the Irish Republic', *op.cit.*
24. Lyne, T., 'Ireland, Northern Ireland and 1992: The Barriers to Technocratic Anti-Partitionism' in *Public Administration*, vol.68 Winter 1990.
25. Farrell, B., *Sean Lemass*, Dublin 1982, p113.
26. *Frontier Sentinel*, 20 September 1947.
27. Farrell, *op.cit.*, p113.
28. 'Economic Relations with the Irish Republic', PRO Cab 129/100, 5 February 1960.
29. PRONI Cab 4/1116, 10 February 1960.
30. 'Economic Relations with the Irish Republic: A Memorandum for the Northern Ireland Government', PRONI Cab4/1115 2 February 1960.
31. See cabinet discussion of Cross-Border Trade PRONI Cab4/1118.
32. 'Economic Relations with the Irish Republic', *op.cit.*
33. He made these comments on a visit to Dublin in June 1963 when he lunched with the former Irish ambassador to London who reported his remarks to the Department of External Affairs, NAD, Department of the Taoiseach, S17400C 15 July 1963.
34. Gailey, *op.cit*, p81.
35. Phoenix, E., 'O'Neill/Lemass meeting caused unease', *Irish Times*, 3 January 1996.
36. 'Partition: Government Policy', letter from W.P. Fay to Secretary of Department of External Affairs' NAD, Department of Taoiseach, S 9361k/63 10 April 1963.
37. *Ibid.*
38. *Irish Times*, 17 October 1963.
39. See his speech to Dublin South Central Branch of Fianna Fail where he invited unionists 'to note the contrast between their economic situation and the dynamism which is developing in the rest of Ireland', *Irish Times*, 13 May 1961.

40. Report of a meeting with Sandys NAD, Department of Taoiseach, S9361K/63, 15 November 1963.
41. *Ibid.*
42. 'Peterborough column', *Daily Telegraph*, 22 March 1965; 'It was he (Lord Longford) who first floated the compromise, now said to attract Mr. Wilson, of a United Ireland within the British Commonwealth.'
43. *Irish Times*, 16 October 1959.
44. Report of meeting with Duncan Sandys, NAD, Department of the Taoiseach 59361K/63 15 November 1963.
45. T.J. McKiernan to H.J. McCann, NAD, Department of External Affairs, P262/1 19 March 1963.
46. *Irish Press*, 17 October 1963.
47. Draft of letter from Mr Havekin to Harold Wilson, NAD, Department of External Affairs, 305/14/ 356, 5 November 1963.
48. C. Cremin to H.J. McCann, NAD, Department of Taoiseach 59361K/63, 5 December 1963.
49. Letter from Patrick McSorley to Sean Lemass, NAD, Department of Taoiseach S19585C/95 , 22 March 1964.
50. Account of Lemass/Wilson meeting, NAD, Department of External Affairs 305/14/30311 16 March 1964.
51. Letter from Eamonn Andrews to Sean Lemass, NAD, Department of Taoiseach, S10739/95, 21 October 1964.
52. Lemass to Eamonn Anderws, NAD, Department of Taoiseach S10739C/95.
53. 'Suggested Civil Service Level Discussions with Six County Representatives', NAD, Department of Taoiseach, S16272E/63, 28 September 1963.
54. Bew, P., Gibbon, P., and Patterson, H., *op.cit.*, pp160-161. See also Peter Rose, 'Labour, Northern Ireland and the Decision to Send in the Troops', in Peter Catterall and Sean McDougall, *The Northern Ireland Question in British Politics*, London 1996. Soskice was 'so pro-Unionist that he would have qualified to be an honourary member of the Orange Order' p88. In fact Soskice had initially questioned the Home Office advice that allegations of discrimination and gerrymandering fell within the range of matters for which Stormont had full responsibility. However, he subsequently informed Wilson that he had 'reluctantly concluded that it would be constitutionally wrong and most unwise in practice, at least for the present.' Quoted in Eamonn Phoenix, 'Sympathy but no action on discrimination', *Irish Times*, 3 January 1995.
55. Memorandum by B Gallagher on discrimination pamphlet, NAD, Department of External Affairs 305/14/303, 12 August 1964.
56. He publicly referred to this in a speech in Belfast after his retirement and provoked an angry reponse from Eddie McAteer, Leader of the Nationalist Party: see NAD, Department of External Affairs 305/14/360, 2 November 1967.
57. Note from P. McCabe to Mr. Nolan, NAD, Department of External Affairs 305/14/360, 5 July 1967.
58. Mr. Nolan to Mr.O'Sullivan, NAD, Department of External Affairs, 305/14/360, 6 July 1967.

59. Note on telephone conversation with Mr. McAteer, NAD, Department of External Affairs 305/14/360 27 October 1967.
60. *Belfast Telegraph*, 27 January 1967.
61. Letter from Patrick J. Gormley MP to Jack Lynch, NAD, Department of External Affairs, 305/14/356 30 January 1967.
62. Letter from Jack Lynch to Patrick J. Gormley, NAD, Department of External Affairs, 305/14/356

2

THE AMBIGUITIES OF THE ANGLO-IRISH AGREEMENT

A key element in the rationale of the 'peace process' that culminated in the eighteen month IRA cease-fire (August 1994-February 1996) was that, since the Northern Ireland moderates had consistently failed to bridge the divide and neutralise their respective extremes, there needed to be comprehensive negotiations to embrace the two extreme poles of the problem. Implicit here was a reference to the various earlier attempts, starting with the Sunningdale Agreement of 1973, to establish a legitimate set of governmental institutions based on 'power sharing' and an 'Irish Dimension'. Such an agreement between mainstream Unionism and the constitutional Nationalism of the SDLP was designed to politically marginalise Republicanism. The collapse of the power-sharing experiment in 1974 under the pressure of the Ulster Workers' Council strike was subsequently read by key British policy makers as showing the virtual impossiblity of a settlement which would have at its heart a set of devolved institutions of government based on an accord between Unionism and constitutional Nationalism.

Some political scientists have given their own academic twist to the judgement by describing British policy in the period 1972-74 as an attempt to apply the 'consociational model' developed by Arendt Lijphart for governing deeply divided societies. This necessarily failed because the various conditions identified by Lijphart for a successful consociational deal – for example, political elites unconstrained by hard-line followers or threatened by more extreme parties in their own electorate – did not exist in Northern Ireland.[1] The various 'solutions' suggested since by these constitutional engineers have varied from support for the Anglo-Irish Agreement (misconceived as an exercise in 'coercive consociationalism'), joint sovereignty and ultimately – until its collapse – support for the Reynolds–Major 'peace process'. Even such a politically astute commentator as Robin Wilson, former editor of the Belfast monthly magazine *Fortnight*, has tended to draw over-simplified lessons from the collapse of the Sunningdale strategy: that it was ultimately unviable because it represented a 'conservative' accommodation between elites.[2]

The Sunningdale strategy collapsed under the weight of a very specific set of conflicting forces and as the balance of forces has changed since then it is not far-fetched to envisage a Sunningdale Mark Two. It is too early to write off a settlement negotiated between mainstream political forces in favour of the ethereal notions of 'new constitutionalism' or a 'turn to civil society' put forward by Robin Wilson.[3]

A key factor which, it is generally agreed, served to undermine support for power-sharing in the Protestant population in 1974 was the Irish government's pushing – largely at the behest of the SDLP – for a Council of Ireland with extensive harmonising and executive functions. As one of the architects of the Sunningdale Agreement has subsequently noted, the only compensating factor would have been a referendum on Articles 2 and 3 of the Irish Constitution (whereby the south laid claim to the north), but the weakening of Lemass's legacy of a more accommodating attitude to the Northern state in Fianna Fáil made this an impossible project.[4] Instead, a court case by a dissident ex-Fianna Fáil cabinet minister, Kevin Boland, forced the Dublin government to argue that their statement on the status of Northern Ireland in the agreement did not acknowledge that Northern Ireland was part of the United Kingdom, nor did it conflict with Articles 2 and 3 of the Constitution. This was, FitzGerald acknowledges, a 'politically disastrous' argument in relation to Unionists.[5]

However, Edward Heath's desire for a settlement which bound the SDLP into structures of government was so strong that he provided no support for Unionist reservations on the Council of Ireland. As the British civil servant who was Permanent Under-Secretary at the Northern Ireland Office when the new Labour administration arrived after the February elections has subsequently noted, the Sunningdale structures were probably well beyond what was possible in the circumstances of the time: '... I thought to myself that this is so complicated and to try and introduce it into one of the most disturbed societies that we can find anywhere must be doomed to failure ... I think the whole thing was too complex, too dependent on people behaving reasonably, and so on ...'

With the benefit of hindsight, he thought that it would have been better for direct rule to have continued for a much longer period before this type of sophisticated constitutional experimentation was tried. However, this, he also pointed out, failed to acknowledge a political imperative 'to say that we want to devolve government again … in order to keep the British population on our side, to keep parliament content and offer a hope to the army that they might not have to sit there for as long as they did in the reign of Elizabeth 1.'[6]

This points up the clear British dilemma. Stormont had been maintained, far beyond its capacity for progressive reform, to avoid direct British reinvolvement in Irish affairs. Though by the time of direct rule a number of senior Tories like Peter Carrington and William Whitelaw were prepared to think along Wilsonian lines that the only ultimate solution was unity, it was recognised that this would be a long-term process. In large part this reflected a degree of disdain for the abilities and capacities of Dublin politicians. A prolonged period of direct rule was rejected as it was at variance with the consensus that this was ultimately an Irish problem. Power-sharing devolution plus the Irish Dimension would, it was hoped, provide interim structures which, while giving stability, would be open to constitutional change. Direct rule and structural reform might have worked but only at the cost of what looked like permanent reinvolvement in Northern Ireland. The problem was how to prevent an unrealistic set of proposals for a Council of Ireland which was seen as a 'vehicle which will trundle us into an Irish Republic'[7] from undermining the realisable project of power-sharing.

As Dr FitzGerald now informs us, there was very little stomach in either the Dublin bureaucracy or the cabinet for such an ambitious vision of the Council. Departmental heads in Dublin, led by the Department of Finance, wanted a minimalist Council of Ireland for a mixture of motives, predominantly those of cost and convenience for existing institutions and practices.[8] Nor was there a burning desire in the rest of the cabinet for significant involvement in the north. The Taoiseach, Liam Cosgrave, had clearly favoured a gradualist approach, warning of the dangers of foregrounding the partition issue; but though such a position could be easily maintained against northern Nationalist criticism in the 1960s this was no longer the case. The government's 'backsliding' on the National Unity issue was upbraided by the SDLP members to the Northern Ireland Assembly and a delegation was dispatched south to pressure for a rethink which came quickly.[9] It was clear that a new combative northern nationalism would do all in its power to hold southern governments to the ideology inscribed in its constitution. The political significance of proposals for north–south institutions had been radically and damagingly altered. For Lemass they were seen as a means for breaking down barriers of mutual ignorance and suspicion, a process which would in time, it was hoped, make a coming together of north and south a possiblity. Now the fevered conditions which existed in the north led to them being seen as having a much more pro-active role and as representing, not a mutually agreed agenda between Dublin and Belfast, but rather a purely Nationalist project.

In reality the ambitious proposals for a Council of Ireland, while dooming the power-sharing experiment, far outran the capacity or desire of the Irish state for significantly deeper involvement in the north. FitzGerald records the growing fear touching on panic in governmental circles in Dublin when they detected an undeclared consideration of the withdrawal option by Wilson's government after the Ulster Workers' Council (UWC) strike:

> Such a possibility had not previously entered our heads, now for a while we felt that we had to take it seriously, especially in the view of the statement by NIO officials on a visit to Dublin on 5 June 1974 to the effect that withdrawal was not *at that time* being considered by British ministers as an option. In the year that followed much of our efforts were directed towards examining how we should handle such a situation were it to arise. At the same time our diplomatic efforts were directed towards ensuring that it did not occur.[10] (emphasis in original)

These efforts included asking Henry Kissinger to intercede with the British against any plan for withdrawal.[11]

In fact it appears that Harold Wilson and his closest advisers had decided that the overwhelming victories of anti-power-sharing Unionists in the February elections had doomed the power-sharing executive, and a committee of four, working out of the Cabinet Office, had been considering a range of radical proposals *before* the Ulster Workers' Council strike, including dominion status and what Wilson referred to as his 'nuclear option' – British withdrawal. The group consisted of Wilson, his press secretary Joe Haines, Bernard Donoghue, head of his policy unit, and Robert Armstrong who was Wilson's Principal Private Secretary. Nevertheless, just as his more radical impulses after 1968 had been overruled, the 'nuclear' option was eventually discarded as likely to make matters worse.

There is some indication that Wilson's interest in radical action on Ireland reflected the exhaustion of his modernisation project in the rest of the United Kingdom, that this was a last desperate search for 'historic' status. Certainly, it came to nothing in the face of the scepticism of his colleagues and his own style of leadership: 'The point about Wilson is that he himself was not the kind of Prime Minister who would grasp any nettles, so if Whitehall was negative he was not going to do it'.[12]

The debate itself did serve some purpose in that it allowed civil servants negotiating the Provisional IRA cease-fire of 1975 to suggest that the government had in fact decided on withdrawal. However, if withdrawal was ultimately ruled out – in part because those who opposed it in London were able to enlist the support of the Dublin administration – the return to direct rule, particularly in the pro-active and implicitly Unionist way it was presented by the Labour Secretary of State, Roy Mason, was not to prove an acceptable long-term means of managing the conflict. This failure in part reflected the negative effects of direct rule on Nationalist politics in the north, where it encouraged the SDLP to shift towards a more traditionalist Nationalism. It also reflected the degree to which the political effect of indefinite direct rule was to alienate the Dublin government, a trend which ran counter to the underlying tendency of the British political elite since the 1950s to seek more amicable relations with the Irish state.

This conciliating tendency was temporarily disrupted by the eruption of northern violence. While on the Irish side this produced a recrudescence of traditional anti-partitionism and put the political legatees of Lemass under pressure, on the British side it encouraged some manifestations of what a former British Ambassador to Dublin termed the 'Isle of Wight syndrome': a tendency to forget that Ireland was an independent state.[13] Wilson was a prime example: from his meeting with the IRA in Dublin in 1972 when he was leader of the Opposition, which caused consternation in the Irish government, to his 'nuclear option', which seems to have given no consideration to Dublin attitudes. Lord Donoghue found this incongruous: 'I must say that the thing that astonished me when I first got into government in early 1974 was all this discussion about Ireland, almost without consideration of the Republic ... to me the idea that you could deal radically with Northern Ireland without involving the Republic astounded me.'[14]

Wilson's policy review did, in fact, look at the possibility of a policy initiative with significant Dublin involvement as well as input from Europe and the United States, although Wilson clung to withdrawal, what Donoghue called 'this barmy solution'. When the UWC strike threatened to destroy the executive, Wilson demanded that Donoghue extract from the Treasury the cost of running Northern Ireland, but apart from indirect use of the information in his television broadcast during the strike, where he referred to 'spongers', his exasperation and urge to withdrawal had no significant policy effects.

Wilson had favoured Merlyn Rees as Secretary of State for Northern Ireland because he saw him as more open to radical options than the former Home Secretary, James Callaghan, or Roy Mason, at that time Minister of Defence.[15] However, the relatively modest conclusions of his policy review group appear to have put an end to Wilson's more radical urges. Even the proposals for bringing in Dublin were ignored as the government relapsed into a fundamental pessimism about the possibility of initative that would not make the situation worse. This was the context for the ill-starred Convention and the negotiations with the Republican movement which led to the cease-fire in 1975. Although the cease-fire proved extremely damaging to the IRA and for a while under Mason it appeared that the British had adopted policy of positive and reformist direct rule, this was more a reflection of Callaghan's own suspicion of grand initiatives than a sustainable policy consensus.

However, semi-permanent direct rule was an unappetising prospect for Britain. Underlying economic tendencies could only discourage this approach. As shown elsewhere in this book the consistent trend since the early 1970s has been for an upward spiralling in the size of the subvention. At the same time the brutally contemptuous attitudes at times taken to the Irish state have been mellowed by the effects of joint membership of the Common Market, while the same process has perhaps encouraged an over-confident feeling on the part of some members of the Irish political elite that while unity was not on – for economic reasons – Europe would provide the context for a system of joint sovereignty in the north. Ironically it would be under the premiership of a politician most publicly associated with the defence of British sovereignty that Irish aspirations were partially satisfied.

THATCHER AND NORTHERN IRELAND

Given the degree to which Thatcherism has been presented as an ideologically-driven project by both left and right commentators, it is not surprising that the signing of the Anglo–Irish Agreement sent out shock waves that extended far beyond the Unionist community. Thus Gaffikin and Morrisey:

> Though, in its present development, the Agreement falls far short of actual joint government, it does unquestionably amount to a qualification of British sovereignty.
>
> As such it was a remarkable decision by Margaret Thatcher. After all, isn't sovereignty this indubitably sacrosanct political substance, for which young soldiers were dispatched to Goose Green ... it is difficult to identify any concept more revered in the lexicon of Thatcherism.[16]

As will be seen in the analysis of the process of negotiation which led to the Agreement, Thatcher's concerns about anything that could be represented as a derogation of British sovereignty, had substantial effects. At the same time other conflicting impulses left their mark: the desire to achieve an 'historic' settlement and secure a decisive blow against the IRA. 'Thatcherism' had a contradictory character: 'Every detailed study of the Thatcher government has revealed the ambiguities that were inherent in the working out of the project'.[17] Her Northern Ireland policy was not immune from such contradictions.

It is impossible to calculate the effect of Thatcher's concerns about sovereignty without first introducing what can be deciphered of her views on the union and the Unionists. Here the conventional wisdom is set out in a quotation from a non-attributable NIO source given by McGarry and O'Leary, who claimed that, up until the negotiations, she had shown only 'the most philistine of unionist prejudices'.[18] When Garret FitzGerald met her new Secretary of State for Northern Ireland in the autumn of 1981, Prior told him that Thatcher was 'really a unionist at heart'.[19] But as FitzGerald's and other accounts show, this 'Unionism' did not extend to much sympathy for Unionism as a political force. Thus, at her first summit with FitzGerald in November 1981, she agreed that the SDLP were a 'courageous' and 'moderate' party in contrast with the Unionists.[20]

In so far as we can use the, admittedly sparse, evidence to reveal her attitude to Ulster Unionism, it does not appear to have departed significantly from the common metropolitan tendency to identify Unionism with its most strident and inflexible manifestations. It is also the case that what Aughey has termed the 'inarticulateness'[21] of mainstream Unionism meant that it was incapable of producing a response to the perceived 'crisis' of a potentially rampant Sinn Fein, which was the apparently 'historic' implication of FitzGerald's approach.

Gamble has noted of Thatcherism that it was 'both highly reactionary in its attachment to traditional constitutional forms and highly radical in its diagnosis of the causes of Britain's malaise'.[22] Here we have an important clue to the ambiguities in the Agreement. Although the Unionists' support for the existing framework of the British state and their perceived status as the victims of IRA violence ensured some sympathy from Thatcher, their, and the whole province's, massive dependence on the support and intervention of central government, meant that there was no instinctive support for the existing forms of the *status quo* in Ulster: the Union might be safe with Thatcher but, given what Riddell has termed her 'self-conscious radicalism', its continued reproduction in Ireland was seen to demand an unprecedented institutional shift to accommodate constitutional nationalism.[23]

In 1979, the Conservatives were elected on a manifesto whose references to Northern Ireland had had a minimalist and integrationist tone, reflecting the approach of their principal Northern Ireland spokesman, Airey Neave. Although a close personal friend and political ally of Thatcher, there is nothing to suggest that, before his assassination by the INLA, Neave had imparted much knowledge of, or interest in, Northern Ireland to the future prime minister.

Thatcher had been forced by a combination of IRA spectaculars – the murder of Lord Mountbatten and his party, and the killing of 18 British soldiers on the same day, 27 August 1979 – and an intensification of American pressure, into the attempt by her first Secretary of State, Humphrey Atkins, to obtain agreement from local political forces on a devolutionist settlement. But, given that the British government ruled out not simply the discussion of Irish unity, confederation, independence or the constitutional status of Northern Ireland, but even the discussion of an Irish Dimension, the response of the SDLP was predictable. An increasingly Nationalist undertow, which had developed in the party during Roy Mason's period in Stormont Castle, reacted strongly against the inclination of the SDLP leader, Gerry Fitt, to accept the British conditions. Fitt was forced to resign and was replaced by John Hume who was convinced of the impossibility of an 'internal' solution.

Hume's accession to the leadership of the SDLP marked the advent of a more openly Nationalist mood in the party as a whole and boded ill for the Atkins initiative. Given that the Official Unionists were boycotting the talks and that Paisley made it clear that what he was interested in was majority rule devolution, it was only a matter of time before, in November 1980, the government formally admitted the collapse of the initiative. Thatcher had shared Airey Neave's sceptical view of the possibility of a power-sharing settlement, and though forced into the Atkins initiative by American pressure, she had made clear her own inclination to a more Caesarist approach in an interview with the *New York Times*: 'We will listen for a while. We hope we will get agreement. But then the government will have to make some decisions and say, having listened to everyone, we are going to try this or that, whichever we get most support for'.[24]

It was thus unsurprising that she embarked on a much more clearly inter-governmental approach within a month of the public collapse of the Atkins talks. But the quick derailing of the Anglo–Irish process by, first the Irish exaggeration of its constitutional implications, and then the imbroglio created by divergences over the Falklands war, seemed to foreclose the terrain which would have allowed the scope for what Young describes as her 'executive compulsion to act'.[25] Instead there was her reluctant involvement in yet another initiative dependent on the accommodationist inclinations of Northern Ireland's local politicians in which she had, not unreasonably, little faith.

The political benefits which the Provisionals were accruing from the Hunger Strikes of 1980 and 1981 – the election of Bobby Sands in a Westminster by-election in March 1981; two more prisoners elected to the Dáil in June 1981; and then, after Sands' death, the return of his election agent, Owen Carron, to the same Westminster seat – produced demands for the most radical reappraisal of existing British strategy. Thus, in a major editorial on 16 August 1981, the *Sunday Times* articulated a powerful if despairing demand for a commitment to a renunciation of British sovereignty, not in favour of a united Ireland, but of an independent Northern Ireland. The analysis of the impasse was highly tendentious:

> The essential point can be simply put. It is that the rival nationalisms of the two Northern Irish factions are both negative … Catholics want an end to British rule. Protestants cannot abide the idea of Irish rule. These are the root impulses, and in a country of long memories they will not

change. Current British policy fails because it flouts the first impulse. A solution must acknowledge both.

We have already criticised this common (among the British political elite) historicist approach to understanding Northern Ireland for ignoring the existence of significant internal divisions within each 'tradition' and also for, conveniently, obscuring the contribution of British policies to the solidification and deepening of communal division.[26] The point here, however, is to bring out the powerful effects such a mindset could have on policy formation. There was little possibility that the British government would seriously consider the positive proposal of the editorial. It would have meant a severe and inevitable conflict with the Dublin government and the SDLP, both of whom, realistically, feared that an independent state would be hegemonised by a supremacist, Protestant regime. However, what was influential was the fundamental pessimism about the possibility of a serious historic compromise between Unionism and Nationalism. This was, of course, compatible with a number of strategic options – including the integrationist impulses of Neave. But integrationism was unattractive because it threatened precisely to deepen involvement in an area which, while Thatcher felt it was juridicially an integral part of the union and had to be defended against terrorism, there is no evidence she felt was anything else than culturally and politically a place apart. Integrationism also failed to deal with her fixation on extracting better security cooperation from Dublin. Also, as the Atkins initiative demonstrated, Thatcher would not have considered any initiative unlikely to win the support of the United States.

Despite the 'special relationship' which had made the US government reluctant to voice opinions on Northern Ireland, and what Irish diplomats perceived as a State Department bias towards London, the mid-1970s had seen a concerted effort by the Irish Department of Foreign Affairs under Garret FitzGerald to reduce support for the IRA in the United States and build a political alliance on Capitol Hill that was sympathetic to the cause of constitutional nationalism.

The success of the Irish effort was first manifest when four influential Irish-American politicians: Senators Edward Kennedy and Daniel Moyniyhan, Speaker 'Tip' O'Neill and Governor Hugh Carey of New York issued an anti-IRA statement on St Patrick's Day 1977. By the beginning of the 1980s the group had become a formal Capitol Hill organisation: the Friends of Ireland. Disturbingly for the British government, one of the earliest manifestations of the new more effective Irish-American presence was the decision at the end of August 1979 by the State Department to suspend the sales of handguns to the RUC. With the change in administration from Carter to Reagan in 1981 there were Irish fears that there would be a regression to a more traditional position. However, by this time the Irish had developed good relations with some senior Republicans. Most significant of these was the prominent Irish-American, Judge William Clarke, a former Californian Supreme Court Judge who was to hold a series of senior positions in the Reagan administration. Initially Deputy Secretary of State, he went on to become National Security Adviser. Sean Donlon who, as Irish Ambassador to the USA was at the core of these developments, has left this description of Clarke's significance:

> No matter what post he held, he was the key player on Irish matters in the US administration in the first half of the 1980s, and his work, combined with that of Tip O'Neill in his pivotal position as Speaker and *de facto* leader of the US political establishment, ensured that there was in Washington a bipartisan network capable of responding to Irish needs.[27]

This more effective presence was clearly a factor that the British had to take account of when calculating which strategy to pursue once the impasse of the devolutionist approach was obvious. Any approach which alienated the Irish government now clearly carried the risk of attracting adverse attention in the US, even with a Republican administration in power. Thatcher's own strong desire to reassert an international role for Britain in junior partnership with the United States, coupled with the warmth of her relationship with Reagan, served to strengthen the Irish position.

Common membership of the EC would have also inclined the British government towards an intergovernmental approach. As Patrick Keatinge has noted, we must be cautious about overplaying the role of the EC: 'Membership of international organisations has moderated the bilateral relationship but there are definite limits to the extent to which it has facilitated the adoption of new policies'.[28] Nevertheless, common membership had meant increased diplomatic contact and a greater facility of communication between British and Irish negotiators. The two civil servants at the centre of the negotiations for the Anglo–Irish Agreement, Robert Armstrong and Dermot Nally, had already worked together in 1979 in preparation for economic summits when Ireland had the presidency of the EC's Council of Ministers.[29] At a basic level of an increasing density of ministerial and bureaucratic interchange, it probably made the British more willing to consider some kind of inter-governmental approach.

NEGOTIATIONS

At the heart of the Agreement, as perceived by one of the key figures on the Irish side, was the creation of an 'intergovernmental mechanism absolutely without precedent, whereby one government (ours) makes all the proposals so far as Northern Ireland is concerned, and the other government is obliged to enter a process of determined efforts to resolve differences.'[30] This refers to the core institution of the Agreement: the Intergovernmental Conference. This body, jointly chaired by the Secretary of State and an Irish minister, was intended to have regular and frequent meetings to deal on a regular basis with a very broad range of issues from cross-border cooperation to 'political matters'. To describe this, as O'Leary does, as the 'formalisation of inter-state cooperation' is to under-estimate its significance.[31] The Intergovernmental Conference was created within the framework of the Anglo-Irish Intergovernmental Council established by the agreement of Thatcher and FitzGerald in November 1981. This deepening of inter-state cooperation represented the return to an approach first developed by Thatcher after her disillusion with Atkins's attempt to develop new devolutionary structures in the province in 1979-80. In her joint communiqué with Charles Haughey after the Dublin summit of 8 December 1980, Thatcher acknowledged Britain's 'unique relationship' with Ireland; she also permitted the establishment of joint study groups to find ways of expressing this uniqueness in 'new institutional structures'. The two premiers agreed to devote the next of their twice yearly meetings to 'special consideration' of the 'totality of relationships within these islands'. But Irish attempts to oversell the significance of the summit angered Thatcher and soured her relationship with Haughey.[32] This was the context in which the leader of Fine Gael and the next Irish Prime Minister attempted to construct an effective rapport with Thatcher. At its core, initially at least, was the principle that 'my enemy's enemy is my friend'.

FitzGerald had bitterly attacked Haughey's nomination as Taoiseach for among other things,

> a narrow and dangerous nationalism ... a patriotism which effectively excludes one million Irishmen and women from the nation as they conceive it ... the patriotism of men and women who do not believe in seeking unity by agreement, but who crave after it by constraint.[33]

By attacking Haughey for attempting to negotiate a deal with Britain over the head of the Unionists, and emphasising that changes in the relationships between the two Irish states could only be brought about by agreement, he was then viewed with a degree of warmth by some Unionists. FitzGerald's reputation in British elite circles was high. He was usually perceived as a major improvement on Haughey and his unreconstructed Nationalism. This reputation was enhanced by FitzGerald's decision to use a radio interview in September 1981 about the first three months of the Fine Gael-Irish Labour Party Coalition Government, to make the case for constitutional reform in the south as a means of transforming north south relations.

> I want to lead a crusade, a republican crusade to make a genuine republic ... I believe we would have a basis on which many Protestants in the North would be willing to consider a relationship with us. If I were a Northern Protestant today, I canot see how I could be attracted to getting involved with a state that is itself sectarian – not in the acutely sectarian way that Northern Ireland was ... the fact is our laws and our Constitution, our practices, our attitudes reflect those of a majority ethos and are not acceptable to Protestants in Northern Ireland.[34]

At this time, FitzGerald was interested in initiating discussions with northern Unionists, which he hoped would accelerate a process of rethinking the traditional Nationalist project. His acerbic comments on the 'illusions of many southerners about the possibility of persuading Northern Unionists to join one day with the kind of state we had become during sixty years of independence'[35] formed part of the basis for a substantial personal rapport with Thatcher. At their first summit in November 1981 she was still smarting from what she considered to be Haughey's opportunistic exploitation of the communiqué published after her summit with him. Then, as later, she displayed a concern for possible Unionist reaction to the institutional deepening of Anglo–Irish relations. Nevertheless this did not prevent her from agreeing to the publication of civil service joint studies resulting from her agreement with Haughey, nor to the establishment of the Anglo–Irish Council, which was to provide a regular mechanism for summits between the two heads of government. Unionist MPs were aghast at the creation of the Council and at what they perceived to be Thatcher's apparent neutrality on the issue of Irish reunification at the press conference after the summit and in the House of Commons. This was the context in which she made her much mis-quoted remark that 'Northern Ireland is part of the United Kingdom – as much as my constituency is'. This is very different in implications from the usual misquotation, 'Northern Ireland is as British as Finchley'.[36]

As FitzGerald points out, the change of government shortly afterwards, and the sharp deterioriation of relations occasioned by the clash over EC sanctions against Argentina in May 1982, prevented a regular pattern of meetings between heads of government from being established.[37] But as he also notes, an important bureaucratic decision was made at a meeting of senior Irish and British civil servants in Dublin on 20 January 1982:

> During this meeting difficulties of cooordination on the British side, due to the different roles of the Foreign Office and the Northern Ireland Office, emerged clearly, and our officials accepted that because of these difficulties the cabinet offices should have the cooordinating role. This development proved of enormous importance for the future development of Anglo–Irish relations.[38]

FitzGerald attaches great importance to the role of the British Cabinet Secretary, Sir Robert Armstrong: '… a man with a sense of history and a deep commitment to Anglo–Irish relations'.[39] This reflects his view that, in contrast to the Irish negotiating team, the British side was characterised by deep internal divisions between different institutional voices and interests. It was therefore only through the intense negotiations within the Steering Committee of the Anglo–Irish Intergovernmental Council, between Armstrong and Dermot Nally, FitzGerald's Government Secretary, that progress was achieved. It may also reflect Armstrong's close involvement in the earlier Wilson attempt to consider radical alternatives to the status quo and his knowledge of Unionist capacity to block any initiative which relied largely on an internal pillar of support.

Discussing the British side of the Agreement negotiations, Brendan O'Leary wrote that it was the outcome of an 'institutional process' dominated by the London representatives of the Northern Ireland Office. This meant a continuation of the 'two track' approach developed since the early 1970s. The 'internal track' was to pursue policies to encourage the broadest possible agreement within Northern Ireland for an internal settlement. The 'external track' was to seek the maximum feasible good relations with the Irish Republic and the USA on the Ulster crisis, while ensuring minimum international embarrasment. The Accord had this approach built into it, according to O'Leary.[40]

Accounts now available from a number of key players demonstrate that this analysis is fundamentally flawed. Garret FitzGerald has noted the deep internal divisions on the British side between the Cabinet Office, the Foreign and Commmonwealth Office and the NIO. It is now clear that the dynamic element in the negotiating process came from the Cabinet Office with the support of the Foreign and Commonwealth Office and that the NIO was seen by both as a resistant force: '... the traditionalists in the Northern Ireland Office' as Sir Geoffrey Howe described them.[41] It is also clear that there was little faith in the 'internal track' at the highest level of British calculation. Armstrong represented a direct continuity with the Wilson policy review group who had given up on the possiblities of power-sharing before the UWC strike and had begun to think the 'unthinkable' or at least to see greater Irish involvement as one way of putting an end to direct and unprotected British involvement.

The success of Sinn Fein in the October 1982 elections for a Northern Ireland Assembly produced alarm in Dublin and some lurid predictions of imminent destabilisation of the position of the SDLP.[42] FitzGerald was also informed that due to frustration at the current stalemate in Anglo–Irish relations some British civil servants were 'speculating' about a new Anglo–Irish approach involving joint action of some kind.[43] This was the context in which FitzGerald radically revised his northern strategy, giving priority to heading off growth of support for Republicanism by seeking a 'new understanding' with the British at the expense of his 'cherished objective' of seeking a solution through negotiations with the Unionists.[44]

In the aftermath of the Westminster elections of June 1983 most Irish commentators found it impossible to focus on anything else but the performance of Sinn Fein, which gained 102,000 votes and 13.4 per cent of the poll as against the SDLP's 137,012 and 17.9 per cent. It was assumed in many quarters that the surge of Sinn Fein was irrestible.[45] This was the context in which FitzGerald and his advisers made strenuous efforts to influence the Irish agenda of Thatcher's new administration. The Irish approach was developed by Michael Lillis, Assistant Secretary in the Department of Foreign Affairs in charge of its Anglo–Irish section. For Lillis the key to tackling Catholic alienation was a radical change in the security and judicial systems, which would provide for 'a full and equal Irish role'. This would ensure that nationalists would 'be brought once again to accept the authority of governmental institutions.'[46]

Lillis was the joint chairman of the cooordinating Commission of the Anglo–Irish Intergovernmental Council. This was the bureaucratic hinge of the negotiating process over more than two years. His British counterpart was Sir David Goodall, a senior Foreign Office deputy secretary, then in the Cabinet Office.[47] It was to Goodall on a visit to Dublin in September 1983 that Lillis revealed Irish thinking. Goodall describes it thus: '... a clear signal from Dr FitzGerald that he was prepared drastically to lower nationalist sights on Irish unification in the interests of promoting stability in Northern Ireland and halting the political advances of Sinn Fein. This meant trying to reconcile nationalists to the Union rather than breaking it; but in Dr FitzGerald's view this could only be done if the republic were associated in some institutionalised way with the government of Northern Ireland'.[48] There is a certain disingenuousness in this evaluation. As was clear from the horror-struck response to the news that Wilson was toying with the idea of withdrawal, the Irish political class had no serious interest in unity. Given this, it might have appeared that FitzGerald was asking rather much in return for giving up such a purely rhetorical aspiration. However, not for the first time, those pushing a line of accommodation with Nationalist Ireland displayed a less than sure grasp of Irish realities – in his account of the genesis of the Agreement Sir David Goodall discusses the collapse of the power-sharing government without any reference to the Council of Ireland issue, which played a central role in stimulating Unionist resistance.

Of course, to have recognised this reality would have made it much more difficult to support the strategy embodied in the Agreement. FitzGerald's willingness to 'accept the Union' in return for what amounted to Joint Authority was not fully discussed at the summit at

Chequers in November 1983 as Thatcher, unnerved by a television programme on Joint Sovereignty, refused to discuss the topic in case it was raised in parliament. Yet she was already persuaded that the status quo was unsustainable, and in the aftermath of the summit, ordered a fundamental review of the government's Northern Ireland policy which examined all the options, including re-partition.

What then was Mrs Thatcher's motivation for embarking on such a radical course? Fear of a Sinn Fein breakthrough figured prominently in Dublin's calculations and would appear to have been central in occasioning a relatively open response from Thatcher. The Hunger Strikes and the subsequent electoral successes of Sinn Fein created an atmosphere in which it was easier for her to be persuaded that a new initiative might be considered. As early as December 1982 she had told Goodall 'If we get back next time I think I would like to do something about Ireland'.[49] (Note 'Ireland' not 'Northern Ireland'.) In her perspective, Dublin was a partner in the fight against terrorism; as Goodall puts it: 'She was interested primarily in finding ways of improving the security situation, and in particular of improving cross border cooperation against terrorism between the British and the Irish security forces'.[50] He adds that the negotiations leading to the Agreement occurred because she was prepared to pay a price, 'but when the negotiations got seriously underway I do not believe she had any clear idea of what the price might be'.[51] Others certainly did. For Armstrong, Goodall and Sir Geoffery Howe, the Provisionals were but a symptom of an intractable and costly problem that demanded radical recasting of both the governance structures of Northern Ireland and of Anglo–Irish relations.

Already in September 1983 – in what Goodall refers to as 'tentative' and 'private' negotiations – the British reassured the Irish that Thatcher was taking the problem of Nationalist 'alienation' very seriously, despite her distaste for the 'Marxist' coloration of the term. The Irish proposal for their involvement in maintaining security and order in Northern Ireland was negotiable, provided that the constitutional position of Northern Ireland was ratified in a way that could not be repudiated by a subsequent government – through action on Articles 2 and 3 of the constitution.[52] It was also made clear that Thatcher was adamant that joint sovereignty was not acceptable.

However, some on the British side were capable of suggesting a greater flexibility on this issue. Thus at the November 1983 Chequers Summit, Geoffery Howe and James Prior, the Northern Ireland

Secretary, met Peter Barry, Irish Foreign Minister, and Dick Spring, the Deputy Prime Minister, to discuss modalities of Irish involvement in the administration of Northern Ireland. FitzGerald claims that in these discussions the British went so far as to say that while Joint Sovereignty was ruled out 'without changes in the constitution' there might be some possibility of joint authority.[53] It does appear that at various times in the negotiations Howe was not averse to encouraging Irish hopes of radical constitutional change.[54]

Thatcher's clear willingness to contemplate a major initiative, the good relations between key British and Irish negotiators, particularly Armstrong and Nally and Lillis and David Goodall, and Howe's ambiguities all encouraged an Irish maximalism.[55] Yet the limits of British concession are clearly visible in FitzGerald's own detailed account of the prolonged negotiations. After the Chequers Summit in 1983 Thatcher outlined her idea of a 'basic equation' which had to be the basis of any new initiative. This involved, on the one side, an acknowledgement of the Union – action on Articles 2 and 3 – and on the other, Irish involvement in the government of Northern Ireland with particular emphasis on security.[56] For the British the radical innovation would be their acknowledgement of *some* role for an Irish government in the administration of Northern Ireland, even if this fell short of joint authority. The British had accepted Lillis's idea that the situation of instability and alienation in Northern Ireland could only be dealt with by an Irish 'presence' within the structures of governance, but they consistently resisted the Irish suggestion that this 'presence' had to take the form of the structures of joint authority. When the Forum Report was published on 2 May 1984, the Irish government was ready to submit its elaborated joint authority proposals to the British. FitzGerald had ensured that joint sovereignty was rechristened as 'joint authority' in the Forum Report and tried to persuade Thatcher that it would not derogate from British sovereignty: it was simply a method by which the British government chose to exercise its authority in one part of the UK.[57] Thatcher clearly regarded this as little more than a semantic distinction.

In their formal response to the Irish proposals on 16 July, the British rejected two of the Forum's three constitutional models – a unitary state and a federal Ireland – but were 'more cautious' about the joint authority model. They really wanted to negotiate on the section of the Report which had expressed an openness to other views.[58] While convinced of the positive results of some Irish involvement in the system of government in Northern Ireland as a way of legitimising the state, it was emphasised that this could not be such as would make it reasonable for Loyalist critics to allege a breach of British sovereignty. It was also made clear that Thatcher, while open to hitherto 'unthinkable' ideas, would not tolerate anything that smacked of joint authority.

This appears to have had some effect on the political ambition of the Irish proposals, which were redrawn before being sent as a new memorandum to the British on 31 August 1984. Now the proposal was for a structure within which an Irish minister would have a right to be consulted by the British on a wide range of security, political and social and economic matters in Northern Ireland. The retraction of political ambition was accompanied by demands for a radical restructuring of policing: an unarmed RUC for Protestant areas, a new unarmed force for Catholic areas, and a new joint anti-terrorist force. These three forces were to be the responsibility of a Joint Security Commission.[59] While these new forces were being created Irish forces would be deployed in Catholic areas.

The next few months were to see Irish optimism about the possibility of a radical initiative severely dented. At a meeting in Downing Street Thatcher appeared to rule out even a formal consultative role for the Irish government for fear of the Unionist reaction, while at the same time rejecting the disarming of the RUC or UDR.[60] At a joint negotiating session on 13 October, just after an IRA bomb destroyed the Grand Hotel in Brighton in an attempt to kill Thatcher, the British emphasised that any Security Commission would be only consultative. Now the British were willing to envisage an arrangement of formal consultation as the core of the political initiative but not in terms which the Irish considered sufficiently strong. But the biggest blow to Irish hopes came when the new Secretary of State for Northern Ireland, Douglas Hurd, visited Dublin on 25 October accompanied by Sir Robert Andrew, Permanent Secretary of the Northern Ireland Office.

FitzGerald detected the retrograde influence of Andrew and a predominantly security-orientated approach in Hurd's negativism during the visit.[61] Certainly it was the case that the NIO would have tended to attach more significance to the possible consequences of any initiative within Northern Ireland. In his largely negative response to the Forum Report, James Prior had clearly articulated NIO scepticism about the Lillis idea that a radical initiative would have substantial effects on the core constituency for Republicanism: 'I am convinced that it would not be easy to get elements of the Catholic community to respect any force of law and order'.[62] In the aftermath of the Hurd visit and the even more dispiriting Chequers Summit in November, David McKittrick summed up the NIO position: 'far reaching moves could be dangerous in that they might stir a backlash without actually solving the problem of the alienation of the minority in the north'.[63] Such a viewpoint reflected not, as FitzGerald argues, some blinkered, security-obsessed orientation but the relatively realistic calculations of those who would have to take most responsibility for running the area after any initiative. As a senior NIO official subsequently put it:

> It had to be an agreement which we could live with in the north. The other negotiators would move on to other tasks when the Agreement was signed; but the NIO would have to make it work in the face of bitter Unionist opposition. In so far as there were differences within the British team, I would submit that it was because the NIO had a more realistic view of what was possible in the North and how far the Unionist majority could be pushed without making the Province ungovernable.[64]

The negotiations that led to the Agreement revealed almost as many intra-British contradictions as Anglo–Irish conflicts. The depth of the division between the Cabinet Office/Foreign and Commonwealth Office axis and the NIO was a reality which surfaced throughout the negotiations and is reflected in the ambiguities of the Agreement itself. It makes it impossible to see the agreement as either the outcome of a relatively harmonious working out of 'external' and 'internal' tracks or – as some 'anti-imperialist' analyses would have it – of a coherent counter-insurgency response to the threat of a rampant republicanism.

Even before Thatcher's brusque dismissal of the three Forum models, the Irish negotiators were dismayed at what they perceived as British recalcitrance. The 'basic equation' on offer was a right for the Irish government 'to contribute', on a systematic and institutionalised basis, to the consideration by the United Kingdom government of a range of policy matters, including security, as a means of strengthening the confidence of the minority community in the institutions of government.[65] It was also argued that such a radical departure would undermine the possibilities of devolution on a power-sharing basis, but that the British would want to consider other possibilities for devolution. Thatcher and Hurd were disposed to raise issues which appeared to question the direction of the Armstrong/Nally negotiations. Thatcher's emphasis was on a security commission with an advisory role for a Dublin representative as something that could be agreed without a referendum on Articles 2 and 3. Her profound doubts about the possibility of an agreed devolutionary settlement were reiterated, and perhaps even more disturbingly, she revealed that she had been considering the feasibility of repartition.[66]

FitzGerald argues that the infamous Thatcher press conference, when she brutally dismissed the three Forum proposals, served to obscure the fact that, for some time, negotiations had been carried on without reference to the three Forum models. The fact remains that, like the Hurd visit to Dublin in October, the summit was a blow to some of the core Irish ambitions. It has been argued subsequently, both by FitzGerald and Sean Donlon, that it was only a successful exercise of Irish diplomatic pressure in the USA that prevented the collapse of the negotiations:

> The situation was serious enough to call for US intervention ... Thatcher was persuaded to modify her position and there is no doubt that US intervention played a decisive role ... The Reagan/Thatcher meeting at Camp David in December 1984 was crucial ...[67]

It is the case that Thatcher appears to have been embarrassed by the effects of her press conference and that this may ultimately have enabled the Irish to extract more than seemed possible during the summit itself. The most substantial concession was to allow Ireland institutionalised consultation *without* a referendum on Articles 2 and 3. Thus when Armstrong met Nally in January 1985 he brought a British package, with Thatcher's approval, that, with one significant omission, exactly prefigured the essential features of the agreement to be signed in Hillsborough. The omission was that the British were not obliged to consult the Irish on matters which could be devolved to a Northern Ireland executive.

This reflected an important difference between the British and Irish approaches to the negotiations. The Irish wished to see formal consultation extended to a range of economic and social matters which could be devolved. This reflected their conviction that if these and other potential devolved powers were exercised with Irish involvement it would provide an over-powering incentive for the Unionists to enter a devolved government with the SDLP in order to lessen Irish involvement. Although the British eventually acceded to Irish pressure on this, there is little evidence that they shared the Irish optimism about the 'shoe-horn effect' of this strategy, i.e., that Unionists could be persuaded to enter power-sharing arrangements with the SDLP, a form of what O'Leary has termed 'coercive consociationalism', in order to limit the influence of the Anglo–Irish Inter-governmental Conference.[68] British scepticism here reflects an approach uncluttered by what was probably considered to be the unrealistic aspirations of FitzGerald's revisionist Nationalism.

The only significant Northern Ireland politician to have an input into the negotiations, John Hume, had a perspective on the process which was far removed from the 'coercive consociationalism' model. As he explained to Thatcher at a meeting in London on 15 January 1985, 'This problem was now such that it could not be solved within the limited context of Northern Ireland: a solution had to transcend the area, and there could not be a solution on the basis of interparty talks alone.'[69] An agreement was possible precisely because both the British and Irish sides to the negotiations were agreed on the need to move beyond the search for agreed devolutionary structures. Its ultimate limitation, however, resided in the totally different strategic perspectives into which a similar rejection of an internalist model were inserted.

For Thatcher and the NIO, the unprecedented ceding of a right of consultation to the Irish was originally conceived as the 'big bang' which would tie the Catholic masses to the state and ensure the political and security benefits which would enable the Provisionals to be finally defeated. There is clear evidence of her fear that by conceding too much she would provoke a destabilising Protestant reaction. From the Irish viewpoint, anything short of joint authority and a referendum on Articles 2 and 3 would fail to end Catholic 'alienation' whilst at the same time destabilising relations with the Ulster Unionist community.

Yet, although the combination of NIO 'realism' and Thatcher's concern on the sovereignty issue ensured a less ambitious Agreement than the one contemplated by Armstrong and Howe, there is no disguising the fact that the debate took place on the ground chosen by those interested in decisively shifting the locus of management of the conflict to an Anglo–Irish one. Direct rule had removed Ulster Unionism's prime bargaining counter with those in the British state most keen to encourage the development of better north–south relations: that, whatever its rigidities, the Stormont regime at least preserved the UK's insulation from the Irish Question. The NIO would provide only a muted articulation of Unionist concerns, which would offer little counterweight against those in London now less encumbered in the search for a means whereby British commitments in Ireland could ultimately be attenuated. Direct Rule had removed Ulster Unionism's institutional strength in negotiations with London: without state power, albeit of a limited sort, it found itself easily marginalised by a metropolitan elite with a long-standing tendency to irritated condescension when faced with Unionist obstacles to a more 'rational' ordering of British–Irish relations. Even those 'natives' most likely to give a modulated Unionist input, like Sir Kenneth Bloomfield, head of the Northern Ireland Civil Service and Second Permanent Under-Secretary of State in the NIO, were excluded from knowledge of the negotiating process until it was virtually complete. He has subsequently recorded his 'days and weeks of mental agony' when he was eventually shown the virtually finalised agreement:

> I knew that the new Anglo–Irish Agreement would be deeply resented, not only by active Unionist politicians but by the whole unionist community, whose sense of outrage would be increased by a realisation that the parties to the agreement had included representatives of one of the two major traditions in Ireland, but not the other.[70]

He considered a direct appeal to Thatcher or Armstrong, but rejected the idea as likely to be perceived as 'nothing more than the death agonies of an old Protestant ascendancy.'[71] Thirteen years of direct rule and a radical diminution of the size and self-confidence of the Protestant bourgeoisie had created a situation where even as perceptive, honest and self-critical an official as Bloomfield could anticipate nothing but exasperated rejection from Whitehall and Westminster. In fact, when he did relate his fears to Tom King, who took over from Douglas Hurd in September 1985, King did make a last-minute effort to express his concerns about the content and balance of the agreement to Thatcher – much to the chagrin of Howe.[72] However, by then the impetus for what had already been agreed was unstoppable.

The historic decline in Unionist leverage would be clearly demonstrated when the proposed initiative was finally revealed to the whole cabinent. Nigel Lawson records that, though he had serious doubts about the proposals, which he articulated, he did not oppose it and nor did any other member:

> I had no doubt that the Anglo–Irish Agreement would be a political liability, in the sense that the resulting alienation from the Unionist majority would far outweigh any accretion of support from the Republican minority, and I could not imagine that any objective observer would believe otherwise. The question, however, was whether the domestic political cost would be outweighed by the military benefits that might be expected from greater cooperation from Dublin in the struggle against IRA terrorism and greater cooperation from Washington in preventing the supply of Irish American money and weapons to the IRA ... I was not sufficiently confident of where the balance of advantage lay to oppose the Agreement.[73]

John Cole's account of a cabinet discussion of the proposed agreement just before the summer recess in 1985 would support the idea that Lawson's reservations were typical:

> The Prime Minister herself, while sharing the scepticism, agreed that it was better to go ahead than to abandon the talks. She wanted to be able to indicate to a sympathetic President Reagan that Britain was trying to cooperate with Dublin.[74]

Clearly while potential Unionist outrage was contemplated as a possibility, it was outweighed by the forecasts of security gains and a stronger position internationally. Nowhere was the logic of the Agreement subject to serious examination. In particular, Thatcher's idea of a basic equation was not probed. This had reflected the two central dimensions of the Agreement from her perspective. The first was the need to 'do something' to respond to the political breakthrough of Republicanism and, by enlisting the support of Dublin, to improve cross-border security cooperation against the IRA and move the management of the conflict onto a new level. The second was to achieve this without provoking too massive a Protestant reaction. For Thatcher and the NIO the rationale behind the agreement was similar to that which had lain behind direct rule: to remove a substantial source of Catholic grievance and thus make it easier to marginalise revolutionary nationalism. For Sir Robert Armstrong, Sir David Goodall and Geoffrey Howe, the agreement was attractive as a means of improving relations with Dublin, fire-proofing Britain internationally especially in the United States, and opening up the possibility of gradually lessening British involvement. Thus, when in June 1985 FitzGerald complained that the Irish were being offered too little, Howe stressed the magnitude of what was implicitly involved: 'It would, he said, concede to us a right of involvement in Northern Ireland that he believed (sincerely, in my view) would be the start of an evolving situation of historic significance'.[75]

In 1988 two of the authors had this to say of what they described as 'two inconsistent impulses within the current British political leadership' in relation to the Agreement:

> Mrs Thatcher sees the Agreement primarily as a device (or necessary concession) to win greater security cooperation from Dublin ... Sir Geoffrey Howe in the Foreign Office, on the other hand, is keen gradually to reduce the British stake in Northern Ireland and is thus mainly concerned that the Agreement, as a first step in this process, is kept in being.[76]

We are now in a better position to consider the Armstrong/Howe approach. It is very clearly part of a long-standing elite disposition to draw the Irish state into a closer and more amicable set of relations, in large part to make Britain's commitments in Northern Ireland more manageable and more politically defensible internationally. Sir Geoffrey Howe said the Agreement was 'as much as can be achieved in one generation'. Sir David Goodall has denied that this meant 'as much as could be achieved towards British disengagement and Irish unification.'[77] What Howe meant, Goodall claims, was 'that by creating a framework for crisis management between Dublin and London and acknowledging the nationalist community's right to an Irish Dimension it had in structural terms done as much as could be done in one generation to facilitate a new (but as yet unclear) accommodation between nationalism and unionism in Northern Ireland and between the island of Ireland and the island of Britain'. The long-term future will evolve new relationships between the North and South, Britain and the Republic, and between Britain and Northern Ireland. As he points out, 'This is not the same thing as aiming simply for British "disengagement" from Northern Ireland.'[78] However, it is certainly a perspective which would be considerably more congenial to mainstream Irish nationalism than to Ulster Unionism.

Despite this, from the Irish government's point of view the agreement was considerably less than what could be hoped to alter radically Catholic attitudes to the northern state. For the British, the possibility of significant improvements in the manageability of the internal situation in the north was hemmed in by the decision not to press for a commitment to the deletion of Articles 2 and 3. Thatcher had been persuaded that it would be possible to allow the Irish government a role within the governing structures of Northern Ireland as a defender and advocate of Catholic interests without infringing British sovereignty. This essentially custodial and petitionary role was clearly at variance with the political project enshrined in Articles 2 and 3. However, while Thatcher was originally determined to extract a Dublin commitment on constitutional change, the fallout, particularly in the US, from the 'out ... out ... out' press conference, forced a reluctant acceptance that the Irish would get their new role in the governmental process with their constitution still intact. The result was a stiffening of British resistance to Irish demands for substantive reformist measures in the key areas of justice, security and policing. For the Irish, a new institutionalised role which fell short of their original proposals clearly opened up the possibility that, in FitzGerald's words, the Agreement gave them 'responsibility without power'.[79]

Yet, despite this, the implications of the Agreement were indeed more radical than FitzGerald appears to imply. This was made clear in Sean Donlon's critical review of Mrs Thatcher's account of the Agreement in her memoirs. Thatcher had claimed that the Agreement was no more than consultative in that it simply allowed the Irish Government to put forward views and propositions on Northern Ireland matters. Donlon then quotes from the 'carefully negotiated' unpublished document which contained the agreed answers to the 60 questions most likely to be asked about the Agreement. The full 'catechism' answer is:

> The Conference will be more than just consultation in that the Irish side will put forward the views and proposals on its own initiative as well as being invited to do so: and there is an obligation on both sides in the Conference to make determined effort to resolve any differences: and one of the functions of the Conference will be to promote cross-border cooperation between North and South in Ireland.[80]

Commenting on an analysis of the Agreement made by one of its Irish architects, a leader in the *Irish Times*[81] commented, 'The Agreement was conceived as a dynamic vehicle for change, not as a bureaucratic instrument for the more convenient governance of Northern Ireland'. This encapsulated both the conceptual and strategic gulf between British and Irish approaches to what was signed at Hillsborough Castle. Fundamentally, the logic of the Agreement from London's vista was a shift away from the strategy of legitimising direct rule by the search for structures of devolved government based on power-sharing. As one senior NIO official has put it, 'Although the Agreement paid lip service to devolution it was really an admission that power-sharing in Northern Ireland had not worked and the Nationalist interest could only be protected by Dublin'.[82] Such a logic – which could be extended to develop an argument for joint authority – would not be publicly articulated, and the very figure who made such a radical departure from existing policy possible also ensured that any extension of that logic was only a distant possibility. It was also the case that the pretensions of the Dublin government to real influence would be subject to the clear British determination – long made clear in relation to the narrow range of powers that were on offer for any devolved government – that its role would be representational and its proposals most liable to a positive hearing when they least disturbed the crucial vectors of governance in Northern Ireland.

The problem for this approach was twofold. First, there was no inclination on the part of the Irish government to accept its allotted role, and the ambiguities of the Agreement legitimised an Irish view of the accord as the beginning of a process from which much could be achieved. At the same time, the very fact that the Agreement yoked together issues of substantive reform and the representational role of the Dublin government within the structures of the Northern Ireland state, meant that Unionist resistance to any policy changes would be intensified – every issue of democratic, legal or economic reform would necessarily be inflected by the 'national question'.

The Anglo–Irish Agreement was a profoundly ambiguous document. In part this reflected the need to reconcile major differences of objective on the Irish and British side. However, it also reflected the existence of deep divisions on Irish policy in the British political elite. Ulster Unionism was economically and politically in a much weaker position than it had been in the 1960s or even in the immediate aftermath of Direct Rule, and this in itself weakened the arguments of those in the NIO who were aghast at the proposals acceptable to the Armstrong–Howe axis. Whether it could be marginalised in the way implicit in the thinking of Armstrong and

Howe, remained to be seen. For ultimately the reservations of the NIO proved to be prescient. The foregrounding of the 'Irish Dimension' of the accord inevitably doomed hopes of devolution. Unionists might be marginalised in the short-term, but in the longer term could British hopes of lessening direct involvement be realised without their participation? The Agreement made the possibilities of a compromise in many ways more difficult to perceive. It encouraged Nationalist maximalism for, whatever Thatcher may have been persuaded, its intellectual logic was joint authority. But precisely because such a radical constitutional innovation threatened a total destabilisation of London's relationship with the Unionists, it was not in *reality* an option to be pursued. The result was – on the British side at least – policy incoherence. Once the very specific configuration of events and personalities that moulded the accord on the British side had changed, as it did relatively quickly, it would be up to their successors to try and rescue some coherence from the conflicting impulses embedded in the Agreement. The task has proved a daunting one.

NOTES

1. McGarry, J., and O'Leary, B., *The Politics of Antagonism: Understanding Northern Ireland*, London & Atlantic Highlands 1993, p197
2. Wilson, R., 'Asking the Right Question' in Democratic Dialogue, *Reconstituting Politics* (Belfast 1996), p51.
3. Both notions are put forward in *Reconstituting Politics*.
4. Garret FitzGerald, *All in a Life* (Dublin 1991), p223.
5. *Ibid.*, p226.
6. Sir Frank Cooper at a witness seminar organised by the Institute of Contemporary British History. These witness seminars are to be published soon under the editorship of Peter Catterall.
7. An SDLP politician quoted in *Reconstituting Politics*, p56.
8. *All in a Life*.
9. Bew, P., and Patterson, H., *The British State and the Ulster Crisis: From Wilson to Thatcher* (London 1985) pp57-58.
10. *All in a Life*, p244.
11. *All in a Life*, p259.
12. Lord Donoghue at witness seminar organised by the Institute of Contemporary British History.
13. John Peck, *Dublin from Downing Street* (Dublin 1978), p18.
14. Lord Donoghue, witness seminar.
15. Lord Donoghue, witness seminar.
16. Frank Gaffikin & Michael Morrisey, *Northern Ireland: The Thatcher Years*, p37, London 1990.
17. Andrew Gamble, 'The Entrails of Thatcherism', *New Left Review*,

vol. 198, March/April 1993, p126.
18. McGarry & O'Leary, *The Politics of Antagonism*, p237.
19. *All in a Life*, p381.
20. *Ibid.*, p381.
21. Arthur Aughey, *Under Seige: Ulster Unionism and the Anglo- Irish Agreement* (Belfast & London 1989),p1.
22. Gamble, *op.cit.*, p126.
23. Peter Riddell, *The Thatcher Decade* (Oxford 1989), p3.
24. Bew & Patterson, *op.cit.*, p115.
25. Hugo Young, *One of Us* (London), p466.
26. Bew & Patterson, pp2-3.
27. Sean Donlon, 'Bringing Irish diplomatic and political influence to bear on Washington', *Irish Times* 25 January 1993; see also Andrew J. Wilson, *Irish America and the Ulster Conflict 1968-1995* (Belfast 1995).
28. Patrick Keatinge, 'An Odd Couple' in Desmond Rea (ed.) *Political Co-operation in Divided Societies* (Dublin 1982), p326.
29. Lord Armstrong, 'Ethnicity, the English and Northern Ireland: comments and reflections' in Dermot Keogh & Michael H. Haltzel, *Northern Ireland and the Politics of Reconciliation*, (Cambridge 1993), p205.
30. Michael Lillis, 'New Coalition must work the Anglo-Irish accord as if starting anew', *Irish Times* 30 December 1992.
31. Brendan O'Leary, 'The Anglo-Irish Agreement: Meanings,Explanations, Results and a Defence' in Paul Teague (ed.) *Beyond the Rhetoric: Politics, the Economy and Social Policy in Northern Ireland* (London 1987) p13.
32. Bew & Patterson, *op.cit.* p116.
33. *Irish Times* 12 December 1979.
34. *All in a Life*, pp377-378.
35. *Ibid.*,p379.
36. *Hansard*, November 10 1981, col.427.
37. *All in a Life*, p383.
38. *Ibid.*, p469.
39. *Ibid.*
40. Brendan O'Leary, *op.cit.*, p25.
41. Geoffery Howe, *Conflict of Loyalty* (London 1994), p420.
42. FitzGerald claims that when he returned to office at the end of 1982 he was told that Sinn Fein could win 3 or 4 sets in the next Westminster election while the SDLP could expect only 1 or 2, *All in a Life*, p462.
43. *Ibid.*, pp463-464.
44. *Ibid.*, p462.
45. Bew & Patterson, *op.cit.*, p124.
46. *All in a Life*, p477.
47. *Ibid.*, p478.
48. Sir David Goodall, *The Irish Question*, Headmaster's Lecture given at Ampleforth, November 1992, *Ampleforth Journal*, vol.XCVIII, Part 1 spring 1993, p130.
49. *Ibid.*, p126.
50. *Ibid.*, p129.
51. *Ibid.*

52. *All in a Life*, p475.
53. *Ibid.*, p478.
54. FitzGerald claims that at a meeting with the Irish foreign minister, Peter Barry, in London on 15 March 1984 Howe said that while joint sovereignty was ruled out, joint authority was not although he would prefer it to be called joint responsibility. *Ibid.*, p496.
55. Goodall's review of FitzGerald's autobiography refers to it as 'undoubtedly the fullest and most authoritative account of these negotiations that is likely to appear in our lifetime.' It was symptomatically entitled 'A Prime Minister of Ireland to do business with. *The Tablet* 1 February 1992.
56. FitzGerald, *op.cit.*, p495.
57. *Ibid.*, p501.
58. *Ibid.*, p502.
59. *Ibid.*, p504.
60. *Ibid.*, p506.
61. *Ibid.*, p511.
62. *Irish News* 26 July 1984.
63. David McKittrick, 'Hopes for new initiative from summit fades', *Irish Times* 12 November 1984.
64. In a personal communication.
65. From a British speaking note quoted in FitzGerald, *op.cit.*, p515.
66. *Ibid.*, p517.
67. Sean Donlon, 'Bringing Irish diplomatic and political influence to bear on Washington'.
68. Brendan O'Leary, 'The limits to coercive consociationalism in Northern Ireland', *Political Studies* xxxvii 4, 1989.
69. *All in a Life*, p529.
70. Ken Bloomfield, *Stormont in Crisis* (Belfast 1994), p254.
71. *Ibid.*, p255.
72. *Conflict of Loyalty*, pp424-425.
73. Nigel Lawson, *The View from Number 11* (London 1992), p192.
74. John Cole, *The Thatcher Years* (London 1987), p192.
75. *All in a Life*, p542.
76. Paul Bew & Henry Patterson, 'Ireland in the 1990s-North and South' in Richard Kearney ed. *Across the Frontiers : Ireland in the 1990s* (Dublin 1989) p80.
77. In a personal communication.
78. *Ibid.*
79. *All in a Life*, p565.
80. Sean Donlon, 'Into battle with Mrs.Right' *Irish Times* 23 October 1993.
81. *Irish Times*, 30 December 1992.
82. Personal communication.

3

'NO SELFISH STRATEGIC INTEREST': THE SEARCH FOR A SOLUTION, 1985-92

In an effort to reassure worried Unionists, both the Prime Minister and the Secretary of State for Northern Ireland, Tom King, argued that the Anglo–Irish Agreement would strengthen the union, presumably by reducing the degree of Nationalist alienation. Interestingly enough, Garret FitzGerald agreed. In his contribution to an Edinburgh document, *Northern Ireland – A Challenge to Theology*, Dr FitzGerald spoke of making the 'status quo work'. The Anglo–Irish Agreement signalled the end of Irish irredentism: it was instrumental in promoting recognition that Irish unity would not come about for two generations and then only by consent (as indicated in chapter two, FitzGerald had rejected his previously more optimistic views on this point as unrealistic). Even more remarkably, in his Edinburgh text Dr FitzGerald acknowledged that the Irish government had responsibility without power in the north and that in that sense 'nothing substantive had changed'.

Yet it remained difficult to see why Britain had any material interest in the strengthening of the union; indeed Mr Peter Brooke, Mr King's successor, insisted in November 1990 that Britain had 'no strategic economic' interest in the union. As argued in chapter two, a section of opinion in Whitehall seemed to see the Agreement as the first step in a process of decoupling Northern Ireland from the rest of the United Kingdom, precisely because Northern Ireland was a drain on the political and economic resources of the British state. The implication was that Britain perceived itself – correctly or not – to have no quarrel with Irish constitutional Nationalism (or the gradual and peaceful extension of its hegemony over the whole island of Ireland) but it was opposed to both revolutionary Nationalism and Ulster

Unionism. It hoped to undermine revolutionary nationalism by political means and security cooperation. Unionism it hoped to weaken by holding it at arm's length and keeping it in a reduced and demoralised condition. The union may well have survived such a process but it was unlikely to be strengthened by it.

The early life of the Anglo–Irish Agreement was dominated by the theme of confrontation: Paisley versus Thatcher. It soon became clear, however, that the Unionist campaign against the Agreement – in its most intense form including strikes and attacks on police homes – lacked the resources to win; in particular, the widespread sense of material dependence on the UK Exchequer was profoundly debilitating and prevented the effective mobilisation of mass popular militancy. The Agreement's fundamental unpopularity with Protestants was to remain one of the core facts of Northern Irish political life but this was to co-exist with a growing awareness that the Agreement was more or less a permanent fixture of the governance of Northern Ireland. In January 1986, the mass resignation of Unionist MPs – by far the most striking of the anti-Agreement strategies – led to only a slight increase in the Unionist vote, though there was clear evidence that a significant section of the non-sectarian Alliance party's electorate (in Antrim and in East Belfast) withdrew its support because of that party's perceived acceptance of the Agreement. Equally, however, it became clear that the breaking of the 'Loyalist veto' on significant political change had not in itself opened up the way to a settlement of 'the Troubles'.

In particular, the Agreement failed to marginalise Sinn Fein; Sinn Fein performed relatively weakly in the January by-election but by May 1986 two crucial council by-elections in Sperrin and Erne East demonstrated that the Sinn Fein vote had stabilised. The general election of May 1987 revealed that Sinn Fein's share of the vote had fallen only slightly in the wake of the Agreement: from 11.8 per cent in 1985 to 11.4 per cent in 1987.[1] Political violence also continued to rise steadily during 1987 with almost 100 deaths as against 62 in 1986 and 54 in 1985. Sinn Fein had in fact already peaked before November 1985; on the other hand, the Agreement offered neither the proof of a final decisive defeat of Unionism nor the concrete economic benefits for impoverished urban Catholic ghettoes which might have sapped 'core' republican support. Ironically the Agreement helped Gerry Adams to win his seat in Belfast because, given the sharp resentment that still remained in the Protestant community, the SDLP was deprived of the necessary Protestant votes which – as in 1992 – were essential if that party was to take the West Belfast seat.

The Agreement also had complex effects on the Protestant community. The Paisleyite DUP had started to weaken in the mid-1980s, having at one key point in 1981 actually outpolled the OUP (with 26.6 per cent to the OUP's 26.5 per cent). Perhaps surprisingly, the Agreement did nothing to strengthen the DUP, which appeared impotent in the face of it. Indeed, the DUP's intransigence could be credibly presented as part of the reason for the imposition of the accord itself. Also, the DUP's resistance to relatively marginal concessions to the Catholic community was rendered futile when a concession as substantial as the Agreement was already in place. Hesitantly the DUP entered a pact with the UUP from which it emerged in a weakened state, shorn of some of its most well known leaders; in the 1992 general election it achieved a mere 13.7 per cent of the poll, though its decline stabilised somewhat (17.2 per cent) in the local government elections of May 1993. The DUP's difficulties went hand in hand with a steady rise in Protestant paramilitarism; Loyalist paramilitaries killed only two people in 1984 but in 1991/92 they became a more active agent of death than the IRA.

For a considerable period, it appeared that the other major feature of pro-union politics in the wake of the Anglo–Irish agreement was the increasing strength of various forms of integrationism. The leader of the Official Unionist Party was believed to be in tacit sympathy with these views, though the Official Unionist Party set itself against the modernised expression of this case (the Campaign for Equal Citizenship, which argued that the British parties should organise in Northern Ireland) by expelling Robert McCartney QC, the President of the CEC, from its ranks. Molyneaux, while ideologically and at heart an integrationist, was, as far as public political strategy was concerned, in essence immobile but tenacious, adhering to a 'steady course' and putting forward only a single new idea (one which was widely ignored) for a 'new Agreement':

> The role of Dublin would be along the lines of proposals we suggested long before the agreement was signed. These provided for improvement in relations between the two nations in the British Isles, which is not far different from what Charles Haughey referred to in his totality of relationships remarks.
>
> In our new relationship, we would not make the same mistake as the

Anglo–Irish Agreement – singling out six little counties in the entire British Isles for special attention. This has defied all logic and has baffled people in Great Britain.

They are asking why it was necessary to have Dublin as a protecting power here in Northern Ireland to make certain the British government fairly treated Roman Catholics who lived in Belfast, but took no account of Irish Roman Catholics who lived in Birmingham.

If the British government, which is responsible for the whole of the United Kingdom, is thought by the Dublin government to be treating Roman Catholics unfairly because of their religion, then this criteria must apply to Roman Catholics in Great Britain, too.

The great mistake is to have this special arrangement of interfering in the administration of six counties out of the large number in the Republic and Great Britain. That doesn't make sense and is a recipe for trouble-making.[2]

The lack of interest in Molyneaux's proposition was not so much on its intrinsic merits as an indication of Molyneaux's relative political marginality for a Tory government with a strong overall majority. Molyneaux responded by deciding to wait for a general election which he hoped would produce a more 'balanced' House of Commons and thus increase his influence. At the time – from 1987 to 1992 – Molyneaux's immobility was widely assumed to have been influenced by other ideological considerations. The Unionist leader was perceived as being prepared to downgrade the power-sharing themes of the Unionist 'Task force' Report; and he was associated with the feeling that devolution might not be 'worth the candle'.[3] In 1988 two polls – one for *Fortnight*[4] and the other for the *Belfast Telegraph*[5] – also seemed to confirm that Protestant opinion, especially in the middle class, was moving sharply in an integrationist direction. The Agreement seemed only to have increased the subjective 'Britishness' of Ulster Unionists and their belief in the value of fuller access to the institutions of the UK state.

However, both these polls showed a widespread acceptance of the principle of power sharing within both communities – 56 per cent of Protestants and 84 per cent of Catholics agreed with the principle – as it became clear that the Agreement simply ushered in a more unstable form of direct rule: direct rule with a green tinge. It was this support for power sharing – in itself simply a reflection of a long-term trend – which the Northern Ireland Office preferred to emphasise. Yet the

government seemed to be aware not only of the increasingly integrationist mood within the Unionist community, but also of an apparent
change of emphasis within the SDLP.

Nationalist politics showed clear signs of movement after the signing
of the Agreement, with a continuing reappraisal of strategy on the part
of both the SDLP and Sinn Fein. In the early phase, from November
1985 to mid-1987, John Hume, the SDLP leader, seemed to believe that
Unionists would accept power-sharing devolution within the
framework of the Anglo–Irish Agreement. This was in line with his
long-stated view that Britain had to confront Unionist obduracy in a
decisive way. Hume's insistence on Britain's role here obscured a key
question: what if Unionist obduracy was due less to British irresolution
and more to the unappealing (sectarian, violent, economically problematical) offer of Nationalism? This lacuna in Hume's thought proved
to be decisive: his prediction that Unionists would negotiate with him
by the end of 1986 remained unfulfilled. Thus SDLP pressure for
power-sharing devolution was not as effective as Hume had envisaged.

Hume's interest in devolution within the framework of the
Agreement declined for two other reasons. The change of government
in Dublin and the re-election of Charles Haughey in 1987 (as opposed to
the pro-devolution Garret FitzGerald) as Taoiseach substantially
reduced Dublin's support for the principle of devolution. Also, Sinn
Fein's electoral resilience in the 1987 Westminster general election made
it clear that the much-predicted Republican electoral melt-down had
not taken place. Significant in this context is the fact that only one in six
Catholics (according to the *Fortnight* poll) felt the Agreement had
helped the minority community.

The combination of these three developments pointed Hume in one
direction: a seven-month-long dialogue with Sinn Fein. This was
facilitated by Sinn Fein's well-established desire to avoid political
isolation and marginalisation – a marginalisation which was a main
objective of the Anglo–Irish Agreement. As early as 1977, the new
northern leadership which had taken control of the IRA and Sinn Fein
had warned their supporters of the need to face up to a long war of
attrition against the 'British presence'. This required a new strategy:
politicising 'the movement', developing Sinn Fein into a political party
of substance, and expanding the 'struggle' into the political system in the
Irish Republic.

Sinn Fein's new approach was massively assisted by the hunger
strikes, which created the conditions for the political breakthrough of

1982 and 1983. However, Gerry Adams recognised that as long as the Sinn Fein vote was limited to around 30-40 per cent of the Catholic electorate – as seemed likely – the impetus of the 1982 electoral surge might well be dissipated. Support for Sinn Fein in the Republic was also not broadly based. To address this, the Sinn Fein leadership was keen to create conditions for a broader 'nationalist coalition', including Fianna Fáil and the·SDLP, aimed at mobilising opinion, domestically and internationally, against the 'British presence'.

The Sinn Fein/SDLP meetings were abruptly terminated by Hume after the accidental killing by the IRA of two of his Catholic constituents. Then the two parties made public a series of lengthy and illuminating documents. These touched on all the most salient points of modern Anglo–Irish politics. The most moving moment in these papers is undoubtedly the SDLP's quotation of Parnell's great Belfast speech of 1891: 'until ... the prejudices of the (Protestant) minority, whether reasonable or unreasonable, are conciliated ... Ireland can never enjoy perfect freedom, Ireland can never be united'.[6] In fact, despite this attractive notion, the SDLP text falls short of acknowledging a Unionist right to say 'no' to Irish unity.

Commentators generally felt there were obvious weaknesses in the presentation of the case on both sides. For Sinn Fein, the weakness was an insistence (based on a rather dated text of Sir Patrick Macrory, a strong friend of Ulster Unionism) that Britain had a continuing strategic interest in Irish division. For the SDLP, the weakness was an insistence that the text of the Anglo–Irish Agreement had, in effect, rendered Britain 'neutral' on the question of partition. In fact, the decision of the Conservative Party to organise in Northern Ireland in 1989 seemed to indicate a renewed commitment to the principle that Irish unity would require majority consent in Northern Ireland.[7]

The Hume/Adams talks therefore left behind a profound question. Many observers have presumed that the SDLP was the power sharing party *par excellence*: the American academic and political scientist, Professor J Bowyer Bell, for example, wrote in this vein as late as 1993: 'Politically the agreement had given the SDLP no role, Direct Rule was still direct rule. There was still no provincial power to share. The SDLP was reduced to the parish pump, the inevitable quarrels over priorities and personalities, the disadvantage of organisation without the returns of office. Only the occasional intervention of London interest kept up SDLP hopes that power-sharing devolution had a future.'[8] But was the SDLP leadership really still committed to power-sharing? What if the SDLP Leadership now felt that Sinn Fein had to be part of a negotiated settlement rather than marginalised (as in the 1974 model) by the coming together of moderate men of good will from both sectarian blocs. This was the key issue of Ulster politics: even supposing a willingness to compromise on the part of the Unionists, were the SDLP still in the market for such a settlement?

This would not in itself have had especially profound implications if the Agreement had delivered – in the terms expected – for the British government. We have seen already that devolution was not central to the government's strategy in November 1985. But it was concerned about levels of violence and these continued to rise: 61 died in 1986 to be followed by 93 in 1987, as against 54 in 1985.

As early as the end of March 1987 the Prime Minister Margaret Thatcher felt that the security returns following the Agreement were inadequate: 'I told Tom King there must be a paper brought forth setting out all the options. I was determined that nothing should be ruled out'.[9] The election of the Haughey government served to cool the atmosphere further, following sharp private exchanges between Thatcher and Haughey in the spring and summer of 1988. Thatcher told Haughey at the European Council in Hanover: 'We knew that the terrorists went over the border to the Republic to plan their operations and to store their weapons. We got no satisfactory intelligence of their movements. Once they crossed the border they were lost. Indeed we received far better security cooperation from virtually all other European countries than with the Republic'.[10] In a tone remarkably similar to that of Nigel Lawson, she concluded: 'Our concessions alienated the Unionists without gaining the level of security cooperation we had a right to expect. In the light of this experience, it is surely time to consider an alternative approach'.[11] This is the context, from the British point of view, of the search for a new and more widely based agreement which began under Peter Brooke, who replaced Tom King as Secretary of State in 1989.

Brooke managed with enormous patience to initiate some talks on the eve of the 1992 general election; a largely 'spurious' suspension of the Anglo–Irish Agreement proved to be enough to get the Unionists to participate. After the general election of 1992, these talks began in much more serious vein with a new Secretary of State, Sir Patrick Mayhew, at the helm. The Unionists approached the talks in a slightly more confident frame of mind: their proposals were certainly considerably more advanced and elaborate. Under John Major, who had succeeded Thatcher in late 1990, the British government gave even more explicit signs that it wished in some way to reduce the Unionist sense of isolation and anxiety. The international benefits of the agreement had been obvious; but the domestic ones, while significant, were less so. The signals seemed to form a pattern: the Foreign Secretary, Douglas Hurd, told the Conservative Party conference in 1991 – no doubt a trifle prematurely for some – that the debate on partition was over. The Anglo–Irish inter-parliamentary tier in early 1992 was presented, by Ken Hind MP, the Secretary of State's Private Secretary, with a critical British analysis of the working of the agreement. In the run-up to the election in April 1992, a Tory Prime Minister rediscovered the union – made up, it was said, of *four* great nations – as a political theme. On the eve of the election, Peter Brooke explicitly attacked the Labour policy of unity by consent.[12] Finally, after the election, came the appointment of a team at the NIO which was about as pro-Unionist as was possible within the current Tory Party at the time. This was a government which lacked Mrs Thatcher's commanding parliamentary majority, a fact carefully noted by Molyneaux.

In the early phase of the talks a significant amount of progress was made. The Alliance Party's document unsurprisingly made the most explicit commitment to a power-sharing local executive. The Unionists tried to avoid such a direct evocation of the 1974 model by proposing a committee system which would ensure SDLP chairmanships in ratio to their percentage of popular support (the DUP) or, more convincingly, from the OUP in ratio to the total Nationalist share of the vote; the point here being that the SDLP share of the vote is about 23 per cent, while the total Nationalist share is around 35 per cent. Some of the SDLP negotiators showed interest in these ideas but in the end the SDLP remained committed to its own proposal: a six-person commission to govern Northern Ireland (three directly elected, one appointed from London; one from Dublin; and one from Brussels). To the Unionists, including here the Alliance Party, this looked like a proposal to turn a local majority (which had just won 65 per cent of the votes in the general election) into a local minority: the Unionists would have had only two sure votes out of six on any controversial issue. The proposal appeared to suggest a form of joint authority with a European flavour. Given the sensitivity of the Maastricht issue, the British government was also dismayed by the SDLP's position: 'The Government's second point was between the SDLP's paper and the EC. Without in any way wishing to appear partisan, it questioned how valuable the EC was as a comparison'. There was a substantial difference between the EC 'club' and a region of the UK having legislative power that it would share with not one, but two external bodies.[13] Thus even in the unlikely event that the Unionist parties had accepted the SDLP proposal, it might well not have been acceptable to the British Government itself.

Despite sympathetic assumptions that the 'European paper' represented only an opening gambit, the SDLP refused throughout the process to move from their original proposal. 'Our models should be sought in areas which have endeavoured to overcome problems of conflict and division. The most conspicuously successful and original has been the EC'.[14] They advanced two very serious and substantive arguments in favour of this stance. In the first place, the experience of 1974 – when the UWC strike had brought down the power-sharing executive – had created a very genuine fear that any similar institutions might fail. 'In the past, parliaments and assemblies had been vulnerable to internal disputes and shifting support'.[15] Hence, the SDLP desired to see new arrangements which would be invulnerable to such pressures. For several of the other talks participants, notably the Alliance party and the devolutionist Unionists, the SDLP's unwillingness to discuss proposals for a local compromise was deeply frustrating. The SDLP fairly pointed out that: 'The UUP had said that it would not even operate its own proposals under Article 4 of the Anglo–Irish Agreement. This demonstrated that Unionists accepted that the context was more important than the content; yet they were asked to participate with a wholly UK context'.[16] Nevertheless, the SDLP's document was the principal rock upon which the talks floundered.

It became obvious that the 1974 power-sharing model now had little attraction for Hume and some others in his party. Formal SDLP comment on the Alliance Party proposals on 12 May 1992 made this perfectly clear: 'The SDLP did not support the idea of a traditional cabinet style executive. In terms of the practical realities of Northern Ireland today, they could not accept that these arrangements would work. The party had taken part in this type of system in the past and it had not worked.'[17] (The Alliance replied that this objection could be applied to every proposed system.) For the SDLP, their commission idea, which embodied the partnership between the two parts of the community in Northern Ireland, had the advantage that it would not collapse if one grouping resigned or withdrew.[18] In later discussions the SDLP leadership was keen to translate its proposals into a concrete form in ways which might have made it more acceptable to Unionists. For example, it was revealed that the SDLP would have no objection if the London nominee was, in fact, a prominent Official Unionist.[19] The difficulty with this and other interesting and reasonable suggestions lay in their conjunctural, short-term nature. Would a future London government elected on a basis of long-term support for Irish unity continue to favour the Unionists in this way? In the end, the fire attracted by the six-person commission idea was simply too great. The UUP insisted, against SDLP's protests, that: 'It would achieve the objective of levering Northern Ireland out of the United Kingdom in any recognisable form … far worse than the present arrangements for direct rule.'[20] (It should be noted, though, that the British government did not accept the UUP's claim that the SDLP proposals were quite simply outside the agreed parameters of the talks.) The DUP asked tartly: 'What if the Commissioners appointed by the Irish government were to be given the portfolio for economic development, and one in which Northern Ireland was in competition with the Republic?' The Alliance Party concluded that the SDLP document failed the basic test of the democratic principle. To whom would the three Comissioners appointed from outside Northern Ireland be accountable?'

Some problems of definition always haunted the talks process. It is possible to sympathise with the British government's reluctance to enter this area: 'Whatever the historic rights and wrongs, Northern Ireland is part of the United Kingdom, Her Majesty's Government exercises full sovereign authority in Northern Ireland and acknowledges a responsibility to all the people there to povide security, stability and good government.' After all, it added: 'Many sources of the inequality between the two parts of the community have been removed.' But it was simply not possible to leave aside broader historical and ideological issues. Both the Unionist parties disputed the SDLP's description of their standpoint. The DUP declared: 'The SDLP suggested that the Unionist rejection of everything from home rule to the Anglo–Irish Agreement is due to the distrust of the nationalist people … [that] is simply false. We are not undiscovered Irish nationalists.' The UUP on 8 July noted, in similar vein: 'There appears to be an underlying assumption that if the fear of Nationalism was removed, Unionists would no longer feel so British. While the fear or distrust attitude may exist, it does not dominate the positive nature of our aspiration to retain our unity with the rest of the United Kingdom.'

Against this, of course, came the SDLP's concern with its own identity. The SDLP document 'Agreeing the Nature of the Problem' (7 May 1992), declared: 'We note that the UUP ... seems to be attempting to put forward a more inclusive definition of Britishness but we are concerned that there is an apparent tendency to subsume the Irish identity within it'. In their 'Analysis of the Nature of the Problem', delivered at the Brooke talks in May 1991, the SDLP had declared:

> From the inception of Northern Ireland until the signing of the Anglo–Irish Agreement in 1985, the nationalist identity was denied political expression and validity, and Nationalists were excluded from effective participation in the institutions of government ...
>
> For the Nationalists the Agreement had gone some way in promoting a sense of just and fair treatment and a diminution of their sense of isolation. The impact of the overall recognition of the equal validity of the nationalist tradition is pervasive and in a sense constitutes the achievement of the Agreement. The Agreement has also registered tangible progress on such areas as fair employment, legalising the status of the Irish language and the repeal of the Flags and Emblems Act, and the establishment of the International Fund for Ireland.

Here, in a sense, is a mature civil rights agenda; 'equality of esteem' is its main theme. However, for the SDLP the logical development of this agenda is an unavoidable one. A year later, 13 May 1992, the SDLP spoke of an 'Irish identity ... the feeling of living in their own country, the common life of which was embodied in the Irish state'. This Irish identity could only be respected under some system of joint authority. A few days before, on 7 May 1992, the SDLP had declared: 'In the new world order, shared sovereignty was commonplace and the approach allowed the accommodation of both identities'.

What lessons could the British government draw from the talks process? The government undoubtedly felt that progress was made on the internal arrangements for Northern Ireland. At an early stage (13 May), the UUP conceded that 'all well-supported constitutional parties would be represented at the highest level of decision making.' Even the Alliance Party felt able to praise the DUP submission (on 13 May 1992) as a considerable step ... 'the UDUP proposal's did not rule out power sharing eventually'. Subsequently the British government produced its celebrated 10 June document, giving a 'possible outline framework for a devolved government', on which the

SDLP reserved its position. The document (published in the *Sunday News* on 20 September 1992) suggested an 85 member assembly (elected by PR), which would control existing government departments in Northern Ireland through committees. Those chairing the committees (becoming in effect the responsible ministers) would be appointed broadly in proportion to party numbers in the assembly. The assembly would be able to debate all workings of government. Local parties were divided on the percentage required in order for a vote to be carried: Ulster Unionists and Alliance proposed 70 per cent, the DUP 65 per cent and the SDLP 75 per cent. The Northern Ireland Secretary of State would retain control of powers not devolved (such as security) and ensure that the Assembly was run fairly but would not interfere in its day-to-day matters. The most novel feature of the plan was the creation of a three-person 'panel' to be elected on the same basis as the European elections and also likely to return one Ulster Unionist, one DUP and one SDLP member. The 'panel' would consult and advise the Secretary of State, inspect and review the assembly and NIO decisions, approve some appointments to public bodies, have some say on how public finances were spent and be responsible for attracting overseas investment. The document also suggested that 'any individuals or representatives of parties who condone the use of violence for political ends' might be excluded from executive power.

It was this document which allowed the talks to make the crucial transition to Strand Two: on 1 July in a 'private' letter to Molyneaux, Sir Patrick Mayhew, in effect, indicated the British government's lack of enthusiasm for the SDLP document and implicit preference for the 10 June document. The Unionists had wanted to reach a firm agreement on internal arrangements for Northern Ireland before making the 'historic trip' to Dublin to discuss north–south relations. No such agreement had been reached but Sir Patrick Mayhew's letter gave the UUP – though not the DUP – the confidence to cross this particular Rubicon on 21 September, when three days of talks opened at Dublin Castle. The Unionists found the Dublin government apparently unprepared; nevertheless, one particular taboo had lost its relevance.

It became increasingly clear that Articles 2 and 3 of the Irish Constitution, which laid claim to Northern Ireland, were now of central importance. Perhaps surprisingly, even the liberal Dr FitzGerald had argued in 1985 that it was only the obsessive paranoia of the Unionist mindset which gave these Articles any role in the political debate. But the ruling of the Irish Supreme Court on 1 March 1990, in the case brought by two Unionist politicians, Chris and Michael McGimpsey, had changed perceptions. The Supreme Court ruled that Articles 2 and 3 are a 'claim of legal right' over the 'national territory'; the Articles are not merely 'aspirational' but rather 'a constitutional imperative'. The clear implication, that Article 1 of the Anglo–Irish Agreement – which accepted the democratic basis of partition – was now devalued, disturbed British policy makers, and there was a feeling that the Agreement had lost some of its balance. It became a theme of British discourse that this matter would have to be definitively resolved. The British paper 'Fundamental Aspects, Common Interests and Themes, Other Requirements' (28 August 1992) argued:

> An outcome to these talks would attract a wide degree of allegiance and support amongst the Unionist community if it were to include agreement among all the participants that Northern Ireland is part of the UK, as well as agreement on the circumstances in which that status could change.

This merely echoed an earlier British statement from Sir Patrick Mayhew on 1 July 1992:

> I believe it is in everyone's interest that the Talks ... should achieve an unambiguous consensus on the constitutional position of Northern Ireland and produce a framework acceptable to all the talks participants and the people. That may have implications for Articles 2 and 3 of the Irish Constitution.

But the key question remained: how to create the conditions in which the Irish government might call a referendum on Articles 2 and 3? The Irish paper ('Identity, Allegiance and Underlying Realities', 28 August 1992) gives a clue here: 'The strength and quality of the proposed links between both parts of Ireland would be one of the most important factors in this regard.' Ideally, they should have 'a capacity to break down barriers of distrust which led to past divisions and lead to unity based on agreement of the people who inhabit the island of Ireland, accepting both the diversity within Ireland and the unique relations between the peoples of Ireland and Britain.' This seemed to be the basis for a mutually beneficial ideal: cross-border institutions of cooperation in exchange for the removal of Articles 2 and 3, or their effective dilution. Thus the British government's 'Fundamental Aspects' paper asks: 'Are there areas where closer cooperation, coordination or harmonisation might add to the strengths of both economies?' In this document – which generated considerable public Unionist hostility – there is even talk of an 'agreed Ireland', but in a clearly defined sense of 'whatever governmental arrangements are widely acceptable and aimed at protecting and forwarding interest of the people of the 'island'.

'Fundamental Aspects' was widely seen as permitting an SDLP interpretation; one SDLP member was reported as saying, 'it proves that the British government really is neutral about the north', while a Unionist source was quoted as saying that it read like a 'cross between something that might be produced by the British Foreign Office, Dublin and the SDLP'. In fact this was a misreading: as the document's reference to the establishment of an Irish government office in the north and a NIO office in Dublin makes clear, the *problematique* of the document rests on the assumption that the problem represented by Articles 2 and 3 can be solved, and the paper indeed is designed to help resolve that problem. The main point of the Strand Two discussions, from the British government's point of view, was that the Ulster Unionist negotiators revealed themselves to be relaxed, well-informed and relatively flexible about the scope for cross-border cooperation – to the extent of allowing these institutions some low level executive powers. The DUP, it has to be said, were much more suspicious on this score; as the talks drew to a close, they felt that the UUP had conceded to a united Irish parliament in 'embryo'.

On 9 November, as the talks collapsed, the Ulster Unionists tabled a series of proposals. The proposals included a Bill of Rights for Northern Ireland to protect minorities; a 'meaningful role' for Nationalists in the administration of Northern Ireland; and, given 'the reality that a significant proportion of the Roman Catholic community in Northern Ireland may aspire to a united Ireland', that there should be an 'Inter-Irish Relations Committee' formally linking members of the Assembly and the Irish parliament. In return the Ulster Unionists wanted Dublin 'to define a means whereby the aggressive and irredentist Articles 2 and 3 in the Irish Constitution would be removed'. From the SDLP they asked 'a *de facto* commitment to a Northern Ireland where all constitutional parties would be able to play a meaningful role'. For the SDLP these proposals were a cynical display of spurious flexibility, a move which came too late to be convincing. This was an understandable response but an inadequate one as far as the NIO was concerned. Although some of the SDLP negotiators displayed substantial goodwill, Hume's adherence to the original six-person Commission concept had been – in the eyes of the British Government – the greatest stumbling block in the way of genuine progress.

As the talks collapsed, press briefings by the NIO referred to the possibility of a change in SDLP attitudes when the ordinary membership realised how much had been on offer. Such a development was, however, unlikely. The Anglo–Irish Agreement had created a context in which it became logical – almost compellingly so – for constitutional Nationalists and the British Labour Party to argue for a form of joint authority, perhaps with a Europe dimension. The talks process had perhaps resulted in a new subtlety in political discourse. Mainstream Unionists now conceded ground on power sharing (preferably termed 'responsibility sharing'), while constitutional Nationalists aimed for joint authority rather than a united Ireland. But it was clear that a widely accepted solution was not yet in sight. It was not so clear, that the new political line of cleavage opened up the possibilities of new alignments – and in particular a change in the DLP/Sinn Fein relationship – which threatened, as 1993 unfolded, to re-write the ground rules of northern politics.

NOTES

1. In Sperrin the Sinn Fein share rose from 40.5 (1985) to 44.8 in May 1986; in Fermanagh Erne East it rose from 37.4 (1985) to 40.8. In short, by the following spring it was perfectly clear that the Anglo–Irish Agreement did not have the capacity to erode the Sinn Fein share of the vote significantly. For the general election figures, see P. Bew, 'How Northern Ireland Really Voted' in *Irish Political Studies*. vol 3, 1988
2. *Belfast Newsletter*, 10 August 1987. At heart Molyneaux was an integrationist. He told his first biographer, Ann Purdy, that Stormont, a 'puppet parliament' as he called it, had not strengthened the Union even when it was dominated by Unionists from 1921 to 1968; hardly surprisingly he felt in the 1970s and 1980s that 'devolution was not worth the candle' if it also involved accepting both the Anglo–Irish Agreement and power sharing. *Times*, 29 August 1995
3. *Ibid*
4. The *Fortnight* poll of April 1988
5. *Belfast Telegraph*, 6 October 1988
6. For the original speech, see the *Northern Whig*, 23 May 1891

7. The Conservative decision to organise was the early indicator of a new and surprising phenomenon – which was to become marked in the 1990s – that of the greater intellectual respectability of the pro-union case within mainstream Toryism.

8. Bowyer Bell, J., *The Irish Troubles: A Generation of Violence 1967-1992*, Dublin 1993, p713

9. Margaret Thatcher, *The Downing Street Years*, London 1993, p402-15

10. *Ibid.*

11. *Ibid*

12. This led some to argue that the SDLP could never trust Peter Brooke again. In the event, they were spared embarrassment by the appointment of Sir Patrick Mayhew. Brooke ironically became a 'folk hero' of Nationalism, see Eamonn Mallie and David McKittrick, *The Fight for Peace: The Secret Story Behind the Irish Peace Process*, London 1996, p97-8. Mayhew, on the other hand, because of his previous responsibilities as a law officer, had already had serious conflicts with Dublin over extradition matters. He was widely rumoured not to be enthusiastic about the Anglo–Irish Agreement – a rumour he did nothing to dispel. On the other hand, he was to prove flexible. At the beginning of the 1992 talks he insisted that, whatever the outcome, the British government would rise from the table committed to the union; by the end of 1993, he supported the Downing Street declaration which explicitly precluded the possibility of his repeating such a declaration

13. This point is made by the British government at the 18 May plenary session of the talks. The 'Talks Papers' will be published by the Cadogan group.

14. 'Agreeing new political structures', submission by the SDLP to the interparty talks, May 1992. See P Bew and E Meehan, 'Regions and Borders: Controversies in Northern Ireland about the European Union', *Journal of European Public Policy*, vol. 1, no. 1, 1994

15. *Ibid.*

16. *Ibid.*

17. *Ibid.*

18. *Ibid.*

19. Private information

20. These and the other quotations below may be found in the Cadogan text

PART II

THE POLITICAL ECONOMY OF NORTHERN IRELAND

4

THE NORTHERN IRELAND ECONOMY: BETWEEN WAR AND PEACE

There is considerable controversy about the performance of the Northern Ireland economy. Virtually every country or region has such a trenchant debate, but in Northern Ireland the difficulty is that exchanges about economic performance have become enmeshed in political conflict. Those of a Unionist inclination tend to be uncritical, painting as rosy a picture as possible of the regional economy. In contrast, those of a Nationalist persuasion tend to be uncompromising in their view that the Northern Ireland economy is a basket-case.

Sharply contrasting views have emerged as a result of these polar positions. On the one hand, some argue passionately that the Troubles have had virtually no impact on the underlying economy. On the other hand, others, with equal zeal, suggest that a war-economy has emerged as a result of twenty-five years of violence. One view is that a big economic bonanza awaits Northern Ireland when peace breaks out. But another suggests that the economic consequences of peace are minimal. This chapter gives an overview of the themes and controversies about the Northern Ireland economy. Our objective is not to offer a definitive analysis, but to give people sufficient understanding so that they can thread their way through the bewildering set of views that currently exist.

THE DEBATE ABOUT THE SUBVENTION

Why the subvention increased
Perhaps the best starting point is to ask: what have been the economic consequences of the conflict? This is not an easy question to answer

since several developments, unrelated to the troubles, have had a profoundly negative impact on the regional economy. De-industrialisation has been the biggest of these negative shocks. In the 1960s, Northern Ireland had a thriving manufacturing sector, employing over 30 per cent of the workforce and returning the highest rates of productivity growth among the UK regions. The engine driving this good economic performance was the large number of multinationals that came to the region in this decade and the still sizeable indigenous industrial base, mainly in shipbuilding, aircraft production and textiles.

These twin pillars of economic success were badly hit by the world-wide economic recession of the 1970s. The large multinationals seemed to leave the region as quickly as they had arrived, and an anorexic shipbuilding industry stands as a visual testimony to the buffeting experienced by local manufacturing. As a result of this industrial collapse, employment in manufacturing fell to about 18 per cent of the overall workforce. Within a decade the longstanding image of Northern Ireland as a dynamic engineering centre had melted away.

A second, more controversial, negative factor has been the rapid annual increase in the labour force caused by Northern Ireland having one of the highest birth rates in the European Union. In the 1980s, for example, about 6,800 people were entering the labour market every year, and at the same time an average of no more than 4,000 new jobs was being created annually. To some extent this gap between labour supply and labour demand was eased by many people emigrating to the UK and elsewhere, but this exodus was not enough to balance both sides of the labour market. Thus, for much of the past twenty-five years, the violence took place against a backdrop of persistently high unemployment caused by lacklustre job-generation in the private sector and too many people entering the labour market. The troubles were not the *cause* of these economic problems, but, crucially, they ensured the adoption of more interventionist policies than would have been the case otherwise. To have allowed an economic crisis to run alongside the political turmoil would have pushed the region into the abyss.

An important consequence of the Troubles, then, has been the adoption of less market-oriented policies. To a large extent, the strategy amounted to increasing the size of the public sector to compensate for the fall in private sector activity. Financing this expansion meant a huge growth in the UK subvention to the region, as shown in Figure 1. The subvention is essentially a fiscal transfer: the

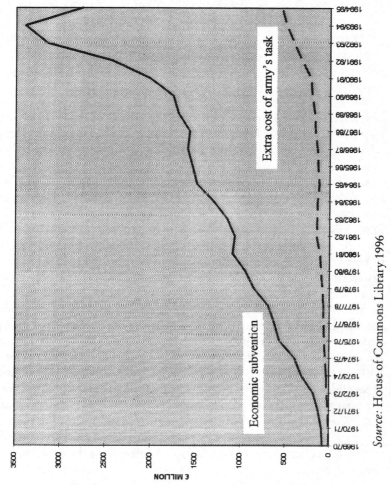

Figure 1: Economic Subvention and the costs of the army's task

Source: House of Commons Library 1996

difference between what is raised locally in taxes and the amount of public expenditure injected into the local economy. It can be seen from the figure that in the early 1970s the subvention was tiny, reflecting the fact that Northern Ireland was nearly economically self-reliant. However, by the mid-1990s it had become huge, standing at about £3.7 billion. Of course this also meant that living standards had become more closely tied to the public expenditure decisions of the UK Treasury than to the commercial activities of firms in the local economy. Whether this subvention has been altogether beneficial to the region has been a matter of some dispute.[1] To make sense of this debate it may be useful to distinguish between the impact of the subvention on economic outcomes, economic structure and economic processes.

The subvention and economic outcomes
In terms of economic outcomes, the subvention has ensured that, even when the UK as a whole has been in recession and the 'underlying' local economy has been under-performing, levels of employment and output in Northern Ireland have remained higher than those warranted by market conditions. Thus, the high levels of public expenditure, by building strong stabilisers into the local economy, have prevented the region from hitting the ropes. That is not to say that everything has been rosy in the economic garden: high levels of unemployment and poverty have been an enduring feature of Northern Irish life in the past generation. Moreover, Northern Ireland has the lowest living standards in the UK.[2] The important point is that the situation could have been much worse. To get an idea of what could have developed in the north we need to look no further than the Republic of Ireland. Because of profligate public spending in the 1970s, the Republic accumulated a mountain of debt and, lacking an external benefactor, Dublin was obliged to enact large-scale cut-backs in public expenditure in the 1980s, similar in scale to the economic squeeze that near-bankrupt third world countries were experiencing at the same time. Inevitably, this deflationary action caused unemployment and emigration to soar. But there was no alternative: in order to remain solvent successive governments had to rip deep into the social fabric of the country.

Fortunately, the subvention saved Northern Ireland from such an unhappy scenario. Thus, the fiscal transfer from Whitehall played the positive role of putting a floor under unemployment and income levels in the region. One qualification must be entered here immediately. Although the fiscal transfer helped buoy up local incomes it has done so in a fairly crude way. Borooah and MacGregor show that economic inequality in Northern Ireland during the 1980s was the highest among UK regions.[3] They suggest that the large public sector, funded in part by the subvention, may have contributed to this situation by encouraging the large number of two-earner families in the region: of all the UK regions, Northern Ireland is in the curious position of having the highest number of two-earner families (on a per capita basis) in the top deciles of the income distribution table and the lowest numbers at the bottom of the scale. It was these research findings that fuelled the popular thesis in the late 1980s that the subvention had created a society of haves and have-nots in Northern Ireland.

The impact on the economic structure

As already stated, the subvention has had a big impact on the local economic structure by enlarging the size of the public sector. In the early 1970s, public sector employment represented about 27 per cent

Figure 2: Non-market/market employment ratio

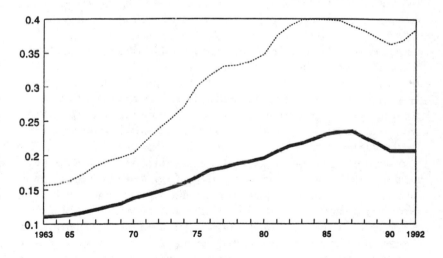

Source: Bradley, 1995

of the total workforce but by the mid 1980, this figure had increased to 42 per cent. This big structural change is vividly captured in Figure 2, which charts the ratio of non-market to market employment in the north and the south of Ireland during the 1970s and 1980s. It can clearly be seen how differently the two economies have developed with regards public employment. During the 1990s, the prominence of the public sector in the local economy has declined slightly. Public sector jobs have fallen back to about 37 per cent of total employment. But this recent decline should not disguise the fact that public expenditure remains a lifeline for the local economy.

Radically different views exist about the impact of the public sector on the structure of the local economy. One less than complimentary perspective is that the big public sector has turned Northern Ireland into a 'workhouse economy'.[4] This analogy is used to highlight that with so much activity centred around the public sector the economy has ceased to work in the conventional way. In particular, it simply sucks in imports from the outside world without exporting anything in return. Meanwhile, those in employment are engaged in either servicing or controlling the local population. This argument rests on the following thinking: the large subvention has resulted in regional expenditure being higher than regional income. Another way of putting this is that regional consumption exceeds regional production, causing imports to outstrip exports. The resulting trading deficit, which amounts to about 27 per cent of regional income, more or less coincides with the scale of the subvention in Northern Ireland's GDP. Thus the subvention ensures that the regional accounts balance, thereby allowing the local population to live beyond its means. Believing that this situation had caused a form of mendacity, Rowthorn was moved to use the term 'workhouse economy'. Clearly, from this standpoint, the subvention has had a malign impact on the local economy.

A contrasting perspective is that the large increase in the amount of money flowing into the local economy from the UK exchequer is neither exceptional nor does it represent an economic distortion. Northern Ireland is part of a UK-wide economic and political union. A key task of a properly functioning economic union is to ensure that a degree of cohesion is maintained within its jurisdiction and that inequalities between different groups and regions do not get out of control. For example, one part of an economic union may have an above average share of mature and declining industries. Left to its own devices this region would probably experience a steep fall in employment and living standards as it coped with the problems of industrial adjustment. But the region escapes such a fate because the inbuilt stability and distribution functions of the union oblige other parts of the territory to come to the rescue. Economists call this procedure fiscal co-insurance and it is a basic operating principle of most nation states and federations the world over.

Thus, year in year out, Newfoundland receives a huge subsidy from the federal government in Canada as compensation for its peripheral position and the lack of resource endowments which places enormous obstacles in the way of it developing a dynamic economy. Similar arrangements exist in the United States and Australia to ensure that all parts of the territory reach a certain standard of living, even though some may be performing better than others. Within the UK, Northern Ireland is not unique in receiving a subvention: London also allows Scotland and Wales to spend more public money than they pay in taxes. Even in southern Ireland the same principle applies as most of the west coast is subsidised by the Dublin conurbation. All in all, this perspective sees the subvention in a benign light, as having maintained Northern Ireland's economic cohesion inside the UK in the face of a triple economic shock: deindustrialisation, excess labour supply and the outbreak of violence.

Debate about the impact of the subvention has been dominated by the head-to-head clash of the two opposite views. It is hard to judge which is the most valid since neither view can be totally dismissed, yet each on its own is unconvincing. Thus, for example, the description of Northern Ireland as having a 'workhouse economy', which to some extent reflects a concern with an underperforming tradeable sector, is ultimately a pejorative caricature. By refusing to recognise that fiscal transfers play a key role in modern federations and nation states, the intention is to portray the region as a basket-case. Unhealthy political and economic consequences can flow from fiscal transfers, but the bottom line question is whether Northern Ireland would have been better off without the subvention. In the context of a low level civil war the answer must surely be no. As a result, the 'workhouse economy' thesis is too harsh a view of the local economy during the years of violence.

Those who remain untroubled by the scale of the subvention actually fall into the opposite trap. This position is too uncritical and at times it seems that the only motivation is to portray Northern Ireland in the best possible light. Certainly most neutral economists would treat such a position with the utmost suspicion. There is a huge volume of professional literature suggesting that negative spillovers may result when a region receives large amounts of financial support from the outside, and, given the scale of the subvention to Northern Ireland, it is fair to assume that this literature would be the first port of call for economists examining the local economy. Regrettably, this kind of survey has not been carried out in any robust or convincing way. The studies that do exist are reviewed below.

Public money and private economic processes
The impact of the subvention on economic processes in the region – the incentive structures in the local economy and the behaviour of economic agents – is controversial. One argument is that the large subvention has created a dependency culture resulting in local businesses as much interested in cultivating a vertical relationship with public institutions to obtain subsidies as with improving their horizontal market position to win new commercial orders. Some evidence supports this view. Comparing profit levels of a sample of Northern Irish manufacturing companies with those attained by similar firms elsewhere in the UK, Roper found that the average profit margins for Northern Irish enterprises were 60 per cent higher than those of their UK counterparts.[5] This divergence was attributed to the generous grant schemes operated by Northern Ireland's economic development agencies. In aggregate terms, the NIEC estimates that the level of public subsidy to local enterprises is five times greater than anywhere else in the UK.

Another claim is that the large subvention has resulted in a distortion of market and business incentives in the local economy. The stylised version of this argument is as follows. One of the most significant direct effects of the fiscal transfer has been to create a circular flow of income in the non-tradeable sector. Through the growth of public sector jobs, many of them governed by UK rates of pay, demand has been generated for a range of private services. A by-product of this development has been to encourage forms of competition that are associated with commercial activity in service-related industries. At the same time, these dynamics may have undermined the competitive influences that encourage industrial activity.

Enterprises in successful manufacturing regions are normally in tune with commercial developments outside the region. This is essentially because if they do not keep pace with technical innovation or the strategies of competitors they will lose market share. Inside the region, companies are supported by a repertoire of economic policies on matters such as training and research and development, designed to ensure that good quality commercial practices are sustained. In addition, enterprises frequently get together and establish cooperative networks in order to help each other. Thus a great deal of effort is made to establish a business environment that allows individual companies to be outward oriented. Different competitive influences tend to emerge in regions dominated by non-tradeable activity. In this situation there is less incentive or even need for many businesses to be outward looking. The orbit of competition is mainly local: a barber in Northern Ireland does not have to be too concerned with the price of a haircut in Manchester since potential customers are unlikely to board a plane to get a trim; the barber's main market rival will probably be less than a mile down the road. As a result, the competitive process is less geared towards connecting local commercial activity with the outside world.

The above argument rests on the notion of externalities frequently used by economists. Externalities arise when individual economic acts or decisions have a wider impact that then in turn influences economic behaviour. They can be either positive or negative: a firm polluting a river is an example of a negative externality whilst a firm sharing research and development innovations is a positive externality. What is being argued in relation to Northern Ireland is that the huge growth of non-tradeable activity has generated negative externalities, locking the economy into low-quality forms of service activity and eroding the scope to pursue high-quality, highly skilled commercial practices.

Intuitively, this thesis is appealing, but it has its shortcomings. One of the problems is that the studies arguing this point of view are underdeveloped and therefore are not fully convincing. On a more theoretical level, it could be argued that the externality approach encourages the type of mind-set within which all sorts of wondrous impediments to doing business can be conjured up. It is also important not to exaggerate the economic influences of the subvention: some developments in Northern Ireland's economy – such as the growth of non-tradeable activity – are not peculiar to the region. Similar patterns of economic development can be found elsewhere in Europe. All in all, more robust and in-depth studies are required of the nature and extent of the negative externalities arising from the subvention. However, it can equally be said that this is beholden on the supporters of the subvention, since it they who claim to show that no negative externalities arise from the fiscal transfer.

THE SUBVENTION IN THE FUTURE

A compelling argument against those untroubled by the size of the subvention is that the current share of public expenditure in regional GDP is widely regarded as excessive and not sustainable in the longer-term, especially if peace breaks out. In other words, the subvention has caused the regional economy to become too dependent on government finance. Here it may be useful to look at recent French writings on *'l'economie des conventions'*. A key theme in this literature is to explore why we regard certain economic categories in the way we do: for instance, why do we not regard domestic work as acceptable paid economic activity. Cutting through much (acrimonious) detail, the French debate suggests that economic categories are invented, then embodied in conventions and codes that help us interpret economic life and guide the formation of economic policies.

An important convention is that a high share of public expenditure in overall economic growth is distortionary and thus should be avoided. Understandably, this convention has been waved in the Northern Ireland case because of the violence. But if peace were ever achieved, then there would be considerable informal pressure to respect this convention. The share of government expenditure in the Northern Ireland GDP is strikingly out of line with the situation of other disadvantaged regions of the EU, which affronts widely shared economic norms. To simply dismiss or downgrade such conventions would be cavalier.

This assessment suggests that the relationship between the subvention, the public sector and regional economic development will change in the future, particularly in the context of any political settlement. Invariably, part of this change will involve reigning in the size of the subvention. This raises the question of how quickly such reform should be introduced. One approach is to argue for a rapid cutback so to allow the region to shake off its dependency culture. In an interesting book, Birnie and Hitchens show that industry in

Northern Ireland suffers from a catalogue of failings, ranging from the under-use of sophisticated machinery to basic, even improvised, marketing and business support services.[6] To pull the region out of this lacklustre competitive performance, they conclude that a 'shock' should be administered to the local economy. In practice, this shock amounts to a dose of old fashion neo-liberal policies, including a drastic reduction in the level of government expenditure in the local economy.

Unfortunately, the authors do not make a convincing economic case for such a drastic programme. If anything, their policy remedy flies in the face of recent developments in economic theory. For the first time in nearly a century economists are in agreement that radically deflationary measures of any type should be avoided since the costs in terms of lost output and employment are not transitory but long-lasting, trends from which it is difficult to recover. This view is corroborated by a study on the consequences of the withdrawal of government money from the Northern Ireland economy carried out by a team of economists at Strathclyde University.[7] They simulated the likely effects of different levels of reductions in public finance on jobs and growth in the region. Their results make for depressing reading: simulating the effects of a complete end of the subvention, they found that employment would fall by about 14 per cent and regional income by about 13 per cent. In other words, any quick withdrawal of the subvention would throw the region into abject poverty. These figures are based on a simulation and thus should be treated with some caution; nevertheless, it is hard to dispute the central message that it would be precipitous, if not downright foolhardy, to administer a shock to the local economy.

In sharp contrast to the above view is the argument that the scale and the possible distortionary effects of the subvention will wither away when peace and a political settlement arrive.[8] According to this view the subvention is the direct result of the violence. It is pointed out that during the 1960s Northern Ireland was more or less a self-reliant economy with little need of any external support. If that were the situation then, so the argument goes, there is no reason for it not to return to self-sufficiency in the future, when peace breaks out.

This view is embedded in neo-liberal economics for it assumes that autonomous market forces will correct structural imbalances. While it is theoretically possible that market dynamics could reduce Northern Ireland's reliance on the subvention, there are good grounds for scepticism. For a start, the experience of Eastern Europe suggests that to rely on the market alone to reduce excessive public subsidies and create a thriving private sector is misguided, sometimes deeply so. Moreover, a key tenet of public economics is that when a country experiences a growth in government expenditure there is a 'ratchet effect' causing the public sector to become an integral part of the economy, a process that is unlikely to be reversed spontaneously. The classic example of this process was the huge growth in public expenditure in the UK during the last war that did not decline in peacetime. In recent times when governments have been obliged to cut public expenditure, they have had to resort to deliberate, and on occasions, draconian measures. This evidence suggests that if Northern Ireland is to operate without a big subvention, planned and possibly unpopular government action will be required. Thus it is perhaps too sanguine to believe that Northern Ireland's over-reliance on external funds can be resolved through a gradual, spontaneous process.

A more level-headed approach needs to be taken about the future role of the subvention in the local economy, particularly if a political settlement is reached. If such a situation were to arise then three important themes will require attention: (1) will a peace dividend arise as a result of the need to spend less money on security or will the UK Treasury claw back expenditure by cutting the size of the fiscal transfer? (2) what improvements can be expected in the private sector as a result of peace? (3) does the present governance structure of the local economy need changing to improve performance? These themes are explored in some detail in the following sections.

Is there a peace dividend to be captured?
During the ceasefires there was wide expectation that a peace dividend would result from the large-scale security apparatus becoming obsolete. Because of a lack of knowledge about the operation of the security budget, some had unrealistically high expectations about the size of the potential dividend. For instance, a common perception was that a withdrawal of troops would allow a huge pot of money to be transferred to other parts of the public sector. However, the costs of maintaining the British army in the region are met by the British defence budget, meaning that any savings made from troops leaving the region simply flow back into Whitehall coffers. Any future peace dividend would be due mainly to the run down of a big police force and the dismantling of other parts of the local security apparatus aimed

at preventing terrorism.[9] With the Provisionals restarting their campaign, any prospect of a peace dividend has virtually evaporated and the relationship between the security machine and the economy will remain unchanged for some time. Nevertheless, it is important to examine the argument about a financial bonanza awaiting the Northern Ireland economy if the violence ends. This view may considerably underestimate the complexities and costs of transforming the Northern Ireland economy into a fully civilian entity.

One problem that has not been given due attention is that of transforming the RUC – the local police force – into a force suited to peace-time conditions. This question has important implications for any potential peace dividend. When violence ends, the RUC will be confronted with two difficulties: (i) it will have too many officers for a peaceful Northern Ireland; and (ii) it will be unrepresentative in that its members are largely drawn from the Protestant community. This last point is important in that redressing the religious imbalance of the police is likely to be part of any political settlement, at least one that is sustainable. Whether the RUC can deal smoothly and easily with these two issues is certainly worth considering.

A rapid expansion occurred in RUC members in response to the outbreak of violence in 1969. Between 1969 and 1975, police numbers increased from about 3,300 to nearly 7,000 (including full-time reservists). A further increase in police personnel occurred in the late 1970s/early 1980s as a result of the British government's adoption of the security policy known as Ulsterisation: British troops were removed from frontline operations against the paramilitaries and a more active role was given to the RUC and the local Ulster Defence Regiment. By 1994, the size of the RUC had increased to an approximate total of 11,500 officers, consisting of 8,400 full-time permanent staff and 3,100 full-time reservists. For every 150 citizens of Northern Ireland there is one police officer, a ratio which is hugely out of line with the ratio in other parts of the UK. Figure 3 compares RUC staffing with two broadly equivalent UK areas in terms of population: Northumbria and Kent. The two British police forces have a staff of 3,600 and 3,100 respectively which suggests that the RUC have recruited about 8,000 people in response to the violence. Or to put it differently, a peaceful Northern Ireland would only require a police force of 3,500 – 4,000; that suggests that an end to violence would threaten about 70 per cent of RUC jobs.

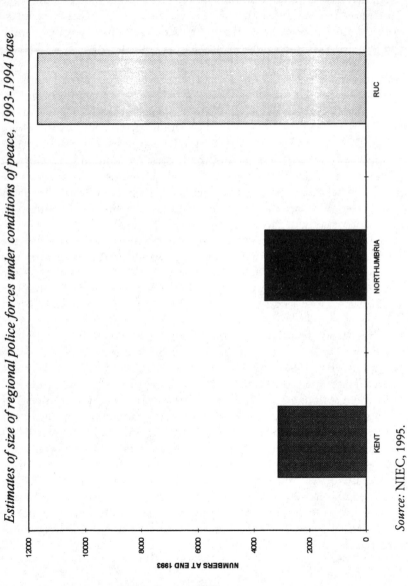

Estimates of size of regional police forces under conditions of peace, 1993-1994 base

NUMBERS AT END 1993

KENT   NORTHUMBRIA   RUC

Source: NIEC, 1995.

This picture is complicated by the religious imbalance in the RUC: about 93 per cent of police officers are Protestants and only 7 per cent are Catholics. In other words, only 800 of the 11,000 are from the minority community. Many argue that the tiny number of Catholic RUC personnel is symptomatic of the lack of social and political integration of the minority community in the region. If it were required that the proportion of Catholics in the RUC should reflect that community's share in the total population in Northern Ireland, then about 40 per cent of police jobs should be filled by Catholics. On present numbers, this means that the RUC should employ a total of 4,600 Catholics, which in turn translates into 3,800 fewer Protestant police officers. If peace were to break out, making the RUC more representative and, at the same time, reducing its size would mean, assuming that no serving Catholic officers were made redundant, 8,500 Protestant officers losing their jobs and between 750 and 1,000 new recruits being drawn in from the minority community.

Assuming that such a scenario was actually carried out, how large would the peace dividend be? The NIEC correctly splits the dividend into short-run and long-run gains.[10] Short-run gains mostly reflect a reduction in the police overtime bill, which in 1993/94 amounted to £84 million. Long-run gains, on the other hand, mainly cover changes in the size and composition of the organisation; if it is assumed that RUC numbers were reduced to 4,000 and that budget reductions were proportional to police numbers, then the police bill would fall from £624 million to about £225 million, a saving of £400 million. Thus peace would bring cumulative savings of £480 million from the police budget that could be released for civilian use. This figure increases by about £50 million if we accept the NIEC estimate of possible savings from the prison budget as a result of the end of violence. All in all, a reasonably accurate estimate of a potential peace dividend from the security budget is £530 million.

All the above is premised on the assumption that the RUC can be recast in a fairly short period. In practice, however, this scenario will be extremely difficult to enact. Losing roughly 7,500 people is a huge downsizing for any organisation and the effects on the RUC would be traumatic. Moreover, job losses on such a scale could well spill over and cause deep alienation in the Protestant community, which in turn could jeopardise any political settlement. Thus, circumstances may dictate a more gradual approach to the rundown of the police force. A slower restructuring could be carried out in two stages. The first stage, spanning a three year period, would consist of phasing out the 3,100 full-time reservists and encouraging voluntary redundancies among the older officers. Early retirement and 'natural wastage' should result in 1,500 officers leaving the force, which means that over the three year period the RUC could shed a total of 4,600 existing members. At the same time, there should be a massive campaign to recruit Catholics, with the objective being to emply 1,000 people from that community. Thus, at the end of the three years, the RUC would be reduced to roughly 8,000 personnel. As we have already seen this is still too high a figure. As a result, a second stage would be required to realise further redundancies. The minimum period for this second stage would be four years since the objective would be to lose 4,000 officers: 1,000 a year. At the end of this time, the RUC would be operating at its minimum efficient scale of 4,000 – 4,500 and at the same time be representative of the two communities. Overall the message is that adjusting the police to peacetime conditions in the future will realistically take at least seven years.

Some may quibble with parts of this arithmetic. Certainly the numbers are not exact; for example we do not deal with civilian jobs in the police and the indirect employment that almost inevitably will be effected by any restructuring. But the figures are not wide of the mark and they highlight an important matter: whether it is done quickly or gradually, police reorganisation will involve compulsory redundancies and severance payments will be a huge financial commitment. In other words, a big part of the money saved from the security budget could be eaten up servicing the redundancy programme. The key point is that adjusting the economy from war to peace is not going to be cheap. Even if the cost of police redundancies were to be met from a specially created restructuring fund, it is still in the balance whether a peace dividend would result. As suggested earlier, when the violence ends, the British government is less likely to be as financially generous as it has been in the past. The stringent public expenditure regimes operated in Britain will no doubt cross the Irish sea; treasury officials will be looking at ways to prune the subvention and the security budget presents a prime target. Political pressure would probably prevent the Treasury from getting its way quickly, thereby giving the region a stay-of-relief of about five years. Then the axe would begin to fall. Thus, the most optimistic scenario is for the the local economy to experience a short-lived peace dividend of about £500 million per annum for no more than five years.

With the Provisionals renewing their campaign, the above discussion is to some extent academic. But it serves the useful purpose of cautioning against extravagant claims that a huge peace dividend from the security budget awaits Northern Ireland when the violence finally stops. Clearly there will be no run down of security force personnel while the threat of violence remains, but the absence of peace should not delay some moves towards reform. Although there are obvious difficulties with such a strategy, a concerted campaign should be launched to increase the numbers of Catholic RUC officers. Making a start to improve the religious balance of the police would not only begin to address a long-standing grievance of the Catholic community, but also it would make any necessary restructuring in the future easier.

IS THERE ECONOMIC LIFE BEYOND THE PUBLIC SECTOR?

The dominance of the public sector in the local economy has tended to push discussion about the performance of the private sector into the background. The stylised view is that the private sector is not particularly competitive and on its own would be unable to sustain existing living standards, provide employment opportunities and offer citizens of the region a bright future. But this perspective is not altogether accurate since there have been some encouraging trends.

For nearly a decade, there has been an impressive growth in local manufacturing, as shown in Table 1. Gudgin argues that, apart from two sectors, regional industrial performance has outstripped that of England, Scotland and Wales.[11] In textile and clothing, Northern Ireland's competitive advantage over the rest of the UK is nothing less than spectacular; compared with the Republic, performance has also been good. Only in chemicals and electrical engineering, did industry in the south outperform its counterpart in the north. All in all, measured in terms of output, there can be no doubt that Northern Ireland's industry has experienced something of a renaissance.

Parallelling this upsurge in manufacturing has been an increase in service sector output. The share of private sector activity in regional GDP has been increasing throughout the past decade or so: in 1984 the figure was 34 per cent, by 1994 this had grown to over 40 per cent. All aspects of service related activities have expanded, but particularly striking has been the growth of retailing and distribution

Table 1: *Industrial output in the recovery period*
(Percentage change 1991 Q3 – 1994 Q4)

	NI	Wales	Scotland	England	Republic of Ireland
MAINLY EXPORT INDUSTRIES					
Chemicals	16.2	1.2	10.9	11.0	49.6
Machinery	43.1	0.0	27.6	1.6	-4.3
Metal Goods	48.1	15.8	-30.9	-5.3	3.0
GB AND EXPORT MARKETS					
Transport Equipment	-18.3	12.5	-8.4	6.9	17.2
Electrical Engineering	18.7	44.6	76.9	13.1	49.5
MAINLY GB MARKETS					
Textiles, Clothing	31.5	0.0	-1.1	0.9	-15.7
MIXED MARKETS					
Food, Drink and Tobacco	2.3	23.4	-2.0	5.4	18.0
MAINLY NI MARKETS					
Paper, Printing	10.6	14.6	0.1	7.6	16.2
Rubber, Plastics	27.4	26.4	-1.1	9.7	7.1
Wood Products	38.5	6.5			12.3
TOTAL	**13.5**	**14.6**	**9.0**	**11.9**	**32.2**

Source: Gudgin 1995.

and financial and business services. These figures will come as no surprise to those who live in Northern Ireland. In the early 1980s, Northern Ireland's social and commercial life was drab, uneventful and underdeveloped. Since then there has been a continuous improvement in these aspects of regional life. Nowhere is this improvement better captured than in Derry. A sustained bombing campaign in the 1970s had left the city a dilapidated backwater. Now it is a thriving, confident commercial centre as a result of ten years of essentially service-led growth. Similar transformations have occurred, albeit on a smaller scale, across the region.

Figure 4
Trends in NI Employment and Unemployment 1985–94
(seasonally adjusted)

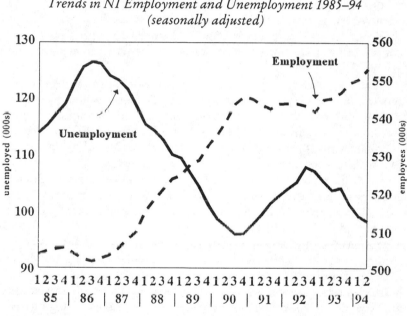

Source: DED

Increased industrial and service sector activity has translated into good job creation performance. Employment growth in the past seven years has been better than any equivalent time in the history of the state. Figure 4 shows there has been an impressive rise in the employment numbers. In the 1980s, Northern Ireland created roughly about 4,500 jobs every year, in the 1990s this figure had increased to between 7,500 and 8,000. At the moment, Northern Ireland is outperforming the UK and the Republic of Ireland, in relative terms, with regard to job generation. The figure also shows that since 1986, apart from a blip in the early 1990s, the local unemployment rate has been on a downward trend. While headline unemployment rates are still too high, this present trend is highly encouraging. Currently, the region has the best short-term unemployment rates in the UK – that means that those who have recently lost their jobs are finding alternative employment quicker than anywhere in Britain. However, the difficult problem of long-term unemployment remains stubbornly and unacceptably high. Concerted government action is needed to tackle this seemingly intractable social and economic problem. The fall in the numbers out of work is not entirely due to the better employment climate. Other factors have also been at play: for example changes to rules in relation to claiming benefits have prompted many not to register as unemployed though they remain economically inactive.

Figure 5 gives a slightly more disaggregated picture of the job generation process over the past ten years. For most of the period, the number of jobs lost in manufacturing outweighed the number of jobs created. Apart from this general trend, the jobs market in manufacturing behaved fairly erratically during the decade: a rollercoaster picture emerges with first a pronounced net loss of jobs, then a slight revival, then another dip and so on. The only glimmer of good news was that between 1993 and 1994, the numbers of jobs created outweighed those lost, which reverses the long standing trend. But nothing too significant should be read into this since the figures have been so up and down over the years. The figure shows that service sector activity lies behind the recent good news on the jobs generation front. Curiously, Northern Ireland did not experience the large boom in market-related service jobs – those in financial and business services, for example – in the mid-1980s that happened in other UK regions as a result of the Lawson boom. But since the late-1980s, and until recently, this area has been the source of exceptionally fast employment growth, increasing in some years by about five and six per cent. Jobs in other service sectors, such as retailing and hotel and catering, have also expanded rapidly. Thus, in the past ten years the private service sector has sharply increased its presence in the region's employment structure. This development simply echoes the common trend experienced by most European regions, but it does reinforce the

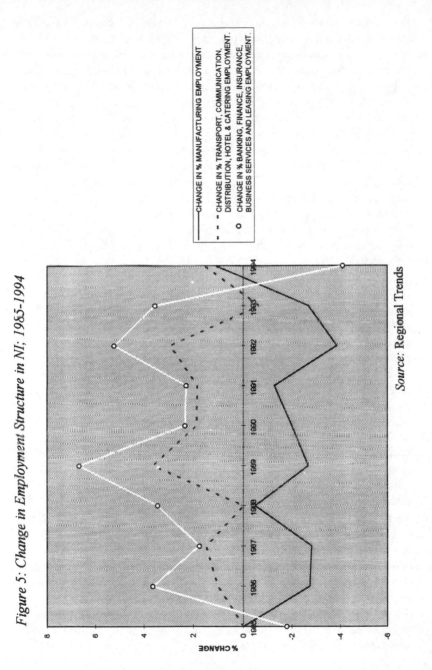

Figure 5: Change in Employment Structure in NI; 1985-1994

Source: Regional Trends

point made earlier that the image of Northern Ireland as a manu-facturing and engineering centre has almost been eclipsed.

All in all, in quantitative terms private sector performance has been good in recent years. If the IRA ceasefire had remained, then future improvements would probably have materialised. An economic consultant's report to the Dublin Forum suggested that a peaceful Northern Ireland would almost immediately result in a bigger tourist sector and more inward investment.[12] This report estimated that a permanent settlement would boost tourist employment by about 11,000, and that new transnationals coming into the region would create about 7,500 jobs. These figures seem about right and, with external funding from the EU and USA also giving a fillip to commercial activity, the total private sector jobs created by a permanent end to violence could be in the region of 20,000–25,000 over a period of years. This slightly upbeat scenario suggests jobs created will outweigh the employment losses that will occur as a result of the rundown of security related activity, which in total could reach 17,000. Thus an end of violence could bring about 5000–7,500 net new jobs to Northern Ireland. Such an employment expansion would be widely welcomed, but it is important to emphasis that such net job gains are insufficient to reduce the local economy's dependence on the public sector.

With the return of violence, the economic transformations that could occur under peaceful conditions may not take effect. At the same time, violence will not put the positive improvements that have emerged in the private sector into reverse. After all, these improvements first emerged when no IRA ceasefire was in sight. Whether the recent rate of increase in private sector activity can continue is hard to predict. In the past, local economic forecasters have been badly burnt when trying to look into the future. On balance, the indications are not good. All economies tend to experience cycles, starting with a spurt of commercial activity, which reaches a plateau and then goes into decline until the process starts again. If this economic law remains true for Northern Ireland, then the current rate of expansion in the private sector will soon peter out. Of course, all efforts should be made to sustain the present situation, but it may be asking too much for the current semi-renaissance to keep going. As a result, it is premature to conclude that the private sector can be the locomotive for the local economy, pulling it towards better living standards and greater prosperity.

THE MOVE FROM JOBLESSNESS TO PENNILESS

A worry, increasingly coming to the fore, is that the quality of the new commercial activity and jobs created is poor. Several different indicators suggest that the region may have become over reliant on low value-added and unskilled forms of economic activity. First of all, many of the new jobs created are part-time or low grade. Secondly, the productivity levels of local industry are unimpressive and remain among the lowest of all UK regions. Since it is ultimately productivity that decides income levels and competitiveness, this is a worrying trend. Low productivity rates translate almost directly into low wages and this has happened in Northern Ireland since the mid-1980s, as shown in Figure 6. In the past decade, wage rates in Northern Ireland have diverged from the UK average after about fifteen years of catch-up. The widespread switch to decentralised collective bargaining in UK industry, together with the growth in low-skilled economic sectors in the Northern Irish economy, are the two main reasons why local wages have become effectively decoupled from other British regions. A third indicator of the growth of low-waged employment is that the share of income from employment in the regional GDP has fallen from 70.4 per cent in 1984 to 65.2 per cent in 1994. Incidentally, the share of gross profits in regional output has increased from 9.4 per cent in 1984 to 12.1 per cent in 1994.

A fourth trend is that job behaviour increasingly resembles that of an 'American'-style deregulated, flexible labour market. In interviews with companies in the food and drink and the leisure sectors it was found that many experienced turnover rates of more than 50 per cent. One company reported that eight out of ten staff leave every year! At the aggregate level, high turnover rates cause unemployment inflows and outflows to be much bigger. Previously in Northern Ireland if a person lost their job it was highly likely that they would experience a lengthy spell of unemployment, if not a fall into long-term unemployment. While the region still has a problem of long-term unemployment, there has been a significant improvement, as already stated, in the rates of short-term joblessness. Thus, a new pattern of labour market behaviour is emerging: while many workers are still likely to experience unemployment, they are more likely to leave the dole queues relatively quickly. People are getting jobs, leaving them more frequently, and returning to another job sooner. This is exactly the pattern of labour market behaviour that exists in the USA. It is

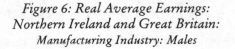

Figure 6: Real Average Earnings:
Northern Ireland and Great Britain:
Manufacturing Industry: Males

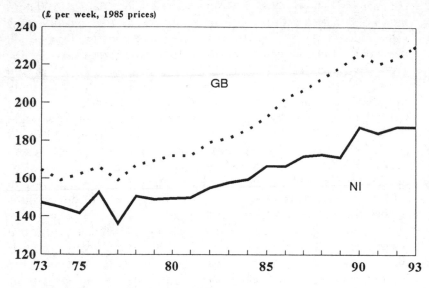

Source: DoE Gazette, New Earnings Survey

closely associated with the widespread availability of low-waged, unskilled jobs. Or to put it differently, economies with more high-skilled jobs display a different pattern of labour market behaviour. Unemployment inflows and outflows are much lower, workers tend to move from job to job directly, and those that fall into unemployment stay there much longer. A key reason for this behaviour is that skilled workers are more likely to prolong their search for work in the hope that they will obtain a good job again.

A fifth, less than positive, development is the current changes to the employment system in the public sector. In the 1980s, it was fashionable to describe those with public sector jobs as privileged, insider employees. Most public sector unions were incensed by the portrayal of their members as some type of new labour aristocracy. But this fury could not disguise the fact that public sector employment was on the whole more attractive than jobs in the private sector: there was a greater level of job security, pay was relatively good due to the continuation of national bargaining, and prospects for training and career advancement were much better. However, the 1990s have seen significant changes in the public sector. In the first place, contracting out and the introduction of quasi-markets through the establishment of Trusts, agencies and the like has put the squeeze on public sector employment. The numbers working in the non-market sector have continually fallen in the 1990s. Moreover, job insecurity has increased, with many people uncertain about whether redundancy is just around the corner. In addition, because of cash limits and meagre pay awards, public sector productivity growth has been rapid. As a result, very few workers are now capturing what economists call insider rents (obtaining wages that are in excess of productivity performance). A more accurate picture now is of public sector workers stretched to the limits. De-regulation and the search for cost minimisation have shattered the relatively privileged position of public sector employees, and the indications are that more of the same is on its way.

Thus, a big question mark hangs over the qualitative dimension of the recent upturn in economic activity. On the surface, the Northern Irish economy appears to have fallen into a low-skill, bad-job trap. In such a situation, workers have little incentive to improve their human capital since relatively high-skilled, high-wage jobs are not available: the private rates of return from training are low. On the other hand, firms do not provide good jobs largely because their productive activity does not require a high-skilled labour input. With such market failures operating simultaneously on the supply and demand side, the labour market gets locked into a low-skills equilibrium that makes it difficult for the economy to compete on the basis of high-skilled, high-value activity. As a result, the process is self-reinforcing, with the trap becoming more pronounced over time. Features of this trap are certainly evident in the Northern Ireland economy. Every year about 12 per cent of pupils leave school with no qualifications and a further 17 per cent with low-level or rudimentary qualifications. Thus, a large part of the workforce is insufficiently skilled.

In some respects the situation is actually more bleak. Like other parts of the UK, Northern Ireland has experienced a large increase in the numbers obtaining tertiary level education. Some regard this development as positive since it equips young people with the skills that are more in line with the new service economy.[13] Thus, side by side with the relatively large numbers of unskilled in the labour market, there is a sizeable pool of well educated people. Without skilled employment, many of these people have been obliged to take bad jobs. As a result, many people in Northern Ireland are over qualified for the jobs they are doing. Moreover, the mismatch between a fairly large pool of well-qualified people and the relative dearth of good jobs, has the effect of pushing down wage rates. As a result, the private return from schooling is lowered in Northern Ireland. It is not only the Troubles but this harsh labour market reality that has encouraged the best and the brightest young people to leave Northern Ireland in search of more prosperous employment elsewhere. Overall, this argument suggests that Northern Ireland has not simply fallen into a low-skills/bad jobs trap, but also into a well-educated/bad jobs conundrum.

It is important not be too indignant about this situation. Many problems emerging in the Northern Irish labour market are merely an echo of similar developments in other European regions and even further afield. Moreover, while some of these trends are not particularly encouraging, they nevertheless are better than the grim, even depressing economic circumstances of the late 1970s and early 1980s although a future of lousy jobs should not be accepted either timidly or passively. Improving the quality of jobs and commercial activity should be made the central goal of government economic policy. Particular attention needs to be focused on solving the inconsistency between creating a mass education system and a job generation process that is resulting in too many bad jobs. Present public policies aimed at attracting inward investment may have to be reexamined. For instance, incentives given to transnationals to come to Northern Ireland may have to be more closely tied to the *quality* rather than simply, as is currently the case, to the *quantity* of jobs created. Secondly, training and skill formation strategies may have to be redesigned in order to encourage firms to create jobs of a better quality. There may even be a case for a minimum wage that puts a floor under pay so that the over reliance on low wage strategies by many firms is challenged. More generally, the present institutional structure of the local economy needs examining to see whether any changes can be made to promote high-skills, high value-added forms of activity.

Improving economic governance
One must not be too starry-eyed about the capacity of economic strategies pursued by regional institutions to effect change. For instance, the traditional instruments of macro-economic policy are not available. Money cannot be made cheaper through the reduction of interest rates to promote investment. Nor can decisions be made to

increase public expenditure to stimulate demand. At the same time, it would be a mistake to write off regional economic policies as unimportant. A highly popular theme in the economic geography literature is that the 'institutional thickness' of a region can have a strong influence on economic performance.[14] Institutional thickness is an umbrella term used to describe the role of local administrations, employer and trade-union bodies, as well as a multitude of other organisations and arrangements such as the churches and training centres, in promoting, enabling and facilitating economic activity. Economic governance is perhaps a better term to use. Many economists are uncomfortable with the heavily qualitative character of this type of analysis. Nevertheless, case studies convincingly show that extra-firm institutions play a decisive role in regional economic performance across Europe, and it would be cavalier to dismiss or ignore this dimension.

This perspective raises some interesting questions about the Northern Ireland economy: in particular, whether some form of regional government would improve economic performance. One fashionable view is to criticise the policy-making process under the direct rule system as inefficient and ineffective. This would be an excessively harsh judgement in the area of economic policy-making. Although mistakes have been made by the local Department of Economic Development, it has shown itself over the years to be sensitive to the needs of the local economy and prepared to be innovative. Consider the matter of targeting social need. Research has shown that the sensitive question of Catholic disadvantage has an important geographical dimension: Catholics tend to live in areas of high economic and social deprivation. In their latest economic strategy document, the local Department of Economic Development recognise this as a problem requiring specific redress. As a result, it has committed itself to targeting special industrial development, training and enterprise programmes on these areas, a stance which radically departs from the neo-liberal economic approach pursued by the government at Westminster.

Thus it would be misleading to suggest that economic policy-making has suffered to any great extent under the Direct Rule system. At the same time, there are flaws in the local economic governance structure that may be improved by some form of regional assembly. One shortcoming is that the public finance system connecting Belfast with London is deeply undemocratic. In 1994/95, nearly £7.5 million of public money was spent in the local economy. The expenditure plans for the various programmes are the result of a long, complex and bureaucratic process, which usually begins with officials in the Northern Ireland Office conducting a mini budget, bringing together and invariably pruning the demands of functional departments in the region. These estimates then form the basis of negotiations between the NIO and the Treasury to decide upon a figure for the block grant: the total annual amount of public expenditure transferred from the Treasury to the NIO. It is important to note that this grant is not divided into specific, earmarked programmes, so when Stormont receives the money, it has a high degree of discretion over its precise allocation and a department can receive more or less than its original expenditure bid.

When the block grant is dispersed across the various programmes, another group of civil servants, usually together with an unelected quango, will sub-divide the money into particular projects and activities. Take health care, for example: each health board – consisting of unelected officials – will receive a financial allocation that it then channels to the various hospitals and programmes under its control. When the hospital receives its share of the pie, yet another unelected body, mostly in the form of trusts, further distributes the money in line with its medical and health plans. An entire chain of financial decisions over public funds takes place every year without any effective democratic controls: civil servants devise and implement plans without being accountable; elected representatives have at best indirect influence over public expenditure priorities and policies. All in all, there is a substantial democratic deficit in the management of public money in Northern Ireland. Like other parts of government decision making, this deficit will only be effectively addressed with the creation of some type of regional assembly. Politicians in such a body would have to account for the financial decisions they make and the policy priorities they establish, even though the ballot box may not be an effective sanction in the short-run, given the polarised nature of local politics.

A regional assembly could also help to bring a touch of fiscal realism to the campaigns of many local politicians. An unfortunate by-product of the large subvention was the expectation, even belief, that economic problems could be solved by government making available extra public money. Elsewhere in the UK and Europe, politicians have had to face the harsher environment of scarce resources, in which the funding of one programme means that another is starved of cash. There is nothing particularly virtuous about politicians having to make such choices, but the essence of modern government is the organisation of competing claims on resources and being able to prioritise between them. Elected representatives in Northern Ireland for the past twenty five years have been in the enviable position of lobbying for extra public cash and campaigning against cut-backs without having to worry about the fiscal implications. A regional government in a peaceful Northern Ireland would change all that. Politicians would have to become more aware of the limits of the public coffers, and would have to face the uncomfortable reality that not everything they wish to do can be done. One beneficial effect of such essentially mainstream democratic behaviour might be to encourage politicians to think less about how the present economic pie is divided between Catholics and Protestants and more how they can collaborate to increase its size.

Another benefit of a regional government would be a greater emphasis on developing policies that are sensitive to the local economic and labour market, and more effective monitoring of such initiatives. Take the issue of employment policy: a consensus has emerged among economists in Europe that benefits systems can distort the labour market in many ways; for instance, the income received by low-paid workers is usually not much more than the benefits they could receive. In Northern Ireland such distortions are particularly acute, as the Northern Ireland Economic Council has shown.[15] To remedy this problem, NIEC suggests that a local pilot scheme should be established to remove disincentives to work from the benefits system: for instance, benefit recipients should be allowed to earn more before some allowances are stopped; and certain benefits like school meals and free prescriptions should continue to be available to people for some time after they have taken a job. Under the present Direct Rule this proposal is unlikely to be acted upon, but if a regional government system were in place, such a pilot scheme would be given closer scrutiny.

Another area suited to local action would be long-term unemployment. To its credit, the Training and Enterprise Agency has developed an innovatory two year scheme for the long-term unemployed known as the Community Work Programme, but first assessments of the programme are not particularly encouraging.

Sheehan and Tomlinson highlight a number of problems: the lack of skill training in many of the programmes, the absence of formal qualifications, and an awkward relationship with the voluntary sector.[16] Under a regional government system, such shortcomings would quickly come under the spotlight and attempts at remedial action could be taken more quickly.

There are, however, many economic problems outside the reach of regional government. Some issues may in theory lend themselves to a regional initiative but these may not be appropriate to the Northern Irish context. Take the matter of regional pay systems, for example: a few years back one of the authors of this book developed a model which depicted the labour market as segmented into a public sector, where wages and conditions were good, and a private sector where the pay and employment situation was more precarious.[17] Clearly this is a stylised picture and exceptions to the rule can be found in both private and public sector. Nevertheless, at the time the model was not widely off the mark. On the basis of this segmentation model, the proposal was made that public sector workers should only receive a proportion of annual UK-wide pay rises, with the remainder being diverted into a regional employment fund. The thinking was simple: the better off in the labour market – the insiders – should show solidarity with the outsiders by helping to create extra jobs. Recently, however, the conditions necessary to make such a scheme operational have evaporated. After several years of little if any pay increases, many public sector workers are not in the financial position nor the political mood to enter such solidarity bargaining. In addition, the big moves towards contracting out and privatisation in the public sector, along with the relentless march towards decentralised pay-setting, have dismantled key parts of the institutional infrastructure to enact such a system. The key point is that careful consideration must be given to every regional economic policy proposal before it is implemented: because it is 'regional' does not necessarily make it good.

A controversial debate about regional government is whether it should have tax-raising powers. In the Framework Documents, the British and Irish governments sidestepped this matter by neither ruling out nor ruling in such a function for a future Northern Ireland assembly. A persuasive case for regional tax-making is made by the Scottish Constitutional Convention. They argue that such a mechanism would enhance the ability of a future Scottish Parliament to develop their own distinctive policies. The same argument has equal validity for the Northern Ireland context and thus a future assembly should be given the authority to raise extra revenue. But the debate about improving economic governance through a regional administration should not be reduced to an acrimonious exchange about whether such a body should or should not be able to tax. Although important, such debates obscure the real purpose of promoting regional level economic policies: to create a thicket of rules and arrangements that animates local commercial activity. Institutions should not be seen as obstacles to doing business, but rather as a source of assistance and help. In more formal economics language, regional government should reduce the pecuniary externalities in local commercial life. Formidable economic challenges lie ahead for Northern Ireland; a regional assembly may not provide all the answers, but it will better position the region to deal with some of these issues.

CONCLUSIONS

While recognising certain positive trends, this chapter is not particularly optimistic about the Northern Ireland economy. It emphasises the barriers that the region will have to surmount if it is to enjoy a prosperous future. This outlook contrasts sharply with the upbeat scenarios that were commonplace during the ceasefires. Understandably, when peace broke out, there was widespread belief that better economic times were just around the corner. Many unfolding developments tended to reinforce this view. After years in the doldrums, the Northern Ireland housing market started to pick up. There was regular news that a new multinational had arrived in town, raising hopes that the region would again become an attractive place for inward investment. The Europeans and Americans reached for their cheque books to provide extra funds, particularly for communities hard hit by the violence. All these were positive and welcome trends, but it would be wrong to conclude that Northern Ireland was on the threshold of a great era of prosperity; many did make this mistake and as a result exaggerated the beneficial economic consequences of peace.

During the 18 months of peace which ended in early 1996, Northern Ireland enjoyed what can be called a phase of expectational growth. This is a term that describes the situation where essentially political changes or developments trigger a self-fulfilling wave of increased economic activity: people believe that, as a result of change, improved economic performance is imminent and thus alter their economic behaviour – spending more or investing more or whatever the case may be. But in reality it is their different pattern of behaviour that fuels the upturn in the economy. Put simply, widespread confidence gives a boost to commercial activity. For example, when Spain made the transition from dictatorship to democracy, there was a huge spurt of economic growth. Similarly, when the the European Commission launched its 1992 programme, economic activity increased significantly across the member states as citizens and firms prepared themselves for the emergence of a completely integrated European market. Invariably, this type of growth, precisely because it is expectational, eventually peters out. After a time, confidence and anticipation fade and the old problems, momentarily camouflaged, come back into view. Thus, as when the magical date of 1992 approached and people and businesses began to realise that the notion of a single European market was a chimera, bullish economic behaviour dissipated and the problems of sluggish growth and high unemployment resurfaced.

This very process took hold in Northern Ireland during the ceasefires. After the years of doom and gloom, the peace fuelled what seemed to be a turn-around in the fortunes of the regional economy. But the odds were stacked against this benign effect being a lasting one: Northern Ireland would lose its novelty value for tourists; inward investors would begin to look elsewhere; the wallets of the Europeans and the Americans would close; and slowly but inexorably the fundamental economic weaknesses would peep out. The brutal reality is that, under peaceful conditions, Northern Ireland becomes just another part of the European periphery, with no particular reason to perform better than anywhere else. Beyond this immutable reality, as this chapter has highlighted, the region will have to deal with two other problems. One is to make the transition from conflict to peace, which is likely to be costly in human and financial terms, particularly in relation to running down the local security forces. The other is to address the trend towards low-skill, low-wage forms of economic activity. At the moment, the immediate prospect involves replacing highly-paid police officers' jobs with precarious employment in areas such as retailing or distribution. This less than optimistic out-look is not to diminish the importance of establishing peace. On the contrary, it is only when the violence ends that the necessary policies and institutions can be put in place to give Northern Ireland a greater opportunity to achieve better economic performance. Without a settlement, the Northern Ireland economy will remain caught between war and peace, dependant on a bloated public sector to save it from the abyss, while at the same time deriving a veneer of normality from low grade private sector activity.

NOTES

1. Teague, Paul, 'Governance Structure and Economic Performance', in *Journal of Urban and Regional Research*, Vol. 18, No. 2, 1994; and Gudgin, G., 'Pulling Ahead: Industrial Growth in Northern Ireland', in *Irish Banking Review*, Summer, 1994.
2. Gudgin, G., 'Regional Problems and Policy in the UK', *Oxford Review of Economic Policy*, Vol. 11, No. 2, 1995.
3. Borooah, V. and McGregor, P., Regional Income Inequality and Poverty in the United Kingdom, Dartmouth, Aldershot 1991.
4. Rowthorn, R.E., 'Northern Ireland: An economy in Crisis', in Teague, P. (ed.), *Beyond the Rhetoric, Politics and the Economy and Social Policy in Northern Ireland*, Lawrence & Wishart, London 1987.
5. Roper, S., *Manufacturing Profitability in Northern Ireland*, Northern Ireland Economic Research Centre, Belfast 1993.
6. Birnie, E. and Hitchens, D., *The Competitiveness of Irish Industry*, Avebury, Aldershot 1994.
7. McGregor, P., Swales, K. and Ying Ya, P., 'Regional Public-Sector and Current Account Deficits: Do they matter? ' in Bradley, J. (ed.), *The Two Economies of Ireland*, Oak Tree Press, Dublin 1995.
8. Gudgin, G., 'Going Boom but Never Going Bust', *Business Brief*, May 1996.
9. Northern Ireland Economic Council, 'The Economic Implications of Peace and Stability for Northern Ireland', Occasional Paper 4, NIEC, Belfast 1995.
10. Northern Ireland Economic Council, 'The Economic Implications of Peace and Stability for Northern Ireland for Selected Sectors: Inward Investment, Tourism and Security', a supplementary paper to the Council's Occasional Paper 4, NIEC, Belfast, June 1995.
11. Gudgin, G., 'Northern Ireland after the Ceasefire', *Irish Banking Review*, Autumn, 1995.
12. KPMG, *et. al.*, 'The Economic Consequences of peace', Report to the Forum of Peace and Reconciliation, 1995.
13. Soskice, D., 'Training and UK Economic Performance', in *Oxford Review of Economic Policy*, Summer, 1993.
14. Amin and Thrift, 1995.
15. Northern Ireland Economic Council, 'Taxes, Benefits, Unemployment and Poverty Traps in Northern Ireland', NIEC, Belfast 1995.
16. Sheehan, M., and Tomlinson, M., 'Long-Term Unemployment in West Belfast', mimeo, Department of Economics, Queens University, Belfast 1996.
17. Teague, P., 'Regional Industrial Relations Systems and the Labour Market Performance in Northern Ireland', *Review of Employment Topics*, Vol. 1, No. 1.

5

CATHOLICS AND PROTESTANTS IN THE NORTHERN IRELAND LABOUR MARKET: WHY DOES ONE GROUP PERFORM BETTER THAN THE OTHER?

8 Claims of discrimination against Roman Catholics go right to the heart of the Northern Ireland problem. The present, bloody conflict has its origins in a civil rights campaign in the late 1960s that demanded an end to Catholic disadvantage. The violence over the past generation has undoubtedly been fuelled by a deep sense of injustice and grievance in the minority community that they have been unfairly treated – discriminated against – especially during the Stormont years. A political agreement has been difficult to reach because the representatives of the Catholic community are filled with foreboding at the prospect of any purely internal settlement that might mark a return to Unionist hegemony. The claim is that Catholics have experienced discrimination in all walks of economic and social life, but that this disadvantage has been most acute in the labour market.

This chapter reviews the evidence of labour market disadvantage where Catholics are concerned, and assesses the competing theories developed to explain unequal status between the two religious blocs. It argues that we should stand back from any single, uni-dimensional explanation for the relatively poor position of Catholics in the Northern Ireland employment system. Certainly, the stereotypical arguments frequently heard in Northern Ireland on the matter– that Catholic disadvantage is the result of Unionist political domination or even oppression, or, conversely, that it is traits within the Catholic community itself that accounts for its underperformance in the labour market – should be rejected out of hand. Such accounts are simplistic, partial, and in some instances, deeply misleading. Labour market outcomes, whether in divided countries like Northern Ireland or in more stable democracies, are the result of complex interactions between social, economic and political influences. Recognising the complexity of the matter does not make Catholic disadvantage any less acceptable. But it should make us wary of those who peddle simplistic explanations of unequal employment performance. More often than not the motivation of these people is to promote a view that one community is in some way superior to the other.

THE DEBATE ABOUT CATHOLIC DISADVANTAGE

Before 1970, due to the absence of reliable data, there was no way of accurately assessing the extent of any Catholic disadvantage in the labour market. Although not altogether satisfactory, the data situation has since improved considerably, and numerous studies have attempted to estimate the degree of religious imbalance in employment. Considerable agreement emerges between these studies on the 'narrow' labour market profiles of the two communities, which could be summarised as follows: that (1) Catholic males are more than twice as likely to be unemployed than Protestant males; (2) Protestants are over-represented in professional, managerial and skilled occupations; (3) Catholics are over-represented in semi-skilled and unskilled jobs; (4) Catholic males are hugely under-represented in security-related employment; while (5) Catholic women are under-represented in administrative and managerial jobs and in clerical, secretarial and sales occupations, they are over-represented in professional jobs; (6) economic inequality within each religious bloc is increasing.

The consensus quickly breaks down however, when it comes to providing explanations for these profiles. The literature on the causes of Catholic disadvantage in the labour market varies greatly in complexion and quality. But it would not be pushing the point to excessively to categorise the debate into (1) political explanations; (2) 'quasi' human capital explanations; and (3) statistical estimations of the unemployment differential between the two communities. Whereas each view throws light on the problem of Catholic labour market performance, none is convincing on its own.

POLITICAL EXPLANATIONS OF UNEQUAL LABOUR MARKET PERFORMANCE

Sympathisers of the Nationalist position frequently claim that Northern Ireland is a 'Protestant State for a Protestant people' which has resulted in endemic discrimination against Catholics.[1] The contrasting perspective held by most Unionists is that: (i) claims of discrimination have been hugely inflated, reflecting simple mischief-making on the part of Nationalists; (ii) any preference shown by Protestant employers towards their co-religionists was caused by the minority community having little loyalty or attachment towards Northern Ireland; (iii) Catholic employers also engaged in so-called discriminatory practices and, as a result, to simply focus on the recruitment practices of Protestant or 'state' organisations is partial and one-sided.[2] To assess the validity of these contrasting views, some political scientists have attempted to assess how systematic the religious discrimination in Northern Ireland has been. Whyte has ably reviewed this literature.[3] He argues that Catholics experienced direct discrimination in many areas of local government and indirect discrimination in other parts of the public sector such as the civil service. With regard to the private sector, Whyte suggests that Protestant employees enjoyed an unquestioned advantage over their Catholic counterparts, particularly at the higher end of the labour market, but he stops short of concluding that systematic discrimination was practised against Catholics. This view is by no means shared by everybody. Reviewing more or less the same data, McGarry and O'Leary were able to conclude that Unionist political dominance during the Stormont years decisively shaped labour market outcomes.[4]

At one level, this political science literature is unsatisfactory. Perhaps the biggest problem is that it exaggerates the role of politics in defining labour market outcomes. In practice, a range of influences independent of the political structure or political decision-making can affect, sometimes deeply so, the relative employment position of different ethnic, racial, religious or social groups. Consider the example of labour market discrimination against blacks in America: between 1940 and 1980 the relative labour market position of blacks continually improved; in 1940, the 'median years of educational attainment', was considerably better for whites than blacks, but by the early 1980s the gap had been more or less closed.[5] Similarly, between 1940 and 1984, the mean weekly wages of blacks relative to whites increased by 26 per cent for males and 56 per cent for females. But during the 1980s, this pattern of continuous gradual convergence with whites went into reverse. In particular, the black–white hourly wage gap has nearly doubled in the last decade from 6.8 per cent to 12.4 per cent.[6] Perhaps the most popular explanation for why the black–white wage gap has expanded runs as follows: in the 1980s, due to the impact of technological change and the globalisation of economic life, the wages of highly skilled workers increased relative to the wages of less skilled workers. Because on average black workers are more likely to be represented at the lower end of the occupational structure, their relative earnings with whites have been adversely affected by the general increase in the price of skill. What this explanation suggests is that spontaneous processes or developments in labour markets can adversely impact on the relative position of different groups, even within the context of fair employment regulation.

We do not have to go to the United States to unearth examples of such endogenous labour market processes; good examples exist within Northern Ireland. One interesting fact to emerge in recent years is the existence of a large number of mainly Catholic or mainly Protestant organisations. Frequently, this religious segregation of corporate workforces is put down to what is known locally as 'the chill factor': the reluctance of individuals from one religion to join organisations where the other religion is dominant because of a perceived threat of intimidation, personal injury, or in the extreme case, death. While clearly an important factor, it is questionable whether the chill factor is the sole influence at play. Even at the height of the violence, there were many trouble-free areas where the chill factor was relatively weak, yet a high number of mono-religious enterprises still existed.

One other factor that must be taken into account is that segregation in employment reflects the growing residential segregation of the two communities. Over the past twenty years, gradual, almost unnoticed, shifts in population have been occurring, resulting in the concentration of Catholics and Protestants in particular parts of the region. For instance, there appears to have been a virtual exodus of Protestants from the border areas and in many residential areas a more pronounced clustering of the Catholic community has taken place. Given that many private sector firms tend to recruit from their immediate surroundings, it may be that religious polarisation in the labour market is being fuelled by these new residential patterns.

Another way of putting this is that many enterprises are 'socially embedded' within their own communities as a result of arrangements like 'extended internal labour markets' (EILMs). Mainwaring suggests that developed EILMs exist where the boundaries between an enterprise and the local community are blurred.[7] A defining feature of EILMs is that recruitment is highly informal. A standard mechanism is for an existing employee to operate as the bridge between the enterprise and the community, so that when a vacancy arises it is filled by somebody from the locality. EILMs are usually beneficial to both employers and workers. For employers, EILMs remove the moral hazard problem from recruitment. Problems of screening and selecting are reduced as new recruits are eager not to compromise the employee who was instrumental in getting them the job or to undermine the operation of EILMs generally by behaving badly. For employees, the advantages of local social relations spilling over into the workplace are considerable.

But Windolf points out that EILMs also amount to a process of labour market closure since job opportunities are monopolised by a local community by erecting social barriers to entry.[8] In the past, there were spectacular examples of local labour market closure in Northern Ireland. The EILMs operated by the shipbuilding firm, Harland and Wolff, and the engineering firm, Shorts, in the predominantly Protestant areas of East Belfast have been cited frequently as examples of the way in whcih Catholics were discriminated against in the region. As these and similar enterprises have declined as a result of industrial change, so the traditional big EILMs have more or less disappeared. But 'micro' EILMs involving smaller firms appear widespread, which accounts, at least partially, for the existence of mainly Catholic or mainly Protestant enterprises.

In other words, over the years a meshing has occurred between the religious profile of some enterprises and the increasingly religious bifurcation of social life in some parts of Northern Ireland. For the most part, this meshing has occurred informally. It has rarely been engineered or orchestrated by the formal political process. The political science debate about labour market imbalance in Northern Ireland tends to overlook these endogenous labour market influences, and as a result, arguments about the unequal labour status of the two communities tend to be incomplete. That is not to say that political science studies have made no contribution. For instance, a great debt is owed to scholars in this tradition for highlighting how the violent sectarian clashes that accompanied the creation of Northern Ireland left an enormous legacy of religious polarisation and prejudice, which in turn hampered the development of liberal-democratic politics. Yet it is a worry that the political science debate has reached a stalemate between those with nationalist leanings, who argue that discrimination has been systematic, those with a Unionist perspective, who maintain the reverse, and compromisers (as Whyte, for example, suggests that whilst Catholics were unfairly treated, this has not been a widespread practice). A fresh agenda needs to emerge so that the discipline can leave behind this stale, repetitive and ultimately fruitless exchange.

QUASI-HUMAN CAPITAL EXPLANATIONS

In Northern Ireland, education is more or less segregated: the overwhelming majority of Catholic and Protestant children go to different schools. Few would deny that separate schooling has perpetuated social and cultural differences between the two communities. Segregated education has also made sectarianism or religious prejudice easier to practise. For instance, a divided educational system made it straightforward for employers to discriminate if they so wished because the religious affiliation of an individual could be immediately detected from the school they attended. An influential view is that separate schooling has had an impact on the quality and quantity of education received by the two communities, which in turn has influenced the respective positions of Catholics and Protestants in the labour market.

Although it is seldom recognised as such, this view closely parallels the theory of human capital. This theory was developed to assess the causes of black–white labour market differentials in the period when racial discrimination became a major political concern in the USA. At root, the human capital approach suggests that a strong and systematic relationship exists between education and personal economic success. According to this approach, the earnings differentials between black and white people are the result of corresponding differences in education between the two groups. In order for the relative labour market position of blacks to improve then, the educational attainment of blacks has to improve. It is this perspective that explains why the debate about discrimination in the USA is so heavily focused on earnings differentials and the relative returns of education. In the USA, there are a number of data sets which have allowed empirical work on these themes. But these econometric studies have not proved conclusive, so controversies rage about the extent to which the human capital approach can explain movements in black–white earnings differentials. For example, Welch suggests that the quality of schooling has had little bearing on the expanding wage gap between blacks and whites, whereas O'Neill takes the opposite view.[9]

With regard to Northern Ireland, there has been virtually no study of the earnings differentials between Catholics and Protestants, largely due to the absence of data which would permit such an examination. As a result, the connection between education and earnings, the key human capital story, remains undiscovered in relation to the two communities. In the absence of such assessments, researchers have adopted the second best approach by examining the education and qualification levels of the two communities. These studies can be called quasi-human capital explanations. From this work has emerged the common explanation that Protestant over-representation in employment and in better jobs is due to the more appropriate and suitable forms of education and qualifications for labour market entry within that community. Another suggestion is that the number of Catholics obtaining 'O' and 'A' level qualifications has always been lower than what might have been expected, especially before the 1970s. Since the 1970s, the gap has reduced but an incongruity still remains between the 'actual' and 'expected' qualification levels of Catholics. Moreover, this body of work suggests that the greater proportion of Protestants at the higher end of the labour market can be explained largely by the fact that Protestant schools specialise in scientific and technical subjects to a greater extent than Catholic schools, where traditionally there has been more interest in the humanities.

There are positive and negative aspects to this line of argument. On the positive side, these studies are a welcome departure from the traditionally sterile political science debate on the matter. Moreover, the quasi-human capital approach has led to the enactment of a range of level-headed and worthwhile policies. For instance, because the Roman Catholic Church wished to remain apart from the state educational system, it received public funding to cover only 85 per cent of the costs of running its own schools. The other 15 per cent had to be found from its own coffers. One argument is that this financial formula may have led to Catholic schools being under-equipped to teach scientific and technical subjects comprehensively and to advanced levels. As a result, Protestant or state schools may have been given an advantage in developing in their pupils skills more directly relevant to high grade occupations in the labour market. However, this financial formula has been recently abolished and Catholic schools are now 100 per cent state funded.

On the negative side, these quasi-human capital studies are exposed to the general line of criticism levied against this approach. One point made by Arrow and Thurow, amongst others, is that lack of information disallows any direct link to be made in practice between the skill or knowledge of a worker and his or her productivity performance.[10] As a result, although some association may exist between these two variables, it is more likely that employers use their knowledge about certain types of education as a 'screen' when hiring certain types of workers. This is known as the screening hypothesis. Some employers may prefer Protestants because they believe that Protestant schools produce better trained pupils. But once screening practices are recognised to be at play, a Pandora's Box is opened about the assumptions and even prejudices which might influence employers' decisions. In other words, while the human capital story has much to say about the supply side of the labour market (the qualities and attributes individuals bring to jobs) it has virtually nothing to say about the demand side of the labour market (the recruitment decisions of enterprises, the way employers structure jobs and so on). Frequently, human capital studies only give a partial insight into why some groups fare better in the labour market than others, and this seems to be the case in relation to Northern Ireland.

At the same time, it would be cavalier to dismiss this approach completely. The supply-side dimension to labour market imbalance in Northern Ireland is clearly important. But the conventional argument that the poorer labour market performance of Catholics is due to inadequate scientific and technical teaching in Catholic schools may need recasting. Underpinning this account is the image of an economy with a large manufacturing sector generating a high demand for people with engineering-related skills, but as a result of structural change this is no longer an accurate portrayal of the Northern Ireland economy: since the early 1970s, manufacturing employment has been in continuous decline while the number of service-related jobs, particularly in the public sector, has increased. Inevitably this structural shift in the economy gives rise to a different occupational profile of the workforce, which may require educational institutions to re-order training and qualification priorities. This development impinges on the 'human capital' story for unequal labour market status of Catholic and Protestants.

Table 1: Change of Socio-Economic Status, 1981–1991

Socio-Economic Status	Men	Women
Employers	+5,326	+2,279
Managers	+7,387	+7,260
Professional Workers	+2,723	+2,311
Ancillary Workers	+3,116	+9,191
Foremen and Supervisors (non-manual)	−1,833	−1,083
Junior non-manual	+3,063	+17,360
Personal Service Workers	+2,122	−6,445
Foremen and Supervisors (manual)	−4,554	+198
Skilled Manual	−5,546	−1,127
Semi-skilled and unskilled manual	−4,915	+14,673
Own account workers (non-professional)	+7,797	+1,252
Farmers and agricultural workers	−5,882	+437
Other	−462	−2,387
TOTAL	+8,342	+43,919

Source: Northern Ireland Census of Population 1981 and 1991.

The 1991 Population Census provides a great deal of detail on occupations. Unfortunately the figures are not directly comparable with those in the 1981 census. Nevertheless, after adjustments, table 1 makes a comparison between the two years. This shows that over the decade, there was a continual decline of those jobs normally associated with manufacturing activity – skilled manual tasks – and an increase in jobs closely related to the service sector, for instance, junior non-manual workers (secretarial jobs). The emerging pattern of an increasing number of jobs at both ends of the occupational structure and a decreasing pool of jobs in the middle can also be seen in other parts of the UK and elsewhere. In relation to the issue of fair employment in Northern Ireland, the big question is whether this new occupational profile is changing the type of skills and thus the type of qualifications and training demanded by employers. Unfortunately, no study has been undertaken on this matter amongst Northern Ireland companies. But the Employment in Britain Survey does present a fascinating analysis of skills developments in British companies, and it can be reasonably assumed that Northern Ireland companies are evolving along similar lines since the occupational changes that are occurring in the two areas are comparable.[11]

This survey found that in two-thirds of the companies surveyed, skill levels had increased during the 1980s in two key ways: one was the growth in demand for people with computer skills and the other was an increase in the demand for social skills. These new skill demands reflect the rapid spread of micro-processors in all spheres of commercial activity and the growing importance of communication and the handling of people in business. Significantly, the survey showed that employers were meeting their skills requirements mostly by employing students with formal educational qualifications. Equally significantly, the survey highlighted that employers showed no clear bias in favour of students with engineering or (technical) computing skills.

These new recruitment strategies have considerable implications for the view that the greater scientific orientation of Protestant schools explains a large part of the religious differential in employment status. To the extent that there is a gap in this area of the curriculum, it may not matter in light of the changing pattern of skills demanded by enterprises. If companies now prefer to recruit on a general basis, then Catholics may not be disadvantaged in terms of educational qualifications. For example, Table 2, which shows the percentage of Catholics and Protestants with 'GCSE', 'A' levels and higher education qualifications, demonstrates that about the same proportion of the two communities is now represented at each tier of the qualifications ladder.

Table 2: Highest Level of Qualification
(economically active persons)

Highest Level of Qualification	Men		Women		Both Sexes	
	P %	C %	P %	C %	P %	C %
Higher[1]	14	13	16	20	15	16
A level (or equivalent)	15	13	11	12	13	13
O level (or equivalent)	17	15	20	20	18	17
Other qualifications	14	10	19	16	16	13
No qualifications	39	48	33	31	36	41
Not stated	1	1	1	1	1	1

[1] Degree level or above, HNC/HND,BTEC (Higher) and equivalents, teaching and nursing qualifications.
Source: Labour Force Survey 1993

Another factor to be entered into the equation here is the high level of unemployment in the local economy, which tends to result in people getting jobs for which they are over-qualified. So if the educational gap between the two communities, particularly at the higher level is closing, and at the same time employers have a preference for generic qualifications while there are only a few good jobs to go about, then the human capital thesis, as it stands, may not be a convincing explanation for continued Catholic disadvantage in many occupations.

This is not to say that the human capital approach is unimportant, simply that we may have to start asking different types of questions. With regard to schooling, for instance, it may be more appropriate to identify differences between the way students from the two communities are taught social skills rather than scientific subjects. In other words, the human capital argument needs recasting and updating so that it is more in line with the huge changes that have occurred to the structure of the Northern Ireland economy and the skill formation strategies of its population. Unfortunately too many people carry around notions about the nature of Northern Ireland's economy and society that correspond more to the 1960s than to the 1990s.

ECONOMETRIC EXPLANATIONS OF THE (MALE) UNEMPLOYMENT DIFFERENTIAL

In recent years, more sophisticated statistical techniques have entered the debate about labour market discrimination. For the most part, studies of this kind attempt to uncover why the male unemployment differential between the two communities has stayed at a ratio of 2.5 for decades. The pioneering assessment was made in 1990 by Smith and Chambers.[12] They set out to estimate how much of the unemployment differential between the two communities was due to either direct or indirect discrimination, by producing a model with controls for the factors identified in other studies to explain poor Catholic labour market performance. Thus, they controlled for location, class and family, dual labour markets, differential educational qualifications and different age and demographic structures. If all these factors taken together had been able to account for Catholic (males) being approximately two and a half times more likely to be unemployed than Protestant males, then their statistical analysis should have resulted in an insignificant residual or none at all (a residual indicates that influences other than those identified by the statistical exercise are at play). But Smith and Chamber's model found a large residual, which suggests that many of the existing studies did not fully explain why Catholics had a worse labour market performance than Protestants. They concluded that much of the residual captured discrimination against the minority.

This conclusion has been heavily criticised on a number of grounds. First of all, people have argued that the statistical methodology of the study was faulty. In particular, the empirical results were regarded as suspect due to certain sampling procedures and the failure of the authors to produce 'a goodness of fit' to test the robustness of the regression equations. Secondly, and more importantly, the study was seen as flawed since security force and black economy variables were not included in the model. Omitting a variable for the security forces was regarded as particularly significant for the following reason. Because of the political conflict in the region, employment in the security forces and related industries has grown considerably in the past twenty years and now stands at 21,000. But almost all these jobs are taken by Protestants. If these jobs were shared out equally between the two communities, Catholics would have 7,500 more jobs and Protestants 7,500 fewer jobs. Assuming that only males would be affected by this hypothetical transfer of employment, Catholic unemployment would fall from about 36,000 to 29,000, and Protestant unemployment would increase from 21,000 to 28,500. As a result, the male unemployment differential between the two communities would virtually disappear. All in all, the argument is that the high concentration of Protestants in the security forces has an important impact on the pattern of employment and unemployment in the two communities. On the surface this arithmetic is convincing, but the big problem is that the unemployment differential existed before the huge increase in security force employment. Overall, although Smith and Chambers' study contained blemishes, their conclusions cannot be dismissed out of hand.

A contrasting statistical study of the unemployment differential was carried out by Compton.[13] He used a method to highlight the difference between 'actual' and 'expected' rates of Catholic unemployment if it were assumed that the Catholic community had the 'structural' properties of the Protestant community. Specifically, Compton's exercise set out to discover whether, if Catholics lived where Protestants do, had the same age structure, had similar educational background and qualifications and worked in the same industries, would their unemployment rate be still twice that of Protestants? His results suggest that if Catholics displayed similar traits to Protestants, then the unemployment differential between the two communities would be 17 per cent. Or, to put it differently, over 80 per cent of the unemployment differential can be explained by factors endogenous to the Catholic community. This conclusion comes close to suggesting that Catholics have only themselves to blame for their unemployment plight.

Almost every aspect of Compton's study has been challenged. Murphy and Armstrong show that the statistical procedure used is constructed in a way that would eliminate the unemployment differential by the maximum possible amount; other equally valid standardisation procedures would yield quite different results.[14] Another criticism is that the study is built upon extreme and unrealistic assumptions. For instance, Compton assumes that the employment structure is bifurcated into Catholic-only and Protestant-only jobs on a permanent basis, but with no justification as to why this should be so. A more fundamental criticism of Compton is that he accepts the 'structural' differences between the two communities as the natural order of things and not the outcome of social and political processes.

Thus, basic yet crucial questions are conveniently ignored, such as why are Catholics crowded into sectors more vulnerable to unemployment shocks, or why are Catholics living in sub-regions with poor employment opportunities? All in all, because of these shortcomings, the Compton study is widely regarded as unconvincing.

Two recent statistical assessments of the unemployment differential reach contrasting conclusions. One was conducted by Murphy and Armstrong.[15] Using a battery of elaborate econometric methods, this study set out to get a clearer picture of Catholic and Protestant male unemployment. The following were amongst the main results: (i) that about half of the unemployment differential between Catholics and Protestants can be accounted for by factors such as age, number of children, housing tenure, qualifications, area of residence. The other half is attributed to personal characteristics or other factors such as discrimination. This conclusion is similar to Smith and Chambers' findings; (ii) that differences in labour force growth were only found to have an effect on the unemployment differential when they were coupled with a range of assumptions about low labour turnover rates, zero or negative employment growth rates and segregation in employment; (iii) that Catholic men are more likely to be long-term unemployed; (iv) that Catholic men are significantly more likely to be economically inactive, and again half of this difference is attributed to religion, while the other half is put down to other characteristics; (v) that Catholic men search less for jobs than Protestants and do so in different ways.

Overall, this is probably the most elaborate and exhaustive study of the unemployment differential. At the same time, because of data limitations and the necessity to base some of the statistical tests on assumptions that would not be widely shared, the authors conclude that their study will not end the controversy about the unemployment differential. This is probably an accurate assessment, despite the high quality of the research. 'Aggregate' assessments of the unemployment differential are perhaps too ambitious given the wide range of influences involved and the interaction between them. Such complex social processes cannot be embodied satisfactorily in an econometric model. A more productive avenue may be to carry out specific desegregated statistical studies.

A contrasting study, both in terms of its methodology and results, was developed by Gudgin and Breen.[16] They set out to explain why the Catholic/Protestant differential has stayed constant at a ratio of 2.5

for over twenty years, even though labour market conditions have varied considerably during this period. In 1971, for instance, the (male) unemployment rate was 7 per cent, while in 1991 it was 21 per cent; a reasonable assumption would be that the differential would be affected in one way or another by these varying circumstances, but this has not been the case. To explain the persistence of the ratio, the authors develop a labour market accounting framework which emphasises flows in and out of employment and unemployment.

For Gudgin and Breen the persistence of the unemployment differential between Catholics and Protestants can be explained by four factors. One is the differential labour force growth rates of the two communities. Between 1971 and 1991 they estimate that the Catholic population of working age increased by 61 per cent (2.4 per cent per annum) compared with 22 per cent (1 per cent per annum) for Protestants. Thus, with more Catholics entering the labour market, they had a higher probability of not finding a job given the rather low level of employment growth. A second factor was the different migration rates of the two communities. Although between 1971 and 1991 roughly 33,000 Catholics left Northern Ireland, as against 17,000 Protestants, the authors argue that the Protestant propensity to migrate in the face of a given level of unemployment is more than five times higher than that of Catholics. Catholics are less likely to respond to unemployment by emigrating than Protestants. A third factor is that Catholics have higher levels of quit rates than Protestants. Fourthly, Protestants are in a better position to obtain a job, given the number of disadvantages experienced by Catholics, such as location, age and qualifications.

In simulations, the authors find that together these four factors can explain the persistence of the Catholic/Protestant unemployment differential. Specifically, they estimate that the 'Catholic disadvantage' factor accounts for about half of the ratio, which coincides with the findings of Smith and Chambers and Murphy and Armstrong and that the other half can be explained by the variables of migration, labour force growth and quit rates.[18] The unavoidable conclusion of this study is that discrimination, direct or indirect, has played no part in the situation where Catholics are 2.5 times more likely to be unemployed than Protestants.

In assessing the Gudgin and Breen paper, it is necessary to distinguish between its technical and theoretical merits. There can be little doubt that it is an elegant piece of technical work, although question marks can be raised about the quality of the data used. For instance, the figures on job turnover are extremely suspect. By contrast, the theoretical aspects of the paper are not particularly sophisticated. Many labour economists would regard their stocks and flows model of the employment system as crude.

Developing 'stocks and flows' models of the labour market is fashionable. A key objective of such models is to obtain a better understanding of the behaviour of job holders and the unemployed. For instance, this approach has thrown interesting light on the problem of European unemployment. In particular, it has been found that those without skills tend to remain longer on benefits than those with skills. Additionally, skilled workers tend to move from one job to another, while unskilled people experience a period of unemployment between jobs. The main message from such studies is that people with different skills and occupational profiles behave differently in the labour market. None of this thinking is taken on board by Gudgin and Breen. Thus the study states correctly that Catholic quit rates are higher than Protestants, but no explanation is offered as to why this is the case. One reasonable conjecture is that, as Catholics are crowded into employment sectors and occupations where lay-offs and quit rates are high, they are bound to leave jobs more frequently than Protestants. Similarly, it may be that Protestants have a greater propensity to migrate because they are more skilled than Catholics and thus in a better position to leave Northern Ireland for a job elsewhere.

Gudgin and Breen fail to address such questions. Their approach is to treat these essentially behavioural factors in the workings of the employment system as accounting identities, which is far from satisfactory. As a result, important questions are left unanswered. Failure to investigate whether it is the labour market position of Catholics and Protestants that determine their respective behaviour in relation to migration and quits, leaves the model premised on a number of implicit but unpleasant assumptions about Catholics. Gudgin and Breen may argue that they take account of the 'structural disadvantage' of Catholics when accepting that half of the unemployment differential between the two communities is explained by such factors. But it is naive to suggest that such structural effects do not influence labour market behaviour. In other words, 'structural disadvantage' cannot clinically be separated off from the stocks and flows of the two communities in Northern Ireland's employment system as Gudgin and Breen have done.

One important implication of this argument is that statistical studies of labour market discrimination or disadvantage must be acutely aware of the assumptions that are being made about factors, such as the social and economic environment, that influence the behaviour of Catholics and Protestants in the labour market. This point can be pushed further to suggest that insights into the question of Catholic disadvantage will not be gained by quantitative studies alone. Equally important will be assessments of a more qualitative type. In the USA, for example, there is a large body of sociological literature which attempts in a non-quantitative way to examine the social processes that lead to different labour market outcomes of particular groups. For instance, attempting to capture the experience of black ghettos and other immigrant communities, Piore suggests that in some social settings norms emerge which reinforce the work habits of those in low-grade occupations.[19] People at the lower end of the labour market develop a low evaluation of work opportunities and rewards, and also tend to regard a whole range of jobs as out of their reach. As a result of 'social feedback mechanisms' these individual perceptions begin to spread across communities, which then promotes a culture of exclusion and entrapment. In essence, Piore is trying to suggest that labour market behaviour may be the result rather than the cause of employment segmentation. Few studies of this kind have been undertaken in Northern Ireland with the notable exception of Howell.[20] This is regrettable since such work provides a necessary balance to more statistically oriented analysis.

DEMOGRAPHY AND FAIR EMPLOYMENT

Perhaps the most important empirical point raised by Gudgin and Breen is the impact of differential population growth on the search for fair employment. Before dealing with this question directly, it is important to point out that solving labour market differences, and in particular the unemployment differential between the two communities, will be heavily influenced by general economic circumstances.

If economic conditions are good, causing employment to grow rapidly, then getting a more balanced labour market will be made easier. Alternatively, if the job generation process is lacklustre then reducing labour market imbalances, such as the unemployment differential, will be more difficult. Employment performance of the Northern Ireland economy over the past seven years has been relatively good. However, this healthy employment performance has not been strong enough to counteract some of the negative features of the Northern Ireland labour market which have a strong bearing on the economic status of the two communities. First of all, in spite of larger numbers in work, unemployment and economic inactivity in the region remains high. Over the past twenty-five years both these rates have increased dramatically for men. In 1971 about 15.5 per cent of males were not in work, but by 1991 this had increased to 32.8 per cent – some 157,000 individuals. Although the Protestant community has not got off scot-free, the situation is worse in the Catholic community. Thus about 41.7 per cent of all Catholic males of working age were not in work in 1991, while for Protestants the figure was 26.3 per cent: clearly adverse trends in the labour market are more acute amongst the Catholic community.

Relatively little of this imbalance can be attributed to employment discrimination. Between 1971 and 1991 the absolute number of jobs held by Catholic males fell by about 4 per cent, whereas the equivalent figure for Protestant males was roughly 14 per cent. In other words the Protestant community suffered the most from the huge shake out that occurred in manufacturing and related activities; Catholics, being under-presented in these sectors, were relatively less affected. But if this is the case, what accounts for the huge increase in unemployment and economic inactivity in the Catholic community? Here the question of differential population growth highlighted by Gudgin and Breen comes into play.

During the period under consideration, there was a big increase in the numbers of Catholic males of working age, much larger than the corresponding figures for Protestant males. Because overall employment was falling, there was no way these increases in population could be absorbed by the labour market proper. As Rowthorn has pointed out, in the absence of sufficient numbers of jobs, people were faced with the choice of either falling into unemployment, accepting economic inactivity or emigrating.[21] Table 3 shows the increase in all three since 1971. The key point that should be stressed here is that the higher growth rate of the Catholic population made it virtually inevitable that the rate of increase for Catholics in all three categories would be higher than Protestants. The laws of arithmetic and not discriminatory practices determined this outcome. This is not to conclude that Catholics have only themselves to blame and that the drive towards fair employment should be halted. Rather it is simply to reinforce the point made earlier; that a range of labour market processes, unrelated to discrimination, can work in a way to cause unequal employment outcomes for the two communities. Furthermore, it is an attempt to highlight the present relatively cold labour market climate in which to secure a more religiously balanced market.

In a recent paper, Rowthorn highlights the difficulties in obtaining a balance between Catholic and Protestant male unemployment rates.[22] First of all, he sets out a pessimistic scenario where the goal of full labour market equality is relentlessly pursued against the backdrop of falling male employment. This situation has highly damaging consequences for the Protestant community as they are likely to loss 35,000 jobs between 1991 and 2011. At the same time, the Catholic share in employment increases, but because of the growth of the Catholic male population of working age unemployment in this community remains high. Thus, although there is religious equality in the labour market neither community is doing very well. Then a more optimistic scenario is outlined in which the goal is to reduce the unemployment differential between the two communities without further squeezing the male Protestant share in total employment. For this to happen 39,000 additional jobs would have to be created for the Catholic community by 2011, and a further 35,000 thereafter. Overall, the Catholic stock of jobs would have to increase by about 36 per cent over the 1991 level. This is a highly ambitious, some would say unrealistic, target which raises the spectre of a zero sum game opening up whereby the position of Catholics in employment improves at the expense of Protestants.

CONCLUSIONS

A range of approaches have been used in an attempt to explain why Catholics perform worse than Protestants in the Northern Ireland labour market. Some focus on the political dimension and argue about whether Catholic disadvantage in the labour market is the result of Unionist political dominance spilling over in the economic arena. Others have examined whether any contrasting educational and skills profiles of the two communities explain differential labour market performance. Yet a further approach has attempted to statistically model particular social and economic characteristics of the two religious blocs to account for the better employment performance of Protestants. Each approach is not without some merit, but all were

Table 3: Population Growth and Economic Activity

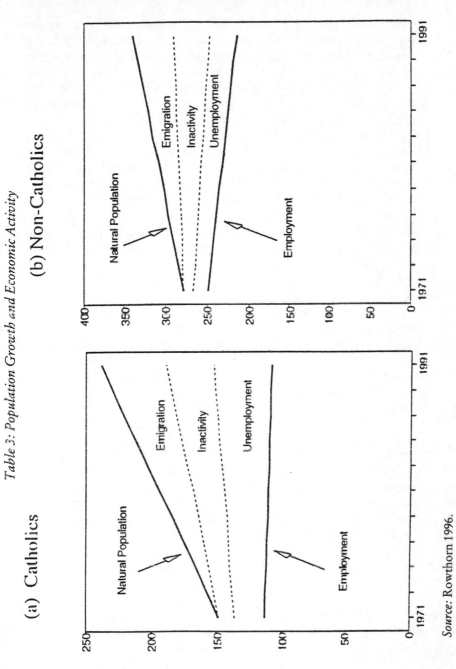

(a) Catholics

(b) Non-Catholics

Source: Rowthorn 1996.

139

found to be defective in one way or another. Perhaps the most unsatisfactory studies have been those that have attempted to explain Catholic disadvantage through the use of statistical and econometric techniques alone. Invariably, these studies make crude assumptions about the social and cultural traits of both communities that devalue the findings that are reached. If the theoretical literature on discrimination and unequal treatment tells us anything it is that labour market advantage and disadvantage is normally the result of a complex range of economic and social factors and cannot be reduced to one or even to a narrow group of factors. Thus we should see religious disadvantage in the Northern Ireland employment system arising from a wide range of influences and this is the key message of this chapter.

While this conclusion is in line with the consensus in the academic literature that urges a multi-faceted approach to explaining inequalities, it is of little comfort for those promoting fair employment in Northern Ireland. Currently the main political trend in the region is a growing polarisation between the two communities. Each religious bloc appears less committed to pursuing a political process that might allow the two communities to resolve the problems of living together in the same territory. In this situation, each community is susceptible to the simple story about labour market disadvantage. On the one hand, Catholics are only too willing to believe that their disadvantage in employment is the result of continued Unionist dominance over local politics. On the other hand, Protestants are more likely to believe that Catholics have only themselves to blame for any labour market misfortunes they may experience. Developing a narrative that argues that labour market disadvantage is a complex and difficult matter, not only to explain but to resolve, is incredibly difficult in such a polarised environment. And of course the more the simple stories are accepted the more the two communities drift apart. This is why attempts at reaching a political settlement are so important. Some type of democratic accommodation between the two communities will allow the political structures to emerge to contain the divisions that exist on the question of Catholic labour market disadvantage. It may also allow the curtain to be pulled down on vulgar, incomplete arguments on the topic.

NOTES

1. Farrell, M., *Northern Ireland: The Orange State*, Pluto Press, London 1980.

2. Hewitt, C., 'The Roots of Violence: Catholic Grievances and Irish Nationalism during the civil rights period', in Roche, P., and Barton, B. (eds), *The Northern Ireland Question: Myth and Reality*, Avebury Press, Aldershot 1991.
3. Whyte, J., 'How much discrimination was there under the Unionist regime', Gallacher, T. and O'Connell, J. (eds), *Contemporary Irish Studies*, MUP, Manchester 1983; and *Interpreting Northern Ireland*, Clarendon Press, Oxford 1990.
4. McGarry, J., and O'Leary, B., *The Politics of Antagonism*, Athlone Press, London 1992.
5. Card, D., and Kreuger, A., Trends in Black–White Earnings Revisited', *The American Economic Review*, Papers and Proceedings, May 1993. *See also* Card, D., and Kreuger, A., 1991, School Quality and Black/White Relative Earnings: A Direct Assessment', NBER Working Paper N3713, May 1991.
6. Boozer, M., Frauger, A., Wolken, S., 'Race and School Quality Since Brown v Board of Education', Brookings Papers on Economic Activity, Microeconomics, 1992.
7. Manwaring, T., 'The extended internal labour market', *Cambridge Journal of Economics*, Vol. 25, No.3, 1981.
8. Windolf, P., 'Structured and unstructured labour markets', Windolf, P. and Wood, S. (eds), *Recruitment and selection in the labour market*, Avebury, Aldershot 1988.
9. Welch, F'. 'The Employment of Black men', *Journal of Labour Economics*, Vol. 11, No. 2, 1990; O'Neill, J., 'The Role of Human Capital in Earnings Differences between Black and White Men', *Journal of Economic Perspectives*, Vol. 4, No.4, 1990.
10. Arrow, K., *Human Capital: A Theoretca; and Empirical Analysis*, National Bureau of Economic Affairs, New York 1959; and Thurow, L., *Poverty and Discrimination*, Brookings Institution, Washington 1969.
11. Gallie, D., 'Patterns of Skill Change: Upskilling, Deskilling or Polarisation?' in Penn, R., Rose, M., Rubery, J. (eds), *Skills and Occupational Change*, Oxford University Press, Oxford 1994.
12. Smith, D., and Chambers, G., *Inequality in Northern Ireland*, Clarendon Press, Oxford 1990.
13. Compton, P., 'Employment Differentials in Northern Ireland and Jobs Discrimination: A Critique', in Roche, P., and Barton, B. (eds), *The Northern Ireland Question: Myth and Reality*, Avebury press, Aldershot 1991.
14. Murphy, A., and Armstrong, D., *A Picture of the Catholic and Protestant Male Unemployed*, Central Community Relations Council, Belfast 1994.
15. *Ibid.*
16. Gudgin, G., and Breen, R., 'Ratios of Unemployment Rates as an Indicator of Fair Employment in Northern Ireland', mimeo, Northern Ireland Economic Research Centre, 1994.
17. Smith and Chambers, *op.cit.*
18. Murphy and Armstrong, *op.cit.*
19. Piore, M., 'Notes for a Theory of Labour Market Segmentation', in Edward, R., (ed.), *Labour Market Segmentation*, Cambridge 1992.

20. Howell, L., 'Unemployment: doing the double and labour markets in Belfast', in Curtin, C., and Wilson, T. (eds), *Ireland from Below: Social Change and Local Communities*, Galway University Press, Galway 1989.
21. Rowthorn, R., 'Inequality and Justice: Male Employment in Northern Ireland', mimeo, Cambridge University.
22. *Ibid.*

6

REALISING FAIR EMPLOYMENT IN A DIVIDED SOCIETY

Whereas the previous chapter examined the debate about the causes of Catholic disadvantage, the focus here is on government-led moves towards fair employment. This is a natural progression, for, as arguments raged about why Catholics fared worse than Protestants in the labour market, successive governments signalled the unacceptability of this situation by pursuing a range of anti-discrimination policies. The purpose of this chapter is to assess the success or otherwise of public policies to eradicate religious bias from the employment system.

Two key conclusions are reached. On the one hand, a strong anti-discrimination institutional regime has been created in the region and progress has been made towards fair employment. On the other hand, neither community appears satisfied with the fair employment system: while Catholics believe not enough has been done, Protestants feel that they are beginning to lose as a result of job recruitment being weighted in favour of Catholics. Together these two conclusions suggest that attempts at reforming Northern Ireland piecemeal run the danger of falling foul of the deep-rooted sectarian divisions that exist in the region. To put the matter differently, realising equity in the labour market, and containing the political tensions that are associated with the issue, would be advanced by a historic compromise between Unionism and Nationalism.

THE LEGISLATIVE MOVES TOWARDS FAIR EMPLOYMENT

In the early years of the Troubles, two influential reports, the

143

Cameron Commission (1969) and the Van Straubenzee Report (1975), concluded that Roman Catholics had been unfairly treated in the labour market. Mainly in response to these findings, the British government introduced the Fair Employment Act (Northern Ireland) 1976, which outlawed employment discrimination on grounds of religious or political beliefs. The Act also established a Fair Employment Agency (FEA) with advisory, research, investigative and enforcement functions to promote fair employment. The Agency was able to pursue individual complaints of discrimination and also to assess the religious composition of workforces in specific organisations in order to ascertain whether or not equality of employment opportunity existed. The Agency was given the authority to take individual complaints before county courts, which in turn had the power to award damages if discrimination was proven. Where enterprises were found to have a religiously imbalanced workforce, the Agency was given the power to oblige them to institute 'affirmative action programmes' which could include the setting of goals and timetables. This was the main enforcement instrument given to the FEA, and as such it was more or less in line with the powers given to the Commission of Racial Equality and the Equal Opportunities Commission in Britain.

Within a short period of time, the effectiveness of the legislation was questioned. A well-organised and highly effective campaign, known as the MacBride Principles, was launched in the United States to ensure that American enterprises investing in the Province adhered to a list of fair employment measures. Furthermore, internal civil service appraisals of the Act reached the conclusion that the legislation was doing little to reduce religious imbalances in the labour market. In an influential paper published in 1983, McCrudden argued that the Act suffered from a number of shortcomings. First, that its emphasis on individuals bringing complaints about discrimination was too limited, as there was no established tradition of individuals seeking redress through the courts in Northern Ireland.[1] Second, that the resources given to the agency were meagre relative to the problem it was charged with solving. Third, that the agency was badly organised and managed. Alongside these criticisms of the legislation, a political campaign got under way for stronger anti-discrimination regulations.

These influences prompted the government to introduce the Fair Employment Act (Northern Ireland) 1989. First, the Act widened the scope of illegal discrimination to include indirect as well as direct discrimination on the grounds of political opinion. Second, it replaced the FEA with the Fair Employment Commission (FEC) which had additional powers and resources. Third, it established a new Fair Employment Tribunal (FET) to adjudicate in individual cases of alleged discrimination. Fourth, it placed new obligations on employers to ensure the active pursuit of fair employment. Under the terms of the Act all private employers with more than twenty-five employees (this threshold has since been lowered to ten employees) are required to register with the Fair Employment Commission. (Public sector organisations were regarded as being registered from the outset.)

All registered employers are required to monitor the religious composition of their workforce and to provide the Fair Employment Commission with the relevant statistics each year. Failure to supply this information is a criminal offence, as is failure to supply it within the prescribed period. In addition, all public sector employers, and those private sector concerns with more than 250 employees, have to monitor the composition of job applicants and return specified information about applicants to the Fair Employment Commission. Summary information about the monitoring returns is published by the Fair Employment Commission on an annual basis; this includes a listing of all individual concerns registered with the Commission, giving the numbers of Protestants and Catholics employed.

The workforce composition of an individual employer is not expected to match the overall composition of the economically active population in Northern Ireland. But, employers are expected to make progress towards a situation where Catholics and Protestants enjoy proportionate representation, taking into account the appropriate catchment area for particular job grades. If such fair participation is not provided, then an employer must take affirmative action measures. These may be undertaken voluntarily, but an employer may also be directed by the Commission, or ordered by the Fair Employment Tribunal, to undertake affirmative action. The type of affirmative action measures set out often involves setting of goals and timetables to measure progress. However, laying down quotas, where specific numbers or proportions of positions are reserved for members of one religion or community, is unlawful.

Each registered employer must also review, at least once every three years, the practices which affect the workforce composition, such as recruitment, selection, training and promotion. This is a major undertaking which involves, for example, obtaining from the Fair

Employment Commission labour market data so that catchment areas can be reassessed, if necessary. Employers are expected to analyse the monitoring returns from the previous three years, compare trends with labour availability data, review affirmative action plans and provide the Commission with a written report on the review. All review reports are audited by the Fair Employment Commission.

Some of the criminal offences identified in the Fair Employment Act have been highlighted above. There are in fact over twenty significant criminal offences in the Act, including failure to respond to enquiries from the Commission about regular review of progress, or supplying false or misleading information to the Commission. Criminal penalties and fines are backed up by stringent, and potentially very punitive, economic sanctions. The Commission has, for example, the power to serve a notice of disqualification on a defaulting employer, leaving an employer subject to debarment from all public sector contracts, as well as from government grants. All in all, the 1989 Act represents a considerable strengthening of the fair employment legislation.

Table 1: Change in the Catholic proportion of the Northern Ireland workforce, 1990–94

	1990 %	Men 1994 %	Change %	1990 %	Women 1994 %	Change %
Managers and Administrators	28.5	32.2	+3.7	36.0	39.1	+3.1
Professional Occupations	29.6	34.4	+4.8	41.4	46.1	+4.7
Associate Professional and Technical Occupations	32.8	34.8	+2.0	45.3	46.8	+1.5
Clerical and Secretarial Occupations	34.9	39.3	+4.4	33.9	36.4	+2.5
Craft and Skilled Manual Occupations	32.2	32.6	+0.4	42.7	43.1	+0.4
Personal and Protective Service Occupations	20.0	22.0	+2.0	40.5	40.5	0.0
Sales Occupations	31.1	36.2	+5.1	34.7	37.0	+2.3
Plant and Machine Operatives	36.5	39.0	+2.5	42.3	46.7	+4.4
Other Occupations	40.5	40.9	+0.4	36.8	39.5	+2.7
Total	32.0	34.2	+2.2	38.5	40.6	+2.1

Source: Fair Employment Commission (1995)

Table 1 shows that since 1989, when the Fair Employment legislation was strengthened, the proportion of Catholic men and women in the workforce has increased. The increase is apparent in every occupational grouping. The most pronounced shifts have occurred at both the top and bottom ends of the labour market. To a large extent, the rising share of Catholics in the plant and machine operatives category has been facilitated by the significant growth in jobs in this area over the period. With more vacancies being created a firm can more easily reduce religious imbalances in its workforce. In the absence of extra jobs a firm has to rely solely on labour turnover to effect change, which can be a slow and uneven process. Thus the reason why the Catholic share of craft occupations only grew by 0.4 per cent over the period is that the total number of jobs in this category declined during the period. But the big increase in the number of Catholics in professional occupations cannot be totally explained by an upsurge in the number of jobs created. Rather this has more to do with the growing symmetry between the occupational structure of the labour market and the human capital orientation of Catholics, as explained earlier.

Thus recent labour market conditions have made it easier to increase the share of Catholics in employment. But conditions have not been so good as to induce any change in the unemployment differential between the two communities; this figure, along with high economic inactivity rates, remains an acute problem. Nevertheless, positive change has occurred since 1989. In addition to favourable labour market conditions, the activities of the two main enforcement institutions have also played an important role in bringing about this change.

THE FAIR EMPLOYMENT ENFORCEMENT AGENCIES

Interviews conducted with employers – fifty in total, drawn from the public and private sector as well as from trade unions and employer bodies – suggest that both the FEC and FET are strong enforcement institutions.[2] For its part, the FEC is widely regarded as being expeditious in pursuing individual complaints of alleged discrimination, thorough in conducting investigations into the religious composition of organisations, and generally efficient at promoting the cause of fair employment. If anything the FET is seen as having a greater impact. The 1989 Fair Employment Act permitted the FET, when a complaint was successful, to: make a declaration as to the rights of both parties; award compensation up to a limit of £20,000; make a recommendation that specific action be taken by the respondent to reduce the likelihood of any recurrence of the discriminatory act. Tribunals appear to make full use of these powers.[3]

FET rulings are probably even more significant than financial awards to individuals found to have suffered from discrimination. In particular, they appear to have a major impact on employer human resource management practices. Take for instance the case of McCausland v Dungannon District Council. The complainant brought a case claiming that an internal trawl system operated by the local authority to fill positions was indirectly discriminatory. The essence of the case was that, as a result of the procedure, a disproportionate share of applications came from Protestants rather than Catholics. The Tribunal ruled, after it was obliged to reconsider its initial decision by the Court of Appeal, that such a practice did constitute indirect discrimination. Most employers have taken this to mean that internal recruitment and even promotions have to be drastically reduced. Thus FET rulings in individual cases have a big impact on human resource management policies in general.

The significance of this spillover effect is that the Tribunal system simultaneously embodies 'individual justice' and 'group justice' approaches to fair employment.[4] From an 'individual justice' perspective, the aim of the fair employment legislation is to reduce discrimination by eliminating from decision-making any considerations based on religion. The model, as implied by its title, concentrates on securing fairness for the individual, and it is 'symmetrical' in that both groups – in this case Protestants and Catholics – are equally protected. In contrast, the 'group justice' perspective places the drive towards fair employment into a wider social context. The basic aim of this approach is to improve the relative position of Catholic men and women by removing social processes that place them at a disadvantage. As a result, it is 'asymmetrical' as it focuses on the betterment of Catholics and is less concerned with the protection of Protestants. The individual justice aspects of the FET work include: the high level of awards that may be made; the restrictions of remedies to individuals; the prohibition of reverse discrimination; and the symmetrical nature of the protection accorded. The group justice model is endorsed by the prohibition of indirect discrimination and the spillover effect of Tribunal rulings. This is reinforced by the monitoring requirement imposed on firms and by the ability of the FEC to conduct investigations without an individual complaint and to impose goals and timetables with regard to fair employment on enterprises.

By performing a 'group justice' role, the Tribunal ensures that there is a large externality to its work whereby one decision will change the behaviour of a whole range of firms. Local employers believe that this externality effect has made the Tribunal too powerful. There is also a feeling that the Tribunal is biased towards the complainant and that its proceedings are overly legalistic and cumbersome. Thus the prospect of a Tribunal hearing is treated with some trepidation by local firms. As a result, more and more employers are preferring to settle cases informally. Many employers attribute this to the high legal costs in preparing and participating in such a hearing. They are also keen to avoid the loss of reputation associated with a fair employment complaint. All in all, the Tribunal has operated as a forceful and potent regulatory instrument.

Whether the FET and the FEC operate as an optimal regulatory regime is another matter. There are a number of grounds for believing that they do not. One problem is that through its rulings the Tribunal may create contagions rather than conventions on fair employment matters. A convention is when fair employment legislation or a ruling of the FET dovetails, or even strengthens, company-level anti-discriminatory policies. On the other hand, a contagion arises when asymmetries exist between regulatory arrangements and the enterprise. It is important to stress that the extra costs enterprises may incur when complying with the fair legislation should not be regarded as a contagion: although these may be burdensome, they may more properly be regarded as the commercial consequences of political decision-making. Thus fair employment legislation can be seen as similar to health and safety legislation or environmental protection regulations: democratic societies always impose boundaries on business activity, which may be constraining but nevertheless have to be complied with. Contagions relate more narrowly to the functioning of the fair employment regulatory environment and whether parts of this regime are causing avoidable or unnecessary distortions.

The scope for the fair employment institutions, particularly the FET, to generate contagions appears to exist. One problem is that the absence of a professional human resource management input into Tribunal proceedings raises the risk that some rulings may give rise to fair employment contagions. It can be persuasively argued that this has already happened in the McCausland v Dungannon District Council case. On the surface the ruling that internal trawls for jobs and certain promotions are unlawful and that such vacancies should be advertised externally appears sound enough. But on closer examination it cuts across a central plank of personnel management: that organisations need to develop internal systems of career advancement, involving promotion systems and the filling of some posts from internal applicants, in order to increase motivation and reduce shirking amongst the workforce. In this instance, there seems to be a direct collision between the thinking of the fair employment authorities and a core practice of most businesses. With a professional human resource management input, the ruling in this case would have perhaps been more circumspect.

The absence of expert human resource management assistance is also a shortcoming of the Fair Employment Commission. The Commission is widely regarded as providing high quality legal advice on fair employment matters. But a criticism levied by a number of employers interviewed was that the body was not so effective when asked to give guidance on difficult human management questions to promote equal treatment. Thus, a gap may exist in the present regulatory regime for fair employment which might cause it to operate sub-optimally. This weakness could be addressed by grafting a human resource management section onto the existing institutions, or by giving the Labour Relations Agency a more explicit fair employment remit.

A second problem with the current regulatory arrangements is that they may focus too much on matching the internal religious composition of a company's workforce with that of the local catchment area. But there are other dimensions to the problem of fair employment which may require different policy interventions. Consider the investigations conducted by the FEC into individual companies. In almost every case these studies adopt the internal workforce/local catchment area framework. Virtually nothing is discovered about the internal labour market processes of the company such as how staff are promoted or how on-the-job training is provided. Yet such arrangements can influence the degree of equal treatment inside the organisation. For the most part, the FEC treats the internal labour market as a black box, which again reflects the absence of a human resource management dimension to the Commission's work.

A third shortcoming in the work of the FEC is that it could work more closely with other agencies, such as the education services and the economic development authorities, since securing equal treatment in the labour market may require more than legal moves against discrimination. Reducing the unemployment differential between the two communities, for example, will require a range of additional policies beyond the law, including innovatory policies for the long-term unemployed, and greater financial assistance to certain targeted localities. The Fair Employment Commission should take on the role of organising powerful lobbies to exhort the government to introduce comprehensive and integrated measures to promote equality.

All in all then, it appears that the Fair Employment Commission and Tribunal are effective regulatory arrangements and that criticisms that these bodies are paper tigers, unable to effect change, are unjustified if not downright misleading. At the same time, these two bodies could improve performance by adopting new policies and programmes that would not require root and branch change. As the current legislation comes up for review, the government has an opportunity to put right some of the present shortcomings. Whether it will do so remains to be seen.

ENTERPRISES AND FAIR EMPLOYMENT

The extent to which a religiously balanced workforce emerges in Northern Ireland will depend crucially on the actions of firms. A range of human resource management policies is open to enterprises when introducing fair employment practices into the workplace. At the very minimum, employers can develop mission statements that declare either that they are an equal opportunity employer or that they embrace the principle of fair employment. These statements are essentially symbolic and their main purpose is to signal to under-represented groups on the outside labour market that applications would be welcome. Mission statements can also be targeted at existing employees of an organisation. For instance, in an effort to promote a 'neutral' working environment, companies may enact mission statements that prohibit sectarian harassment or intimidation. More specific policies could be put in place to ban the display of any flags or emblems such as the Union Jack or Tricolour so that particular groups of workers do not feel threatened or alienated.

A tougher approach is to pursue what might be termed 'soft' human resource management policies for fair employment. Such policies are mainly designed to remove potentially discriminatory practices from employee relations systems without compromising the merit principle. One set of soft human resource management initiatives is designed to promote equal treatment at the point of entry into an enterprise. If a firm has an imbalanced workforce, it may gain the reputation of being a Catholic-only or a Protestant-only employer. As a result, individuals from the under-represented community may be deterred from applying for a job at the enterprise. Active outreach policies by the enterprise may be required to break down these community barriers to entry. In concrete terms, managers from the company establish contracts with local schools and community groups from the under-represented groups to emphasise that they recruit on the basis of merit and not religion.

Removing potential bias from the recruitment and selection process is another target of soft human resource management policies. Invariably this involves introducing a greater degree of formality into the employment system. While the extent of the formalisation can vary, the basic requirements include the use of application forms, the writing of precise job specifications, and a more careful and systematic approach to the selection of candidates for interviews. Some organisations do more and conduct competency tests as part of their recruitment procedures. Another common practice is to give those who sit on selection panels a considerable degree of training to ensure that any bias, latent or otherwise, is removed from the decision-making process. For instance, interviewers are taught that hiring decisions should not be based on informal screening procedures, particularly those based upon deportment during interviews. Greater formalisation is an attempt to make the decision to hire or not more transparent so that it can be easily seen that no religious or discriminatory influence has been at play.

The soft human resource management approach also attempts to remove policies that may thwart moves toward a religiously balanced workforce. For example, an enterprise attempting to redress religious imbalance in its workforce could be stalled if it has to make redundancies under the last in/first out principle. To prevent such a situation arising, an organisation could adopt an alternative human resource management system, using 'efficiency' criteria such as disciplinary records and productivity performance when determining lay-offs. Overall, soft human resource management strategies reorder formal procedures and establish new arrangements to eliminate barriers to equal treatment of Catholics and Protestants at the workplace.

A defining feature of soft HRM policies for fair employment is that equal treatment is promoted without recourse to positive discrimination. In contrast, hard human resource management policies, while not completely jettisoning the merit principle, are more far-reaching measures to reduce religious imbalance inside the enterprise. From this perspective, deliberate and targeted initiatives, which amount to favouring one religious group over another, are required if equal treatment is to be secured in the short to medium term. Thus, for example, if Catholics are under-represented in certain occupations, enterprises could develop 'on-the-job' training programmes particularly for that religious group to reduce the skills gap. Another initiative in this mould is for firms to introduce fast-track promotion schemes whereby Catholics could bypass a number of 'job ladders' inside the organisation and assume senior positions quickly in order to redress any religious under-representation in higher tier levels. Such schemes have been used by American firms to increase the number of blacks in senior management positions inside an organisation. But it should be stressed that those admitted to the fast-track schemes have considerable ability and would in time have progressed through the organisation: the scheme simply sets out to accelerate this upward mobility in the interest of equal treatment.

A further measure under the rubric of hard human resource management is relocation. If an employer is situated in a predominantly Protestant or Catholic area, it is likely that the majority of the workforce will be of the same religious composition. As a result, the enterprise may have an image of being a mono-religious concern. To shed this image, the enterprise could move parts or even the entire operation to an area where the other religious group is in the majority, or to a neutral site, thereby putting it in a better position to achieve a religiously balanced workforce. Larger organisations are perhaps more likely to pursue such relocation strategies than smaller companies. For instance, some parts of the public sector have considerable opportunities to enact a policy of decentralisation and move 'back office' jobs to specific locations.

A number of employers were interviewed on the question of fair employment.[5] As would be expected, large private sector companies as well as public sector organisations have adopted radical human resource management innovations to secure a more religiously balanced workforce. One enterprise, for example, has pursued a corporate decentralisation strategy with the explicit aim of increasing its presence in predominantly Catholic areas. Others are quite prepared to develop 'Catholic only' training courses but are unable to do so because such action is illegal under the provisions of the Fair

Employment Act. Most big companies with a religious imbalance in their workforce are undertaking outreach programmes to attract applications from the under-represented community. Across the public sector far-reaching changes have taken place to organisational structures and procedures to ensure that Catholics are not in any way disadvantaged. Thus the evidence from interviews is that large organisations have changed the rules and processes governing internal labour markets to squeeze out the potential for religious discrimination. Most of the changes made have been of the soft HRM variety: none of the companies interviewed adopted the hard HRM strategy in any systematic way.

Table 2: Proportion of companies adopting broad good employment practices and the religious composition of their employees.

	Sample	Adjusted	Employees	Protestant	R. Catholic
Written equality of opportunity policy					
Yes	91.6%	89.3%	92.9%	[65.2%]	[34.8%]
No	8.0%	9.6%	6.5%	[54.4%]	[45.6%]
Equality of opportunity senior member of staff's responsibility					
Yes	93.7%	91.4%	94.8%	[64.7%]	[35.3%]
No	3.5%	4.2%	2.7%	[62.0%]	[38.0%]
Policy on flags and emblems					
Yes	91.6%	90.7%	92.4%	[64.6%]	[35.4%]
No	5.9%	6.2%	4.8%	[67.2%]	[32.8%]
Discrimination / harassment disciplinary offences					
Yes	82.5%	84.5%	85.4%	[65.4%]	[34.6%]
No	11.9%	11.5%	8.7%	[61.3%]	[38.7%]
Don't know	5.6%	4.1%	5.9%	[55.3%]	[44.7%]
Joint declaration of protection					
Yes	22.0%	16.1%	26.4%	[71.4%]	[28.6%]
No	67.1%	71.1%	61.3%	[61.8%]	[38.2%]
Don't know	10.8%	12.8%	12.4%	[62.6%]	[37.4%]
Fair employment support scheme					
Yes	61.9%	60.6%	63.9%	[65.5%]	[34.5%]
No	19.9%	20.9%	16.7%	[67.3%]	[32.7%]
Don't know	18.2%	18.5%	19.4%	[58.5%]	[41.5%]

*Source:*FEC survey, 1995

Table 3: Advertising Methods

Method	% Companies using by type of post			
	Management	Clerical/Admin	Manual	Other
Daily Press	69.7	51.9	37.8	47.0
Local Press	36.3	62.8	63.5	51.1
T & EA Offices	20.6	62.3	74.4	56.8
Internal notices	35.0	39.4	35.8	31.0
Informal	35.0	11.1	20.9	13.6

Recruitment Practices

Method	% Companies using by type of post			
	Management	Clerical/Admin	Manual	Other
Job description	74.9	76.2	62.4	60.4
Personnel Specification	56.1	55.7	44.5	46.9
Application Form	80.9	86.8	75.7	70.0
Interview Assessment Sheet	68.3	69.5	56.5	54.5
More than one interviewer	61.8	54.8	46.7	36.4

Source: FEC, 1995

Other evidence suggests that firms are diffusing fair employment HRM policies. For the first time, the FEC has analysed a sample of employers' own three yearly reviews which are required under Section 31 of the Fair Employment (1989) Act. Since the sample covers 31 per cent of private sector concerns and includes 60 per cent of the total private workforce, the picture is fairly comprehensive. As Table 2 shows the overwhelming majority of companies have adopted what has been called symbolic policies. Written equality of opportunity policies were implemented in over 90 per cent of organisations: a similar proportion of companies had policies governing the display of flags and emblems. There is also evidence that there has been a significant adoption of soft human resource management policies with regard to recruitment and selection. Table 3 gives some information on these issues and it shows that a majority of employers have taken steps to formalise recruitment and selection procedures and practices. This finding accords with another survey conducted in 1992, which found that staff recruitment procedures was the area that companies had changed the most as a result of the 1989 Act (CCRU 1993). Thus the evidence suggests that the fair employment legislation has caused employers to adopt new human resource management policies, mostly of the soft variety, to promote equal treatment.

THE SOCIAL PARTNERS AND FAIR EMPLOYMENT

In broad terms both the trade unions and employers' organisations are supportive of the fair employment legislation. Over the years trade unions in particular have received wide acclaim for being the most robustly and consistently anti-sectarian institution in the region. More than any other body, they have been able to keep the workplace largely free from religious strife and conflict. Since the early 1970s, the Northern Ireland Committee of the Irish Congress of Trade Unions (NIC-ICTU) has launched a number of anti-sectarian initiatives: the 'Better Life for All' and the 'Peace, Work and Progress' campaigns for instance. While not always a complete success, these campaigns highlighted the importance trade unions attached to opposing bigotry and violence. In relation to fair employment, the trade unions have been active on the matter since the beginning of the Troubles. Trade unions played a leading role in the establishment of the Van Straubenzee Committee, which paved the way for the Fair Employment Act (1976), and they were in the vanguard of campaigns to strengthen this legislation in the mid 1980s. For their part, successive governments, or at least ministers at the Northern Ireland Office, recognised that organised labour could play a crucial role in the diffusion of anti-discriminatory practices inside companies. As a result, in return for trade unions' active support in implementing fair employment measures, the Conservative government did not introduce much of its new industrial relations legislation into the province.[6]

More recently, NIC-ICTU has established 'Counteract', a voluntary organisation committed to anti-intimidation. It organises seminars for shop stewards and union officials to help them promote a 'sectarian free' workplace. In addition, it conducts research into the scale of religious harassment in companies. Discussions with ICTU officials suggest that they are pleased with many aspects of the current regulatory regime for fair employment. At the same time, they feel still more could be done. They would like contract compliance introduced in a way that would encourage employers to adopt best practice; and they would like to see further regulation of the measures employers are obliged to take if they are found to have a religiously imbalanced workforce.

For their part, employers have supported all government steps towards fair employment, though perhaps not as wholeheartedly or enthusiastically as the trade unions. Emphasising the high costs that strong fair employment legislation imposes on companies, the Northern Ireland Committee of the CBI has argued for a weaker regulatory arrangement. At the moment, as already mentioned, they feel that the Fair Employment Tribunal is excessively legalistic, slightly biased in favour of the complainant, and over-powerful in performing a group justice role. When the present legislation is reviewed, the employers' organisation will argue for a streamlining and dilution of the current system. In particular, it would like to see the Tribunal system weakened considerably, if not abolished altogether; the ceiling for potential awards to be lowered; and the FEC to focus more on educational activity and less on investigations and legal matters. All in all, the CBI would prefer a loose regulatory regime for fair employment. Self-regulation by enterprise rather than external institutional pressure is what employers ultimately want to see.

Some of the more sector-based employers' organisations have played an active and positive role in helping individual organisations to adjust to the requirements of the fair employment legislation. Take, for instance, the district councils. For some time these organisations have had a reputation for being fair employment laggards. Thus, the majority of individual complaints of employment discrimination are from local councils. However, the Local Government Staff Commission for Northern Ireland has gone a considerable way in reducing such malpractices. Through an intensive programme of education, and on occasions even exhortation, it has succeeded in getting all the district councils to agree to a code of procedure on recruitment and selection which makes it much more difficult for discrimination to occur. It also provides an active service of advice and assistance on fair employment questions to individual councils. Although the tawdry image of discrimination still lingers, the Staff Commission has been instrumental in moving district councils within the parameters of the fair employment legislation.

In addition to this sector-related activity, an informal group known as the Employer's Equality Group has been established. This body brings together senior human resource managers from key organisations in the region. These managers exchange views on the type of policies they are introducing to promote fair employment and the problems they encounter in the process. As a result of this activity, a greater degree of expertise and competence is being introduced into company level fair employment policies. They also share experience of the Tribunal hearings and are developing active policies for this area to help enterprises to prepare for such proceedings. All in all, although not altogether happy with the present system, employers' organisations are doing a considerable amount of work to ensure that individual organisations comply with the legislation in a professional and imaginative manner.

CONCLUSIONS: TOWARDS POLITICS OF COMMON UNDERSTANDING

In a brilliant book about economic development, Albert Hirschman developed the schema 'exit, voice and loyalty' to highlight that societies have two basic ways to deal with social and economic problems.[7] This schema is best illustrated by choices individuals continually have to make. On the one hand there is the exit route whereby an individual severs a social or commercial relationship: for one reason or another the unhappy couple divorce; the dissatisfied diner goes to another restaurant; the disgruntled employee quits the organisation. On the other hand, there is the voice path whereby the individual uses dialogue or communication to resolve a problem: the unhappy couple discuss their marital problems before going to the divorce courts; the dissatisfied diner complains about the quality of food; the disgruntled employee joins a union in an attempt to improve working conditions. Hirschman argues that if societies are to function as democratic and cohesive entities then they must develop voice mechanisms such as voting, bargaining, conflict resolution procedures and so on, to encourage loyalty and attachment from citizens to the political institutions that govern them.

Exit, voice and loyalty can be used to throw light on the drive towards fair employment in Northern Ireland. For the most part, the introduction of a legal and institutional apparatus to promote equality of employment opportunity can be seen as an attempt at creating a voice mechanism to reduce Catholic alienation or exit from Northern Ireland political life. By creating tough anti-discrimination laws it was hoped that the loyalty or attachment of Catholics would increase, thereby removing a key grievance that has fuelled the political conflict over the years.

In this chapter we have seen that since the enactment of the 1989 Fair Employment Act the Catholic share of employment in virtually every occupational grouping has increased. Most of this increase is the result of fairly favourable labour market conditions and the active role of the fair employment enforcement agencies. At the same time, some problems remain; for example, the question of the unemployment differential between the two communities is still as great as ever. Despite the big strides that have been made towards fair employment, the matter has still to be fully resolved. The chapter also shows that the corporate world has absorbed the fair employment legislation without great difficulty. Although more could be done, companies have adopted new policies and procedures to ensure equal treatment of the workforce. Moreover, trade union and employer organisations outside individual firms have done much to help the diffusion of human resource management policies to promote equality. Thus the strengthening of the Fair Employment Act in 1989 has brought about decisive changes in enterprises and labour markets that now makes it much more difficult to practise discrimination.

This fairly positive assessment does not accord with the responses of the two communities towards fair employment: neither appears to view the anti-discrimination regulatory regime as operating as a voice mechanism. On the one hand, although many individual Catholics have benefitted from the anti-discrimination laws, most political representatives of this community argue that more needs to be done, particularly in terms of Catholics as a group. It is this view that has given rise to the demand for 'parity of esteem'. On the other hand, there is growing unease amongst Protestants that Catholic advances under the fair employment laws have been at the expense of members of their community. These contrasting views suggest that the anti-discrimination legislation has not promoted social and political integration between the two communities. To some extent it can be argued that the fair employment initiative has been prone to sectarian capture: instead of being a bridge to transcend community divisions, the initiative may have fallen foul of the sectarianism that keeps both religious groups apart. This is not an argument for a repeal of the fair employment laws, but a commentary on the complexities of establishing democratic politics in the region.

If political stability is to be secured, an inclusive form of citizenship will have to be established so that each person enjoys equal political and civil rights in some formal sense, and feels free to take an active part in governing that society. Most modern democracies practise citizenship in the liberal individualist sense. From the perspective of liberal individualism, citizenship is about setting out in a Constitution or legislation a plinth of rights and entitlements that upholds the sovereignty and autonomy of the individual. The vision is of individuals having a status that allows them to stand above state and even society. More concretely, the liberal version of citizenship emphasises ideas such as freedom of speech and association, the right to vote, the protection of property rights, the defence of pluralism, the separation of church and state, and so on.

In accepting the arguments for a Bill of Rights to protect the rights of individuals in Northern Ireland most political parties have clearly been influenced by this conception of citizenship. But it would be heroic to claim that a Bill of Rights will by itself create a ·liberal-democratic society in Northern Ireland. This is essentially because the political and social life of the region is dominated by two communities within which a truncated form of the 'civic republican' version of citizenship prevails. The civic republican model of citizenship stands in sharp contrast to the liberal individualist version. In particular, it places more emphasis on the idea of the collective good and the social duties and responsibilities of individuals. Thus civic republicans are strong advocates of political communities. The notion that citizenship is simply some type of legal status that confers on individuals certain rights against the state is rejected as impoverished. Individuals are regarded as only being fully enriched through social co-operation and in circumstances where they play an active role in public life and abide by community norms and rules.

Civic republicanism is widely seen as having been left behind by industrialisation: today's society and economy are regarded as too complex and varied to be organised along the homogenous and highly ordered lines implicit in a tradition which was at its height during the middle ages, particularly in the Italian republics. But a civic republican form of citizenship is as much at play in Northern Ireland as any liberal individualist version. Since the formation of Northern Ireland, political and religious divisions have always prevented the full emergence of a normal western-style civil society. Moreover, one of the effects of the past twenty-five years of violence has been a hypertrophy of community or group life.

This important social change has taken a number of forms. As mentioned earlier, the most tangible sign has been significant population shifts which have turned sub-regions into mainly Catholic or mainly Protestant residential areas. Other less tangible factors also point to the communal bifurcation of Northern Irish life. Missing are the shared symbols that bond citizens together, even in an 'imagined' sense, as in other western societies. A simple but striking example is the Northern Ireland soccer team. Almost everywhere else the national football team is a unifying force, but in Northern Ireland it is the source of division, with Protestants actively supporting the team while Catholics are either indifferent or actively opposed to it. Pursuits that are exclusively associated with one community or the other have experienced an upsurge. In the Catholic community, Gaelic games are now more popular than ever and increasing numbers are learning the Irish language. For its part, the Protestant community appears to be under a cloud of uncertainty and apprehension, reflected in many school leavers from middle-class families being encouraged to go to universities in Britain. All in all, the co-existence of two distinct communities is a key feature of Northern Ireland society.

At the same time, it would be misleading to push the 'two communities' thesis too far. The Catholic or Protestant community is less cohesive and integrated than, say, the historical example of primitive tribal groups in stateless societies or modern intentional communities like the Israeli kibbutzim. Neither religious bloc in the region is so well developed that it has its own mechanisms to maintain social control – despite the barbaric efforts of the paramilitaries. In highly developed communities, social order is secured through such devices as sanctions of approval or disapproval, the withdrawal of reciprocity, and in extreme cases feuds and vendettas: all these instruments are absent from Northern Ireland in any overt and developed form. Thus, following Hannah Arendt, the French political philosopher, Catholic and Protestant communities cannot be regarded as *communities of action*, through which decentralised collectivist solutions are found to the question of order and authority. But they do come close to what Arendt describes as *communities of meaning*.

According to Arendt, communities of meaning are established by the interaction between individuals and a wider group. This interactive process involves individuals defining themselves and their identities in the context of a community, which in turn defines its identity within the wider social context. Thus, communities of meaning are akin to elements of civic republicanism, which emphasises the social setting of individual behaviour or action. They can take a negative or positive form – or both. On the one hand, they can create support structures that reduce the uncertainties and difficulties of individual life. On the other hand, they can degenerate into self-absorbed worlds in which individuals and the nature of their group are defined without engagement with other communities. This introspection causes separate communities to lose not only interest in communicating with each other, but, gradually, also the capacity to do so. In the end, each community develops a politics more or less based on its own identity and becomes reluctant to engage in a wider political process that sets out to reach a democratic accommodation between different groups.

Such a scenario appears to have risen in Northern Ireland. The collapse of civil society into competing religious blocs has led to the emergence of Protestant and Catholic-based politics. Little wonder that the compromises and concessions necessary for the two groups to resolve the problems of living together in the same territory are proving so elusive. To a large extent, the fair employment laws have not been able to operate as a voice mechanism because they have clashed with the emergence of communities of meaning in the region. Each community approaches the matter of equity in the labour market from their own perspective. Take the idea of parity of esteem for instance. A wide range of policies fall under this catch-all term, but it is primarily concerned with the enactment of group justice measures which set out to reduce structural imbalances between Catholics and Protestants, and initiatives to give equal validation to Gaelic culture. In the abstract, 'parity of esteem' can be seen as a fulcrum to create an equilibrium between two different traditions in Northern Ireland. But, in the context of self-absorbed, antagonistic, community politics such notions may not take such a benign form, but rather become a malign campaign for the triumph of one group over another.

To prevent the two communities from becoming excessively inward-looking, it is necessary to promote a politics of common understanding that attempts to make each bloc sensitive to, and aware of, the demands of the other. A politics of common understanding is not about attempting to break up each community. Rather, it is about encouraging a dialogue between the two camps, which leads people to reflect on their experience in ways that ultimately alter the interpretative framework of their own community. It is about making communities more outward-looking, more amenable to change and compromise. Clearly such a political dialogue would impact favourably on the fair employment question. On the one hand, it might promote a greater awareness that progress towards a more religiously balanced labour market will involve compromise and flexibility on the part of both communities. On the other hand, it could promote a realisation in both religious blocs·that they would be better off collaborating with each other to maximise employment growth rather than clashing over the distribution of the existing stock of jobs. But the bottom line is that there can be no retreat from the principle of fair employment since this is one of the cornerstones upon which the creation of an inclusive citizenship in Northern Ireland depends.

NOTES

1. McCrudden, C., 'The experience of the legal enforcement of fair employment', Comack, R. and Osborne, R., *Religion, Education and Employment in Northern Ireland*, Appletree Press, Dublin 1983.
2. Central Community Relations Unit, Employment Equality Review, Research Report No. 1, *The Fair Employment Legislation – Survey of Employer's Experiences*, CCRU, Belfast 1993.
3. Hegarty, A. and Keown, C., 'Figuring Out Equality: An Analysis of Tribunal Remedies in Individual Complaints of Discrimination', *Review of Employment Topics*, Vol. 2, No. 2, 1994.
4. McCrudden, C., Smith, D. and Brown, C., *Racial Justice at Work*, London Policy Studies Institute, 1991.
5. CCRU, *op.cit.*
6. Cradden, T., 'Trade Unions and Fair Employment in Northern Ireland', *Industrial and Labour Relations Review*, Vol. 31, No. 1, 1992.
7. Hirschman, A., *Exit, Voice and Loyalty*, Harvard University Press, Cambridge, Mass, 1971.
8. Arendt, H., *The Human Condition*, Doubleday, New Jersey, 1959.

7

POLITICAL STABILITY THROUGH CROSS-BORDER ECONOMIC COOPERATION

A key part of the debate about the future direction of the Northern Ireland economy is the question of the possible benefits that may arise from deeper economic and business ties between the north and south of the island. Some argue that cross-border commercial interactions have not been fully developed, and as a result a range of positive economic benefits are being left untapped. Others take a different position, suggesting that the potential gains from greater north–south economic cooperation are minimal. This chapter reviews the debate about the merits or otherwise of deeper all-island economic connections, and argues that, while some gains can be realised by intensifying business flows across the border, these should not be overestimated. Certainly the gains are not of the magnitude to decisively impact on economic performance either north or south. Nevertheless, given that it may prove an effective means of integrating Catholics into a new Northern Ireland, cross-border cooperation is deemed to be a crucial part of any overall political settlement.

This chapter does not deal with the economics of Irish unity, an issue frequently conflated with the debate about cross-border economic cooperation. These are two distinct issues and should be dealt with separately: many passionate advocates of greater commercial ties between both parts of the island are not supporters of Irish unification. In any event, the debate about the economic feasibility of Irish unity is now almost obselete since virtually every political party and group on the island appears to accept that such an arrangement is a non-starter for the foreseeable future. Those with an interest in this debate are referred to the work of J. Bradley.[1]

IS CROSS-BORDER TRADE THE ROUTE TO PROSPERITY?

In the 1980s the idea that deeper trade connections between the two parts of the island would bring economic benefits was widely criticised, if not openly ridiculed. The consensus view was that both economies stood on the periphery of Europe with only each other's dismal performance to share. By the 1990s, however, this consensus view had fragmented and a large, mainly business, lobby had emerged, arguing that big benefits were to be gained by establishing one trading zone in Ireland. A Confederation of Irish Industry (CII) Report, 'A Single Market on the Island', pointed out that manufacturers from the Republic sell only one-third as much per capita in Northern Ireland as they do in the Republic; and manufacturers from Northern Ireland sell only one-sixth as much per capita in the Republic as they do in Northern Ireland.[2] The employers' organisation went on to argue that the value of trade between the two parts of the island could be trebled, resulting in 30,000 additional manufacturing jobs and 75,000 jobs in total. With the backing of the main employers' organisations on the island, this argument has gained a high profile.

At the time, most professional economists treated the document with a great deal of scepticism, regarding the calculations as crude and the estimates reached as wildly optimistic. Subsequently, there have been a number of assessments which have poured further cold water on the idea that increased trade integration on the island will generate an employment and commercial bonanza. Scott and O'Reilly point out that the level of cross-border trade existing between the north and south more or less conforms with the level that exists between small, neighbouring economies in other parts of Europe.[3] Another study by Gudgin argues that the north trades more on a per capita basis with the south than Scotland does with England. Although the data used in these studies is not the most reliable and there are conceptual difficulties with the methodology – using per capita figures as a measure of trade intensity, for example, would not be every economist's cup of tea – these assessments are broadly accurate in arguing that increased trade on the island is unlikely to yield big employment gains.

Other valid arguments point in a similar direction. First of all, the Republic's status as a *super-trading economy* (and perhaps the need for the north to become such an entity in the future) restricts the extent to which cross-border trade can deepen. Countries where exports account for more than 50 per cent of GDP are called 'super-trading economies'. This is a relatively new development in international trade and is closely associated with economies in the far east like Singapore and Hong Kong, where exports actually exceed national output. But such nations are also emerging elsewhere and Ireland is one of the most prominent examples in Europe. Fuelling the creation of super-trading economies are the international production strategies of transnational companies – what Krugman refers to as 'slicing up the value-added chain'.[5] By fragmenting productive activity so that many different countries are involved making a product, transnationals are causing the level of trade in total production to be higher than the value added activity in the process. The implication of supertrading status for a small open nation like the Republic of Ireland is that a big part of the tradeable sector is locked into international value added chains. This reduces the scope for many of these companies to deepen exchange relations inside the island. In other words, the high external orientation of much industry in the Republic's economy places a constraint on the development of all-island trade connections. Although this argument is not presently applicable to Northern Ireland, the situation may change if the level of inward investment increases in the region.

A further reason to doubt that large benefits would arise from more cross-border trade is the size of the two markets. Because the two economies are relatively small it is unlikely that the dynamic gains normally associated with trade integration will arise. One argument is that deeper trade will intensify competition between market rivals, encouraging them either to merge in order to obtain economies of scale, or to look externally for new markets, or to become more competitive by reducing costs. At a distance, this perspective seems plausible, but on closer examination it becomes less so. Take for instance the argument that trade will encourage the formation of bigger firms. In an economy as small as the island of Ireland this effect is unlikely to happen on any widespread basis, not least because many of the industrial sectors are dominated by transnationals, which are by and largely insulated from market rivalry in the domestic Irish market. Moreover, it may be misguided to encourage indigenous firms north and south to come together in search of economies of scale. O'Malley points out that most industries in the Republic of Ireland – and thus, by implication, in the north as well – are not located in sectors where such corporate strategies are the route to competitive success.[6]

Attempting to get bigger firms on the island may lock productive activity into inappropriate and outmoded commercial strategies. The important competitive goals for much of Irish industry are to diffuse new technologies, make a decisive shift to flexible production and improve product quality, which have very little to do with the capturing of economies of scale.

The thesis that increased competition on the domestic Irish market will oblige firms to be more outward looking is also not persuasive. In theory, this is possible, but in practice it depends on the attitude of managers and company owners.[7] In the face of increased competition, managers can adopt an offensive approach and attempt to improve company performance by capturing extra market share through making improvements to products. Alternatively, they can adopt a defensive approach and try and maintain existing commercial orders by pursuing cost based competitive strategies. In light of the criticisms made of their present business outlook and behaviour, it is not at all certain that the offensive route would be adopted by managers in Irish companies.[8] If the defensive route were widely adopted, then the most likely outcome would be a fierce competitive battle between enterprises in the north and the south for each other's markets. In other words, rather than creating new jobs or adding to economic growth in the short to medium term, greater cross-border trade could simply amount to a redistribution of existing commercial activity, with gains made by some firms being matched by the losses of others.

Thus claims that cross-border trade will usher in a virtuous circle of new commercial activities, leading to more jobs and better growth rates, are excessive and unjustified. A more realistic approach is needed. Such an approach would start from the position that more than seventy years of separate development and a quarter of a century of political conflict may have caused some cross-border commercial opportunities to be left untapped. Without over-hyping their potential, a range of initiatives should be put in place to counteract these market failures; for example, measures to improve information about market opportunities on both sides of the border. Indeed such strategies have led to increased levels of trade between the north and south in recent years. But there should be no pretence that these developments, though welcome, will improve the fortunes of either economy in a significant way. Upgrading the performance of the two Irish economies will require much more than deeper cross-border trade connections.

EXTERNAL ECONOMIES OF SCALE AND THE BELFAST-DUBLIN CORRIDOR

Establishing an economic corridor between Belfast and Dublin is another popular proposal to strengthen cross-border commercial connections. Sir George Quigley, the Chairman of the Ulster Bank and the Northern Ireland Economic Council, is widely regarded as the originator of the idea. In a lecture in Belfast in 1992 he gave an insight into the thinking behind this proposal.[9] According to Quigley, a key dimension of contemporary business life is the concentration of commercial activity in particular geographical areas: the 'M4 Corridor' in the south-east of England, Silicon Valley in California, and the Emilia Romagna region in Italy for example. Through this process, known as the 'pearl oyster syndrome', companies try to capture the benefits of commercial clustering or networking and gain access to sophisticated or specialist infrastructure. Since good economic performance and the geographical concentration of business seems to go hand in hand in Europe and elsewhere, Quigley argued that forging cross-border cooperation may be the ideal opportunity for some similar dynamic to be created in Ireland, hence the idea of the Belfast-Dublin corridor. Although only outlined in broad terms, the proposal immediately became a key item on the cross-border cooperation agenda.

But how plausible is the idea? To answer this question adequately means first saying something about how and why commercial clusters can create a dynamic economic effect. Economists frequently make the distinction between internal and external economies of scale. On the one hand, internal economies of scale normally arise as a result of firms deciding to expand. In so doing, they can more fully utilise capital investment, which results in production costs falling even though output is rising. When a firm experiences this situation it can be said to have captured *internal* economies of scale. On the other hand, external economies of scale refer to the situation where a range of dynamic economic influences exist outside individual firms but at the same time are internal to the region or territory. Thus the geographical location of an enterprise can greatly enchance its competitive performance.

Territorial commercial complexes of this kind can take a variety of forms. In some cases, they consist of relatively small firms, normally in the same productive sector, closely collaborating with each other. They may work together on the same commercial contract, or share the same capital or labour, or exchange market and business information. As a result, although the specialisation of each enterprise may be relatively narrow, inter-firm collaboration increases the operational scale and scope of individual units and the productive system as a whole. Thus commercial activity in the territorial complex becomes greater than the sum of the individual parts. Just how these geographical clusters of business activity – often called industrial districts – are created and sustained is a matter of some debate. But the most popular view is that industrial districts arise from the *social embeddeness* of economic activity. Although a rather fancy term, it essentially means that bonds of loyalty and trust generated in the social and political spheres of a region spill over into the economic arena and influence the behaviour of firms and individuals. This blurring of the boundaries between the community and enterprises encourages an approach to commercial life which combines cooperation with competition.

The highly successful industrial districts of the Emilia Romagna region of Italy are frequently attributed to the common religious and political traditions of the locality (Catholicism and Communism). A strong sense of community identity creates an 'industrial atmosphere' where different firms are prepared to tie their own prosperity to that of others. In addition, relations between managers and employees inside the firms are underpinned by an informal social compromise whereby employers agree not to pursue exploitative practices and in return workers comply with the flexible deployment of labour and machinery. All in all, the bonds of commitment and trust that are forged allow external economies of scale to emerge.

Other regional commercial complexes are less amorphous and more hierarchial in character. In many instances, geographical production systems revolve around and to a large extent are coordinated by a few large firms. For example, the success of the Baden-Württemberg area of southern Germany is attributed to the activity of a number of key big enterprises. Such large firms can play an important role in forming regional economic systems by setting the rules of the commercial game in such a way as to ease the vagaries of market life for small firms. Thus, for example, they can enter into long-term sub-contractual relationships that not only ensure the delivery of high quality intermediate products but also create incentives for small firms to invest in new technology and skill formation. As a result of such coordination, the core large firms can upgrade the productive capabilities of other enterprises around them. In turn, this enhances the commercial performance of the entire area.

A third way that external economies of scale can emerge is through the activities of public institutions. Universities, and other government-funded organisations, like military complexes, frequently generate commercial activity in a manner that improves local economic development. The successful high-technology complexes of Silicon Valley, Route 128 around Boston, and more recently Grenoble in southern France, are examples of this form of regional development. In these cases, the universities have played a central role in helping researchers bring pioneering scienitific and technological innovations to the market. Moreover, they have often done so in a way that has transferred the highly collaborative ethos of the university laboratory into business enterprises. Once established, these complexes attract the best engineers and computer people, giving firms ready access to a highly skilled and appropriate external labour pool, a benefit that many of the enterprises would not enjoy if located elsewhere.

Other forms of regional economic systems housing external economies of scale no doubt exist, but the three typologies outlined above represent the most common patterns of such arrangements. Although quite different in institutional detail and indeed economic character, each pattern tends to generate similar influences and have the same qualities. First of all, each has a commercial infrastructure that tightly dovetails with the needs of individual enterprises. Thus for instance, as already indicated, the local labour market has a large stock of the right type of skills for the particular productive activity that is going on. Banks and other parts of the financial system are frequently organised in a way that promotes the long-term interests of the region. Loans, for example, are given to firms without undue emphasis on short-term profitability. Non-market external institutions contribute positively to the local business environment, whether they are training establishments, marketing support centres, chambers of commerce or whatever. Second, each region produces a low transactions costs environment. Information about market developments as well as up-to-date production techniques is widely shared, putting all enterprises in a better position to do business. For the most part, unruly commercial behaviour such as defaulting on payments or poaching staff and orders is shunned; cooperative commercial behaviour tends to be the norm. Third, the presence of external economies of scale ensures that each region is a learning community. By sharing knowedge and experience about all aspects of business, enterprises are better positioned to make continuing improvements and innovations to their operations.

Of course, not all regions where firms in the same productive sector congregate, or where a few big firms dominate, or where a powerful university exists, generate external economies of scale. For example, Saxenian shows how the science park developed by Cambridge University, and made up of high-tech enterprises, failed to replicate the collaborative commercial behaviour found in areas like Silicon Valley.[10] In a similar vein, Amin and Thrift argue that attempts by many regional authorities to replicate the industrial districts found in Emilia Romagna have not been particularly successful.[11] Thus, although there are impressive examples of some regions forging ahead by capturing external economies of scale, there are also many areas that have found these effects elusive. Another cautionary note that needs to be sounded is that the benign picture of successful regional economies representing an offensive response to competitive markets may not always be accurate. In some instances, external economies of scale arise in regions as a result of the defensive behaviour of enterprises. This is particularly the case when firms move to areas where they can be alongside enterprises that operate in similar product markets in order reap the benefits of regional economic concentration.

The big question is whether any of the three models of external economies of scale outlined above can be generated inside a Belfast-Dublin commercial corridor. The dispassionate answer is that it is unlikely: at best only fragments of specific models will emerge. The scenario of industrial districts is the least likely to unfold: none of the necessary conditions appear to exist for this model. At the moment there are no significant clusters of enterprises operating in the same production sector inside the corridor. Although very little is known about corporate behaviour in the area, there is no evidence of a high level of collaboration or co-operation between enterprises. If anything, anecdotal evidence points in the other direction, with many stories of opportunistic behaviour by enterprises, particularly when it comes to cross-border commercial dealings. The social conditions that have been the bedrock of successful industrial districts elsewhere in Europe are absent. There may be harmonious social relations in specific areas each side of the border, but there are no deep bonds of loyalty or any sense of mutual interdependence on a cross-border basis. At present there are no social foundations on which to build a Belfast-Dublin corridor.

At first glance the big firms model looks more promising. Many of Ireland's largest companies are situated inside the corridor and the hope is that efforts to develop internal business activity may encourage them to adopt new commercial practices. In particular, promoting the idea of inter-firm cooperation may prompt these enterprises to re-evaluate the type of relationships they have with sub-contractors. No doubt the architects of the corridor idea would be delighted if southern firms started to look northwards for sub-contractors, and vice versa. If German style sub-contractual relations were to enter Ireland on the island's eastern seaboard, then the initiative would be an unqualified success, but this seems unlikely.

First of all, far from being laggards, some big firms inside the corridor are already doing a lot to orchestrate commercial activity in particular areas. For example, in recent years Shorts in Belfast have made great strides in developing a sophisticated supplier network and they are unlikely to jeopardise the gains that have been made simply to respond to the creation of a corridor. Second, as is the case in the area of trade, the fact that many of the big firms located in the Belfast Dublin area are subsidiaries of multinationals locked into international sourcing arrangements reduces their capacity to coordinate local commercial activity. Third, to the extent that the corridor is successful, it may not encourage new offensive forms of enterprise calculation on the part of large firms, but rather defensive commercial strategies. Companies situated in other parts of the island may move to the zone in search of agglomeration or concentration benefits. Such corporate moves are not likely to lead to any aggregate increase in economic activity: the first order effects will be to accentuate the already unbalanced economic geography of the island; east will once again win over the west. Thus the prospects for big firms triggering a virtuous wave of commercial activity are not good.

A similarly down-beat assessment applies to the potential economic role of universities in the corridor. A number of universities in the area are making important efforts to promote the commercial exploitation of innovations in science and technology. But these initiatives are not of the scale or quality to have a decisive impact on the economic zone between Belfast and Dublin. All in all, the evidence suggests that a Belfast-Dublin economic corridor is not likely to be a thriving, bustling, dynamic commercial centre. The corporate, social and institutional infrastructures are simply not in place to allow this to happen. With sufficient government intervention this situation could change, but such intervention would have to be far-reaching given present commercial circumstances, and to embark on such a policy would be costly.

In particular, as Bradley points out, if the public authorities, north and south, were to concentrate economic policy on building up the capacity of the Dublin-Belfast corridor, then long-standing approaches to economic development would have to be abandoned.[12] For decades each jurisdiction has pursued a policy of dispersing manufacturing activity so that different parts of the island receive some level of employment and industry. This policy is particularly evident with regard to inward investment projects. To make the Belfast-Dublin corridor a success would mean concentrating a disproportionate amount of economic activity there in the future. Whether such a policy reversal could be pushed through the political system either side of the border is questionable. In the south, where clientist politics are still widespread, opposition to such a plan from such places as Cork, Clonmel and Galway would be formidable. Opposition might not be as strong in the north, but the consequences are potentially more far reaching. A persistent claim of Nationalists is that the relative economic prosperity of the mainly Protestant eastern part of the region has been at the expense of the poorer, mainly Catholic, western areas. A Belfast-Dublin corridor could easily widen this divide within Northern Ireland and thus, perversely, an initiative designed to improve north–south economic connections could have the effect of further bifurcating economic divisions between the two religious blocs inside Northern Ireland.

On paper, the idea of a Belfast-Dublin corridor is attractive, but once unpacked many drawbacks can be found. This negative assessment does not mean that no schemes should be enacted to improve economic and commercial life on the eastern seaboard of the island. Efforts should be made to improve road and rail links between the two capitals. In addition, more targeted schemes to improve business links along the border, particularly between Newry and Dundalk, should be established. But such initiatives, rather than being dressed up as a grand plan to create a corridor, should be presented as part of a panoply of measures to improve economic performance both north and south. The last thing Ireland needs is yet another over-hyped economic programme which proves to be ephemeral.

HARMONISATION AND CROSS-BORDER ECONOMIC CONNECTIONS

One shortcoming of the debate about north–south economic cooperation is that it has become a catch-all term for a wide range of programmes and policies. One claim made under the banner of cooperation is that many of the rules and regulations governing commercial activity each side of the border need to be harmonised to bring the two economies closer together. So far there has been hardly any serious thinking on this matter. As a result, little is known about whether large-scale harmonisation is possible, or even desirable for that matter. This section sets forth the argument that the task of achieving closer economic and institutional harmonisation on the island is seriously underestimated. The important area of the labour market is used to highlight this argument.

Table 1 sets out the degree of convergence/divergence in several parts of the labour market. The working proposition is that harmonisation will be easier to obtain if there is a large measure of convergence or similarity between the two employment systems. Alternatively, if there is considerable divergence it is difficult to see how the two labour markets can be brought together in any meaningful way without highly disruptive policies, which in the end may not yield beneficial results. The diagram itself needs a little explanation: the black dot in the middle represents the situation of complete convergence whereas the circumference of the outer circle constitutes total divergence. Overall, the table shows that the two labour markets operate in different ways. Consider the matter of wage formation. On every score there is considerable divergence between the north and south: in the Republic, a centralised system of pay determination is in place, while in the north fragmented, decentralised bargaining is the norm in the private sector, and increasingly in the public sector too. The wage structures, involving such things as pay relativities between occupations and wage dispersion rates, are also quite different. The systems of income tax and social charges on labour are yet a further source of divergence.

Secondly, consider the area of training. Here once again we find considerable divergence between north and south. In the north, a twin-track approach is being pursued. On the one hand, like other parts of the UK, decisive moves have been made towards a mass education system which will equip young people with generic

WAGE SYSTEMS

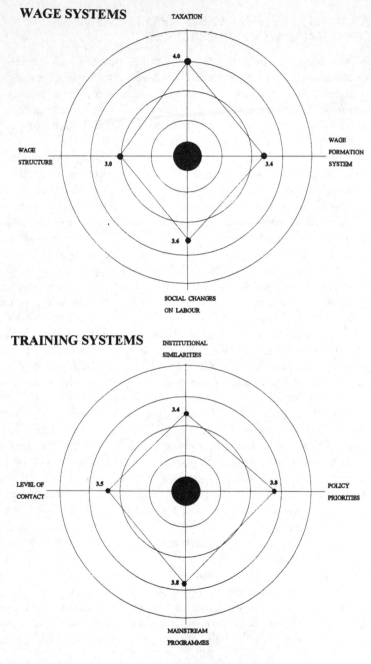

TAXATION

4.0

WAGE
STRUCTURE

3.0

WAGE
FORMATION
SYSTEM

3.4

3.6

SOCIAL CHANGES
ON LABOUR

TRAINING SYSTEMS

INSTITUTIONAL
SIMILARITIES

3.4

LEVEL OF
CONTACT

3.5

POLICY
PRIORITIES

3.8

3.8

MAINSTREAM
PROGRAMMES

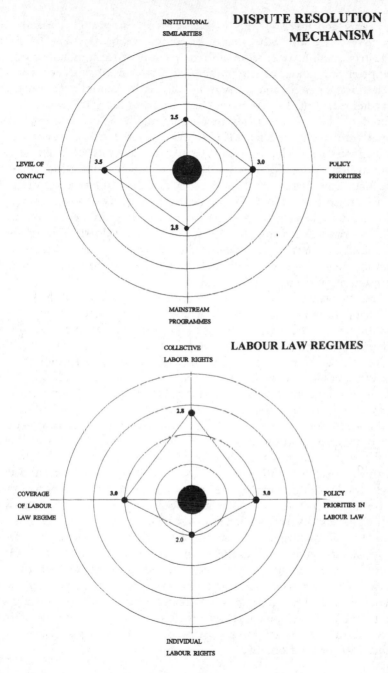

DISPUTE RESOLUTION MECHANISM

INSTITUTIONAL SIMILARITIES

LEVEL OF CONTACT

POLICY PRIORITIES

MAINSTREAM PROGRAMMES

LABOUR LAW REGIMES

COLLECTIVE LABOUR RIGHTS

COVERAGE OF LABOUR LAW REGIME

POLICY PRIORITIES IN LABOUR LAW

INDIVIDUAL LABOUR RIGHTS

numeracy and literacy skills in line with the new skill demands of employers. On the other hand, attempts are being made to shift industrial training away from craft-based apprenticeships and towards competence training, which combines a modicum of skills acquisition with tuition on social and behaviour skills. In the Republic the situation is rather different. In particular, the training authorities remain committed to the traditional apprenticeship model. Furthermore, only tentative moves have been made to reform the rather elitist and academic education system. The fact that the two training systems on the island are travelling along different paths has important implications for the occupational structure in each economy and the form of economic and social citizenship in place. On top of this divergence, the organisations formulating and delivering skills-formation programmes – FAS and T&EA – operate in distinctive ways, which is not helped by the present low level of contact and exchanges between the two bodies. Thus, prevailing circumstances are hardly conducive for the enactment of a harmonisation strategy with regard to training.

The same story emerges when the areas of labour law and the system of dispute resolution are considered; so it is hardly necessary to set out the full details. What is true for the labour market is equally valid for other important sections of the economy and public policy; health, industrial policy or whatever. On the surface, because the two economies face similar problems, such as unemployment or poorly performing indigenous companies, it seems plausible to argue that scope exists to pursue collaborative or even joint schemes to remedy such shortcomings. But on closer examination it is apparent that each jurisdiction has developed contrasting policy and institutional responses to these problems, which narrows the ground for harmonised initiatives. A further, frequently underestimated, obstacle to harmonisation is the high level of interdependence across different parts of national governance structures. Consider the labour market area again. Employment policies covering such things as wages and training are closely linked with other aspects of economic management, particular macroeconomic strategies. As a result, any attempt to obtain greater harmonisation of employment policy would very quickly run into the problem of having to synchronise fiscal and monetary policy too. Labour market structures arise from complex interdependencies of national social and economic systems, which places severe constraints on the scope for cross-frontier harmonisation. Again this conclusion also applies to other parts of the economy.

This suggests that full-scale harmonisation may be difficult to achieve, but is harmonisation necessary or desirable? In principle, a certain level of harmonisation makes trade and commercial interactions across nations easier. If different regulations are hampering cross-border trade in Ireland – a case which remains to be proven – then something should be done to address this distortion. But rather than pursuing time-consuming and cumbersome harmonisation strategies, a tidier and easier solution might be to use the mutual recognition tactic employed by the EU. For the past decade, the EU has been busy implementing the programme to complete the internal market which aims to remove the remaining non-tariff barriers against trade between the member states. To by-pass the administrative nightmare of attempting to unify the diverse regulatory regimes in the EU, the member-states opted to recognise each other's standards and rules. Since both parts of the island are in the EU there is no good reason why this mutual recognition procedure should not be used to create an all-Ireland trading zone. In other words, the matter of removing regulatory distortions becomes not one of developing elaborate harmonisation strategies but of enacting intensely and deeply the measures set out in the EU's internal market programme.

Thus the evidence suggests that there is neither much scope nor need for cross-border harmonisation to promote greater commercial connections on the island. This conclusion does not foreclose the possibility of encouraging policy coordination between the the two economies. By pooling resources or planning policies more closely together, greater benefits may arise. Some of this type of activity is already going on. For example, health authorities on each side of the border are beginning to share equipment and other resources. Such collaboration makes good sense and should be extended. The areas of transport, environment and agriculture are obviously ripe for such coordination, given the inter-dependencies between both parts of the island. Encouraging policy coordination does not necessarily mean the the creation of all-Ireland institutions, but it does require closer policy communities to be established between the administrations in Dublin and Belfast. At present the policy contacts between the two administrations across a wide range of government functions are not of the frequency or depth to allow for the full exploration of all possiblities for coordination.

179

THE EU AND CROSS-BORDER COOPERATION

The role of the European Union in promoting cross-border cooperation is a matter of much debate. For some the EU could actually be a wedge preventing more intimate economic relations emerging between the two parts of the island. Others hold the opposite view and suggest it is the most appropriate framework for forging links between the north and south. These two views are examined below, but first something must be said about claims that the EU should play am important role in the future economic and political governance of Northern Ireland.

In recent years, the idea that the European Union could play a decisive role in bridging the deep political divisions in Northern Ireland has become more prominent. For instance, the Social Democratic and Labour Party argued at the beginning of the 1990s that 'the European Community institutions offer an accessible and persuasive model of how new arrangements for Northern Ireland might be shaped'.[14] More specifically, the party argued that the EU should have a representative on its envisaged six-person Commission that would operate as a type of collective presidency in the region (see pp76-77).[15] Another proposal was that Northern Ireland should become a 'European region'.[16] The thinking here was that a recasting of the economic and political foundations of Northern Ireland was required to weaken engrained Nationalist and Unionist beliefs. The European Union, standing once removed from the conflict but yet growing in authority and competence, was seen as a suitable setting within which these long-standing, and on occasions fanatical, loyalties might atrophy.

At a distance, proposals of this kind have a certain appeal, not least because they display an innovative and fresh approach to a complex political problem, but under closer scrutiny, however, they look less convincing. First of all, it is highly questionable whether the EU could operate as the economic exoskeleton for Northern Ireland. At the moment, the EU transfers about £200 million annually to the region, most of this in the form of structural fund money. This amounts to only about 6 per cent of the fiscal transfer flowing from the UK exchequer. In other words, the EU's financial transfer would have to increase by a factor of 18 before it could replace the UK in the role of Northern Ireland's benefactor; under existing budgetary conditions it is difficult to see how the EU could do so. For the period 1994–99, the annual EU structural budget is approximately ECU 28.3 billion (at 1992 prices). For the EU to service the Northern Ireland subvention at present levels about 25 per cent of this money would go to the region on a recurrent basis. The only way this could be done is if other 'less favoured' regions experienced a huge cutback in European money. It is extremely unlikely that Spain, Portugal or any other current recipients of funding would accept such cutbacks, and the very suggestion would probably provoke a political uproar.

Another possibility might be to divert money from another part of the EU budget, but again, obstacles would be thrown up by potential losers. Realistically the EU could only take financial responsibility for Northern Ireland if the European budget were enlarged, or if some special fund were established by the member states. On an annual basis, the EU budget would have to be increased by roughly ECU 7.5 billion if Brussels were to service the subvention. If this extra financial contribution were to fall on the seven richest member-states, each would only have to find about ECU 1.1 billion each year which in absolute terms is a lot of money, but in the context of national public expenditure is relatively insignificant. Thus those who argue that it is financially impractical for the EU to assume responsibility for the Northern Ireland subvention may be overestimating the fiscal burden.[17] Financially it is not beyond the bounds of credibility; the problem is more of a political one.

For a group of member states to hand over about £500 million each year on an indefinite basis would require a high degree of political commitment. Whether such a commitment exists in relation to the Northern Ireland subvention is a moot point. Although a resolution to the conflict is clearly important for EU member states, they are at the same time confronted with other equally serious problems that also need addressing: easing the transition to market economies in what used to be the communist bloc and resolving the crisis in the former Yugoslavia for example. Faced with these competing claims on the EU's resources, many member states would query why they should divert an extra ECU 7.5 billion to cover the Northern Ireland subvention which is currently being met by the UK.

More importantly, until now the EU has assiduously avoided intervening in the internal affairs of a member state. Operating the Northern Ireland subvention from Brussels would mark a dramatic reversal of this policy and it is doubtful whether any European capital would be in favour of such a move. Thus the political conditions do not appear to exist for the EU to take over financial and economic responsibility for Northern Ireland, and for a considerable time to come; it is fair to assume that the region will remain tied to the UK subvention. In an otherwise fairly fluid situation this is one economic variable that is almost certain to remain unchanged.

In terms of the prospect of significant EU involvement in Northern Ireland's political affairs, again the EU centre, as well as the member states, are loathe to break the principle of non-interference in the internal affairs of a EU country. In fact, when the SDLP proposed that a EU nominee be a member of the six-person Commission which would effectively govern the region, the European Commission moved fast to squash the suggestion. In a speech in Belfast in 1992, Jacques Delors ruled out any direct EU involvement in the governance of Northern Ireland. Another ill-considered idea on the political front is the notion that any new decision-making structures devised for Northern Ireland should resemble in some form those of the EU itself. Kennedy has carefully dissected this argument, but some of its limitations are immediately obvious.[18] For example, it is perhaps too sanguine to believe that a locally elected assembly would be prepared to accept a role similar to that of the European Parliament. Moreover, it is hard to see a body like the European Commission or the European Council functioning in any coherent or sustainable way in the Northern Ireland context. Very quickly the democratic legitimacy of such an arrangement would be called into question. Thus the scenario of the EU playing a pivotal role in the political governance of Northern Ireland is unconvincing. Even if the internal opposition to the EU playing such a role, particularly among Unionists, is left to one side, this position simply overestimates the capacity of Brussels to function as an agent of government in the region.

THE EU AS A WEDGE BETWEEN THE NORTH AND SOUTH OF IRELAND

The double hegemony and cross-border economic cooperation
Countering the above position is the argument that the EU may actually impede moves towards closer economic cooperation between the north and the south. In support of this view, some point to the sharply contrasting approaches to European integration held in Dublin and London. On the Irish side, there is strong support for moves towards monetary union and greater economic supranational

decision-making. On the British side, the approach is more cautious and equivocal. One calculation is that cross-border collaboration may be hampered because of the two capitals' polarised views on a European single currency. To fully answer whether this assessment is accurate, some of the economic background needs to be understood.

The Anglo-Irish Settlement of 1921 (mostly) achieved a political divorce, but economically the two countries remained intimate: Irish monetary policy continued to be set in London and the bulk of the Republic's exports went to the British market. In the 1960s and 70s the sense of an unfinished revolution was widespread and Europe was seen as offering the opportunity of complete liberation from British influences. The decisive economic reorientation came in 1978 when the Republic joined the European Monetary System (EMS) and the parity between the punt and sterling was broken. In the Republic this decision was greeted somewhat naively as economic emancipation. In reality, however, the country had managed to escape from the monetary tutelage of one hegemonic power, only to find itself exposed to a double hegemony – with Frankfurt setting monetary policy and Britain remaining the main trading partner.

In the 1980s this double hegemony actually worked in Ireland's favour. At the time, the country stood at the edge of the economic abyss due to the scale of public debt. The authorities had no alternative but to introduce a far-reaching austerity programme. Part of this disinflationary exercise involved using the exchange rate mechanism of the EMS to appreciate the punt against the Dmark. This move was a variant of the 'Hard ERM policy' pursued by several of the member states during this period, in an attempt to help reduce domestic inflation. Coupled with the big cutbacks in public expenditure, this policy caused a huge disinflation of the Irish economy, leading to high unemployment and emigration. But the situation would have got much worse were it not for the 'Lawson boom' in the British economy during the mid-1980s. Prosperous times in the UK ensured there was a large market for Irish exports as well as its people, many of whom were leaving the country in despair. Thus, for the 1980s, the double hegemony worked in tandem: Europe was a vehicle for austerity while Britain in essence provided an economic and social safety net.

In the 1990s, the reverse situation emerged as Irish economic interests were squeezed due to divergent policies being pursued in Bonn and London. At the start of the decade, the UK decided to pursue a 'hard ERM' policy by pegging sterling to the Dmark at a higher rate. This parity rate proved unsustainable in the face of the huge turmoil in the currency markets in 1992. In fact, the turbulence was severe enough to cause the UK's ejection from the ERM. The immediate effect of this withdrawal was a massive depreciation of sterling against the Dmark. With the punt maintaining its Dmark rate, the Irish currency appreciated against sterling, making the country's exports more expensive on the British market. The Dublin government was put on the horns of a dilemma: should it continue with its long-term economic objectives of being a member of a European core and keep the punt/Dmark exchange rate? Or should it give immediate relief to Irish-based firms exporting to the UK by depreciating the currency, thereby saving jobs and market share? In the end, the financial markets made up the government's mind by forcing the devaluation of the punt inside the ERM. But the episode highlights that when German and UK economic policies travel in different directions, severe strains are placed on the Irish economy.

Table 2: Ireland's Trade Dependency with the UK

	Imports % from UK	Exports % to UK	trade Ratio
1970	53	66	60
1975	49	54	52
1980	51	43	47
1985	43	33	38
1990	42	34	38
1992	42	32	37

Source: CSO, Trade Statistics of Ireland

This episode had a profound impact in Dublin for it punctured the widely held belief that the Republic had broken free from British economic influence. One response was to call for a redoubling of efforts to reduce economic connections, particularly with regard to trade with the UK. Whether the Republic can ever find itself in a position where events in the UK have few spillover effects on its economy is open to doubt. Consider the matter of trading relations. Since 1970 the Republic has succeeded in considerably reducing trade flows to and from Britain: For example, as Table 2 shows, in 1970 about 60 per cent of total Irish exports went to the UK market; by 1994 this figure was only 32 per cent. But it will be difficult to get this figure much lower, given the well-established commercial connections that exist across the Irish sea. Moreover, if exports from the indigenous sector are considered alone then the percentage of the total going to the UK market shoots up to 45 per cent. Geographical proximity creates a social underbelly to trading relations that will be hard to disrupt from the political centre.

It seems likely that close economic ties will remain between Ireland and Britain for the foreseeable future. As a result, the Irish economy is likely to remain in the grips of a double hegemony. Acutely aware that the country is caught mid-stream between Germany and Britain, the Dublin policy elite is beginning to worry that European integration could potentially disrupt moves towards greater connections between the north and south. Consider the scenario of the Republic joining a European monetary union whilst the UK stayed out, reflecting the creation of a two-speed Europe, with Ireland in the core and the UK in the periphery. The outcome would be that the economic and political orientation of the Republic would be tied to Germany as the dominant power in the new first division Europe, while the priorities of the north, like the rest of the UK, would be those of outer Europe. As a result, the scope to build meaningful economic and political links between the two parts of the island could be radically reduced.

In Dublin it is popular to blame a reckless and opportunistic approach to the EU on the part of the UK political establishment for making European integration a potential wedge between the two parts of the island. But this argument that the monetary union project may block deeper economic connections between the north and the south is overblown. In fact such a scenario is unlikely to arise. First of all, the emergence of a two-speed Europe, even if by default, must be regarded as a long shot, especially as the key member states – Germany, France and the UK – appear to have set their faces against this option. Secondly, even if a European core were to be established, it is far from certain that Ireland would be a member. On a number of occasions in the recent past, German officials have cast doubt on the ability of

Ireland to function properly in a first tier Europe. Thirdly, despite the ambivalent position of successive governments in the UK, it is hard to see a European monetary union being established without the UK. Britain's economic interests are too bound up with Europe for the country's powerful financial and commercial lobby to allow that prize to get away. Fourthly, it is even harder to visualise a European monetary union that includes Ireland but not the UK: the economies of the two islands are too entangled for the monetary authorities of Europe to allow such a highly dysfunctional situation. The message from Frankfurt and Brussels is that if Ireland joins so must all of the British Isles.

Dublin is in fact in the position to take the most decisive action to prevent the single currency issue from placing a wedge between the two parts of the island. Not to put too fine a point on it, because of the double hegemony problem, Germany does not want Ireland without the UK. One way out of this conundrum for an Irish government would be to ease the double hegemony by back peddling and re-establishing orderly economic ties with Britain by rejoining a sterling area. Economically, such a course would prevent the Irish punt being buffeted by the ebb and flow of sterling and the Dmark. Moreover, if the assessment here is accurate, it would not seriously damage the country's chances of joining a European monetary union in the future; in some respects it could actually improve the prospects.

Politically, the implications would be far reaching. A common perception amongst Unionists in the north is that Nationalist irredentism is still widespread in Irish political life, with the UK seen as a jailer, imprisoning the country's economic fortunes. Rebuilding close links between Dublin and London would be a clear and unequivocal signal to the Unionist community that the Republic is truly committed to a historic compromise between the two traditions on the island. Although it would involve a gamble, the Irish government could give the peace process a shot in the arm, ease the double hegemony and at the same time not overly damage its desire to become part of a European monetary union. Whether such a course is pursued or not, the bottom line is that European monetary integration will only pose a threat to deeper north–south cooperation if Dublin allows it to do so.

COMPETITIVE INTERDEPENDENCE AND AN ALL-IRELAND SOCIAL DIMENSION

Concern has also been voiced in the past that, since the Republic signed the Social Chapter while Northern Ireland, due to the UK opt-out, remained outside it, a schism could develop between the two Irish labour markets, causing a regime of competitive interdependence to open up on the island. If this had happened, then the climate would be cold for any kind of positive cross border cooperation. The worry was that a cost-based incentive structure could emerge between the north and south. In other words, firms in the Republic, might move to the north to escape the constraints of tougher EU labour market regulations. If a regime of competitive interdependence were to open between the north and south, then a strong lobby would emerge for some type of all-Ireland social dimension. With the election of a Labour government committed to signing the Social Chapter, this problem has lessened. However it is still worth looking at the argument.

The possibility of what would essentially be a form of social dumping occurring as a result of north–south cooperation is unlikely for a number of reasons. First of all, the argument over-estimates the impact of the legislative programme that has emerged to enact the Social Chapter. Table 3 outlines this programme and shows that virtually every measure applied to the UK, and hence to Northern Ireland, as well as to the Republic. Only in the case of the European Works Councils Directive did the British government find it necessary to use its opt-out clause. But the general view is that the UK will cannot insulate itself from the effects of this directive and will have to comply with its contents. In most other instances the UK's administration was quite content with the provisions of proposed directives, or able to secure important concessions from Brussels: the controversial directive proposing a maximum working week of 48 hours being a good example of the latter.

Two pieces of the legislation programmed to be considered by the European Council relate to the regulation of a-typical employment. The Conservative government was opposed to these draft directives but it is unlikely that Britain will escape from EU legislative influences in this area, even if the opt-out is evoked once again. As a result of a number of rulings by the European Court of Justice, the UK will be obliged to concede certain rights to part-time workers that closely

Table 3: Social Action Programme Arising from the EU Social Charter

Legislative Issue	Applicability Republic of Ireland	Northern Ireland
1 Employment and Remuneration Directive (1991)	Yes	Yes
2 Improvement of Living and Working Conditions Directive (1991)	Yes	Yes
3 Equal treatment for Men and Women (1992)	Yes	Yes
4 Health protection and Safety at the Workplace Programme		
a) Medical Treatment on Board Vessels Directive (1992)	Yes	Yes
b) Exposure to Asbestos at Work Directive (1991)	Yes	Yes
c) Safety Requirements on Temporary or Mobile Construction Sites Directive (1992)	Yes	Yes
d) Provision of Safety and/or Health Signs at Work Directive (1992)	Yes	Yes
e) Safety and Health Standards for Workers in Surface and Underground Mineral Extracting Industries Directive (1992)	Yes	Yes
f) Health and Safety on Board Fishing Vessels Directive (1993	Yes	Yes
5 Protection of Young People at Work Directive (1994	Yes	Yes
6 European Works Council Directive 1994	Yes	Yes
7 Imminent Directive on Working Conditions	Potentially Yes	Potentially Indirect

Figure 1: Labour Productivity in Manufacturing:
Republic Ireland and Northern Ireland

Erratum

Due to a printing error, this graph was omitted from p189.

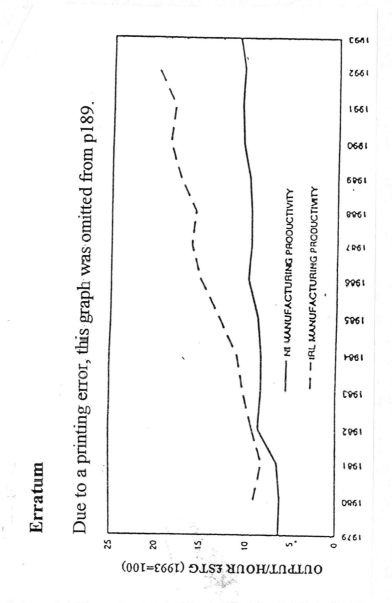

echo those in the draft directives. Thus, in practice the highly vocal UK opposition to the Social Chapter amounted to precious little. Since almost all of EU social legislation is applicable in the north and the south, it is unlikely to be the source of divergence between the two labour law regimes on the island.

Ground level economic conditions also suggest that the regime of competitive interdependence should be treated with a high degree of scepticism. Even if the argument that the Social Chapter put the south at a cost disadvantage in relation to the north were accepted, this extra burden was unlikely to be enough to trigger any form of social dumping practices between the two parts of the island. This is largely because a substantial productivity gap exists between the two economies. Figure 1 compares labour productivity in the north and south.

It shows that on both scores the south is clearly out-performing the north. In fact, industry in the south is so much more competitive that it would have required the costs imposed by the Social Chapter to be huge before companies started to look northwards for some type of regulatory liberation. Thus it appears misleading to suggest that EU employment policies could actually drive an institutional barrier between the two Irish economies. Little if any inter-regime competition will arise in Ireland as a result of European integration and there is no ground level justification for an all-Ireland social or employment protection programme.

The EU and north–south policy collaboration
The main conclusion to be drawn from the above discussion is that the various claims that the EU could play a big role in the future governance of Northern Ireland – and that it could jeopardise (or accelerate) north–south economic cooperation – should be treated with caution. Both views exaggerate the authority of the EU as a political and economic institution. It must be remembered that member states remain firmly in control of the decision-making system in Brussels. This system, known as intergovernmentalism, does not lend itself to big policy initiatives but rather to a gradual process of integration where the emphasis is on developing programmes based on compromise and consensus. When seen from this perspective, it becomes clear that the EU could play an important role in building all-Ireland policy and economic connections largely because many of its programmes and policies actually set out to facilitate, enable and

improve collaboration across nation states. But its involvement will not amount to a surreptitious project to cause the border to wither away, contrary to Nationalists' hopes and Unionists' fears. The EU simply represents a ready made institutional structure for improving all-Ireland relationships while keeping present constitutional arrangements intact.

Labour market policy offers a good example of how the EU could help promote north–south cooperation. As highlighted earlier, the two labour markets on the island function in highly distinctive ways, reducing the scope for any ambitious programme to create a single employment system on the island. At the same time, existing divergence does not mean that *no* collaborative measures can be enacted. A number of EU social policy programmes could kick start this collaborative process. Consider the area of labour mobility. Ever since the formation of the Common Market in 1957, Brussels has continually pushed for the removal of barriers to the free movement of labour. At the moment, policies in this area include: obtaining the mutual recognition of diplomas and qualifications across frontiers; the portability of pensions across national boundaries; and revisions to social security systems that would encourage search activity among the unemployed in different member states. Promoting such policies on an all-Ireland basis appears worthwhile, particularly as labour market flows between the north and south are relatively small.

The EU already has a considerable presence in the health and safety dimension of the labour market, largely because this was the first area of European social policy in which the member states conceded the principle of qualified majority voting. As a result, much of the health and safety policy agenda in Dublin and Belfast has its origins in Brussels. Implementing such schemes jointly or in cooperation would not only bring the labour market institutions on both sides of the border closer together, it would also help to level the commercial playing field, since all business would face the same regulations. Equal opportunity measures is yet a further area where the EU could operate as a conduit for greater north–south cooperation. Encouraging groups in the north and south to work together on equality issues would simultaneously give rise to concerted all-Ireland action on such matters and create important social foundations to the entire collaborative exercise. Other examples from the labour area include: higher education; labour law; and long-term unemployment. The EU could play a similar role in other policy areas like transport, the environment, or Structural Fund allocations. But the key point is that the EU could act as a catalyst and focal point for stronger links and collaboration between the two policy communities on the island.

The political implications of north–south economic cooperation

Arguing that the EU could be a conduit for closer policy ties between Dublin and Belfast raises directly the question of the political implications of north–south economic cooperation. Reflecting a widely held nationalist expectation, Rowthorn suggests that closer economic cooperation between both parts of the island will induce the Unionist community in the north to shift their loyalties away from Britain and towards the Irish Republic.[19] As a result of this gradual process, the political foundations will be laid for the unification of Ireland. This view is best described as the 'rolling integration' scenario and it closely resembles the neo-functionalist account of integration inside the European Union. Neo-functionalism sets out to explain the process whereby political actors in separate national settings are persuaded to shift their traditional loyalties, expectations and activities from a well-established political formation towards a new constitutional order. A key proposition of this literature is that once different national political and economic elites decide to deepen cooperation between themselves, even in fairly prescribed policy areas, they will find that the scope or boundaries of the integration agenda expanding quickly.

Haas, the intellectual founder of neo-functionalism, used the concept of spillover to capture the idea that a cross-country integration process is inherently cumulative and dynamic.[20] At the start, the integration process is seen as involving governments horsetrading to conclude package deals. Essentially such deals oblige some governments to take action in a certain field in return for other governments agreeing to do something in a different policy sphere. Because these reciprocal actions invariably have unintended consequences in unrelated areas, governments feel compelled to spread the integration arena in response. After a time it is not only the political and administrative elites that are engaged in the integration process, but also citizens too. According to Haas the spillover dynamic, by creating new centres of decision-making, will encourage citizens to turn away upon from existing political jurisdictions. This is largely because their general well-being will be increasingly tied to the integration process. Eventually citizens are persuaded to regard the institutional apparatus associated with integration as representing a legitimate new political community, thereby rendering the old jurisdictions obsolete.

The similarity between the Rowthorn line of argument and neo-functionalism should be apparent. Nationalists expect that cross-border cooperation will set in train an integration process that will cause the economic and political connections between the north and mainland Britain to atrophy and similar linkages with the south to hypertrophy. Good grounds exist to be sceptical about such a neo-functionalist scenario emerging in Ireland. First of all, although a neat scenario on paper, it is doubtful whether neo-functionalism has fully emerged in any actual integration experiment. Consider the case of the European Union, for example. It is certainly the case that the policy-making capacity of the EU has increased considerably since its inception in 1957. At the same time, it would be heroic to claim that forty years of European integration has dented, to any great extent, national identity across the member states. Rather than progressing along a smooth integration conveyor belt towards an ever closer union, the EU has evolved in 'fits and starts': like an erratic marriage where love, loathing and lethargy are embodied in the one relationship.

Above all else, the EU experience shows that the relationship between politics and economics in an integration process is unpredictable. In the mid-1960s, for example, when economic interdependencies were rapidly being forged between the original six member countries, political relations between them were thrown into turmoil by De Gaulle's behaviour in the Council of Ministers. More recently, the Maastricht plan for monetary union, rather than deepening connections between the member states had the effect of weakening the political commitment to the EU among European citizens. In other words, a negative process of spillback which causes the weakening or even rejection of the integration process amongst national elites and citizens, is as likely to arise as a positive spillover dynamic.[21] Efforts to deepen interdependencies between nation states seldom travel down a one way street.

Those who argue that cross-border cooperation in Ireland, involving a strong EU dimension, represents the stepping stones across a river from one constitutional arrangement to another should take note of the European integration experience. The unavoidable message is that it is specious to believe (or hope) that economic cooperation between both parts of Ireland will cause the political border to wither away.

Another lesson is that to present cross-border connections as essentially a neo-functionalist project runs the big danger of triggering a spillback process. Given the intense loyalty the Unionist community has to Britain, deep suspicions exist about whether closer economic ties between the north and south might serve as the backdoor route to the political unification of the island. Portraying cross-border institutional connections as exactly that type of process will almost certainly cause the Unionists to withhold their support.

Another reason to be sceptical about a neo-functionalist scenario is that the institutional arrangements conducive to rolling integration are unlikely to emerge on the island. For a start, the theory tells us that neo-functionalism is more likely to happen when the integration programme has an autonomous institutional structure whose policy capacities are not tightly ring fenced.[22] This situation increases the scope for political and policy entrepreneurship on the part of the 'integration centre' to push forward the depth and breadth of collaborative measures. Another favourable condition is if the integration project has a legal dimension. Establishing economic and policy interdependencies through the law has the effect of creating a new legal order outside domestic judicial systems. As a result, tensions frequently emerge between the extra-national and national sources of law over which takes precedence. Resolutions to such disputes can strengthen the extra-national legal order. Moreover, citizens of the participating countries may explore ways to use the extra-national source of laws within the domestic setting, thereby deepening ground level support for the integration process. Finally, if the integration process has a budgetary process, then the scope for side payments – one country getting compensation for agreeing to go along with deep forms of integration – increases.

It is questionable whether any such structures will be built to house cross-border collaboration in Ireland. Certainly, neither the British nor Irish governments regard this type of arrangement as appropriate, if the proposals in the Framework documents are anything to go by. These documents do not envisage the setting up of an all-Ireland institutional structure with independent policy-making or budgetary powers. Furthermore, they do not foresee the need for an all-Ireland legal order. If anything the two governments seem to have gone out of their way to prevent the creation of institutions that could be used to push a neo-functionalist or rolling integration project.

Political stability and cross-border economic cooperation: a new symbiosis

To pour cold water on the Nationalist vision of rolling integration is not to support the Unionist position on cross-border cooperation. Unionist politicians are signalling that they are prepared to accept closer economic and policy ties between the north and south. But this acceptance appears conditional on there being no overarching cross-border institutions, the Irish Dáil and any local assembly established in Belfast being the sanctioning authorities for proposed initiatives. Frequently this stance is called the 'good neighbours' model. It is highly questionable, however, whether this position can command widespread support. In a nutshell, northern Nationalists – of no matter what hue – would feel short-changed by such an option. The likely response from the SDLP and others would simply be to make such a plan unworkable. Just as rolling integration is constrained by the political sentiment of the Unionist community, so the 'good neighbours' model runs up against the opposition of Nationalist opinion. A fact that must not be overlooked is that, in addition to the Unionist veto, there is now a Nationalist veto over political change in Northern Ireland. If a sustainable political settlement is to emerge that represents a genuine equilibrium between the two traditions, the Unionists will have to give a little on this issue.

The Unionist position is ultimately a rather unsophisticated zero sum approach to matters such as sovereignty, identity and pooled decision-making. For most Unionists, any transfer of authority or responsibility to cross-border economic arrangements means an equal diminution of Northern Ireland's economic and political status inside the UK. But such a direct one-to-one trade off is unlikely to happen in practice. For one thing, not all – indeed very few – initiatives designed to bring different countries closer together through economic cooperation mechanisms compromise the identity, cohesiveness or citizenship of the respective nations. Here it is important to distinguish between inner and outer sovereignty. Most nations have three key pillars of inner sovereignty: defence arrangements, internal law and order procedures, and taxation. If a system of cross-border cooperation or coordination breaks into the arena of inner sovereignty to any great extent, then the distinctive character of a national economic and political formation comes under threat. At the same time, cooperation is possible on inner sovereignty, but this normally involves low-grade matters. Outer sovereignty refers to those government policies and other economic and social arrangements that are important but not pivotal to the distinctiveness of a nation: industrial policy, agricultural arrangements and so on. Considerable interdependencies can be established in the realm of outer sovereignty without compromising national identity.

Examples from the European Union may make the above points clearer. For about ten years the member states have worked within an arrangement known as the European Political Community to promote collaboration on defence arrangements. This arrangement proved utterly ineffective when the war in Bosnia broke out as it failed to get the member states to take decisive action on the matter. Cooperation existed in an area of inner sovereignty, but when it really counted this amounted to very little.

Another example is monetary coordination. Since 1978 most of the member states have agreed to coordinate exchange rates through the ERM. Participating in this currency corset, however, did not result in member states presiding over the atrophy of their national economic and political life. But when the governments (apart from the UK) agreed to the plan for monetary union at Maastricht, almost immediate opposition emerged from the citizens of the EU. Whereas the regulation of exchange rates was regarded as compatible with the continued existence of nation states, the creation of a single currency in Europe was widely interpreted as an invasion into inner sovereignty: the distinctiveness of national systems was perceived to be under threat. A third example is agriculture: for twenty-five years Brussels has controlled the agricultural industry in Europe but this has not dented national sovereignty to any great extent. To be sure people in rural parts of Northern Ireland do not seem any less Unionist or Nationalist because of the operation of the Common Agricultural Policy. Thus the history of the EU suggests that despite all the integration that has taken place, member states remain stubbornly intact as political, economic and social units. The lesson for Unionists is that economic cooperation does not necessarily mean that Northern Ireland's position within the UK or the Protestant identity will be compromised to any great extent.

A second lesson from European integration questions the current Unionist position on cross-border cooperation even more profoundly. In a brilliant study, Milward argues that, far from undermining nation states, European integration has actually strengthened them.[23] Thus he shows how Belgium was able to deal more easily with the problem of huge over capacity in the coal industry by the creation of the European Coal and Steel Community in 1953. Similarly he shows how the provisions relating to the free movement of workers in the Treaty of Rome, establishing the Common Market in 1958, helped Italy deal with the chronic unemployment problem in the southern part of the country. Milward, in effect, is suggesting that European integration is a symbiotic process, whereby a strong EU centre and national political systems are actually mutually reinforcing rather than in collision. In the same way, if properly designed, cross-border economic cooperation and a new Northern Ireland could exist in a symbiotic partnership of mutual dependency. In the context of European integration, this process operates primarily in the economic field, but in the Irish context, it would have more of a political dimension, the most likely effect being that north–south economic cooperation would strengthen the political stability of a new Northern Ireland. By giving institutional and policy articulation to an important aspiration of the Nationalist community in the north, the full political commitment and support of that community to an eventual peace settlement is more assured. This is the true significance of moves towards closer economic cooperation between the two parts of this island. Unionists ' appear to have neglected this possibility, which is to be regretted.

Of course whether or not symbiotic co-operation actually emerges between the north and south very much depends on the architecture of any all-island institutional, commercial and policy arrangements. It would be inappropriate to attempt a blue-print for such an architecture here. Invariably, it would be a multi-layered structure with separate segments having different functions and autonomy. At one level, it is quite possible to see all-Ireland bodies emerging in trade and agriculture, even with executive powers. We have already pointed out how the EU could be the catalyst for closer policy coordination across a range of government responsibilities. A special programme could be established to improve the lot of the border areas, both north and south. A new all-Ireland consultative body could be established to help shape the agenda for cross-border commercial and policy collaboration. Policy communities could be created to further improve communication and exchange between business, social and voluntary groups. A whole range of permutations are possible, but the key objective is to increase the social, commercial and economic interdependencies on the island, within an overall institutional structure which respects existing constitutional boundaries.

CONCLUSIONS

The arguments presented in this chapter are fairly straightforward. Rallying calls for the north and south to march onwards and upwards to an all-island economy should, for the most part, be ignored. Economic theory and calculation tell us that there is no pot of gold at the end of the all-island rainbow. A more level-headed and realistic approach needs to be taken on the matter. Without exaggerating the gains to be captured, north–south collaborative policies and initiatives should be put in place to improve business performance on both sides of the border: the Dublin–Belfast road and rail connections should be upgraded; joint action should be taken to improve economic and social conditions in the border regions; and there should be cooperation between the two capitals to develop a better quality 'soft' infrastructure for commerce. These and similar initiatives should be pursued, but they should not be overburdened with the fanfare and razz-ma-tazz that has been stoked up about building a new island economy. This type of sloganising is unhelpful to economic policy-making as it falsely raises expectations and puts on the agenda a goal that cannot be properly achieved without the political unification of the island.

This raises the question of the politics behind the move towards north–south economic cooperation. Some hope that by promoting greater cross-border commercial connections a process of rolling political integration will be put in train with the final destination being an all-Ireland republic. For these people, the demand for an island economy is not made to improve the economic lot of people on either side of the border, but to secure a political triumph for Nationalism and Republicanism. This chapter has been deeply sceptical of such a project. It argues that a rolling integration strategy is more difficult to enact than is generally recognised. Furthermore, it suggests that the Irish and British governments shied away from this option when drawing up the Framework Documents. More profoundly, the chapter has been critical of such an approach because it highlights that strong irredentist influences are still widespread in Irish Nationalism. There is still a deep reluctance to fully accept that over a million Protestants in the north do not want to belong to a united Ireland and that economic and political programmes should be built upon that reality.

At the same time, Unionists are not exactly falling over themselves to forsake traditional values and positions. The chapter has been equally critical of the 'good neighbours' model held by many leading Unionists: a sparse and begrudging position which is also not particularly intellectually coherent. It reflects an unwillingness on the part of many unionists to face up to the changed nature of northern Nationalist politics. No longer are these people simply interested in democratic reform inside Northern Ireland, they also want some institutional expression of their Irish identity. This is as much a reality as Protestants not wanting to join an united Ireland. So when Unionist leaders make dismissive remarks about the Republic of Ireland being as foreign as France or Germany they too are wanting to triumph, and if stable government is to return to Northern Ireland then this position has to be abandoned.

Herein lies the true significance of north–south economic cooperation: it may represent a way of squaring the circle between Nationalism and Unionism. Through north–south economic and policy linkages, Nationalists may feel that an important part of their identity has been recognised and thus feel more committed to an entity called Northern Ireland. Since such linkages can be built in a way that does not threaten Northern Ireland position's inside the UK, Unionists do not have to worry about being on a conveyor belt to Dublin. North–south economic cooperation may not bring a business bonanza, but it could help capture the biggest prize of all – a reconciliation between the two opposing traditions in Ireland.

NOTES

1. Bradley, J., *An Island Economy*, Report prepared for the Forum of Peace and Reconciliation, Dublin 1995.
2. C11/CBI, Confederation of Irish Industry, Newsletter, C11, 1990.
3. Scott, R., and O'Reilly, M., 'Exports of Northern Ireland Manufacturing Companies', Northern Ireland Economic Research Centre, Belfast 1992.
4. Gudgin, G., 'The Potential for North–South Trade', Paper to Dublin Office of the European Commission, 1995.
5. Krugman, P., 'Growing World Trade: Causes and Consequences', *Brookings Papers on Economic Activity*, No. 1, 1995.
6. O'Malley, E., 'Ireland', in 'The Impact of the Internal Market by the Industrial Sector, The Challenge for the Member States', the Commission of the European Community, Brussels 1990.
7. Porter, M., *Competitive Advantage of Nations*, MacMillan, London 1990.
8. Birnie, E., and Hitchens, D., *The Competitiveness of Industy in Ireland*, Avebury, Aldershot 1990.

9. Quigley, G., *Northern Ireland: A Decade for Decision*, Annual Sir Charles Carter Lecture, Regent 95, Northern Ireland Economic Council, Belfast 1992.
10. Saxenian, A., 'The Cheshire Cat's Grin: Innovation, regional development and the Cambridge case', *Economy and Society*, Vol. 18, No. 4, 1989.
11. Amin, A., and Tift, N. (eds), *Globalisation and Regional Development*, Oxford University Press, Oxford 1995.
12. Bradley, J., *op.cit.*
13. Teague, P., and McCartney, J., 'Big Differences that Matter: Labour Market Systems in Ireland, North and South', in Bradley J.(ed.), *The Two Economies of Ireland*, Oak Tree Press, Dublin 1995.
14. SDLP, *Agreeing New Political Structures*, SDLP, Belfast 1992.
15. Bew, P., and Meehan, E., 'Regions and Borders: controversies in Northern Ireland about the European Union', *Journal of European Public Policy*, Vol. 1, No. 1, 1994.
16. Kearney, R., and Wilson, R., 'Northern Ireland: A European Region', in Pollock, A. (ed.), *The Opsahl Commission: A Citizen's Inquiry*, The Lilliput Press, Belfast 1991.
17. Gudgin, G., 'The Economics of the Union', in Wilson-Foster, J. (ed.), *The Idea of the Union*, Belcouver Press, Belfast 1995.
18. Kennedy, P., 'The European Union and the Northern Ireland Question', in Roche, P.J., and Barton, B. (eds), *The Northern Ireland Question: Perspective and Policies*, Avebury, Aldershot 1994.
19. Rowthorn, R.E., Foreword, in Munck, R., *The Irish Economy*, Pluto Press, London 1993.
20. Hass, E.B., *The Uniting of Europe, political, social and economic forces, 1950–1957*, Stanford University Press, Stanford 1968.
21. Hoffman, S., 'Obstinate or Obsolete: The Fate of the Nation-State and the case of Western Europe', in Nye, J.S. (ed.), *International Regionalism*, Ballinger Press, Boston 1968.
22. Pollock, M., 'Creeping Competence: The Expanding agenda of the European Community', *Journal of Public Policy*, Vol. 14, No. 2, 1994.
23. Millward, A., *The European Rescue of the Nation State*, Routledge, London 1986.

PART III

PROSPECTS FOR PEACE

8

A FRAMEWORK FOR PEACE?

Following the failure of the 1992 talks, both the British and Irish governments contemplated a new approach. The key concept here was 'inclusiveness'. In short, it was decided to make an effort to bring in the political extremes of Republican and Loyalist paramilitaries. The Irish belief in this principle, however, was always more rigid and wholehearted than that of the British; also, the British were only willing to pay a decidedly limited price to bring about this objective. The first indication of the British side's approach came with Sir Patrick Mayhew's intellectuall complex 'Identity and Culture' speech at Coleraine in December 1992; supplied in advance to Sinn Fein – as briefings on the 1992 talks had been – the speech stressed yet again British neutrality. But as this theme was in itself no novelty, a decision was made to add a dose of green rhetoric. Thus the speech was replete with flattering references to a rather ill-chosen gallery of violent Republicans, such as Ernie O'Malley, and less than conciliatory Nationalist heroes such as Joe Devlin, all safely dead. (Embarrassingly, the recently released British intelligence reports of 1921 (PRO CO 904/156/58) describe O'Malley thus: 'His salary as IRA staff captain was 6.10s a week, augmented by any perquisites that he could obtain from the pockets of murdered cadets.' Joe Devlin was hardly a suitable role model for democratic Nationalists either; it is true that in 1916 he belatedly embraced the notion that northern Unionists could not be coerced into a united Ireland, but for most of his time as a northern Nationalist leader from 1900 onwards he was a bitter, and even violent, opponent of those Nationalists who sought to understand the Unionists. Thus there was an attempt to disguise the basic lack of any concrete concessions to the Nationalists in a camouflage of meaningless – and insensitive to Unionist feeling – rhetoric.

It was said that Sir Patrick Mayhew came to regret some of the rhetorical flourishes if not the substance of the speech. 'Identity and Culture' certainly surprised local Unionists – if only because some formal account of the recent talks process had been expected. Earlier in the immediate aftermath of the failure of the 1992 talks, NIO sources had praised Unionist flexibility – one source even implied that grass-roots Nationalists, when they realised how much had been on offer, might exert pressure on the SDLP to be more responsive. But the Coleraine speech contained no such themes; rather it was dominated by the attempt to encourage Republican 'revisionism': once again, a British government assured Republicans that, in the event of peace, attention would be paid to their concerns. For most Unionists this was a pointless exercise; hence the widespread dismay and irritation in the aftermath of Sir Patrick's effort.

Coleraine did not signal an irreversible change in British policy. In 1993, it is true, secret contacts with the Provisionals were maintained by the British government who informed the IRA leadership on 23 March that 'Mayhew had tried marginalisation, defeating the IRA etc, that's gone ... Mayhew is now determined. He wants Sinn Fein to play a part, not because he likes Sinn Fein, but because it can not work without them'.[1] But these same secret contacts also revealed a British determination *not* to act as a persuader for Irish unity: the cardinal demand of the Republican movement. The longest of the secret communications (May 21) makes it clear – surprisingly clear in the context – that the British government could not do otherwise than act in accordance with the principle of consent; they ruled out any attempt to 'educate' the Northern majority that their best future lay outside the United Kingdom.[2] Thus the Coleraine speech had heralded no real consensus to Nationalists.

The summer saw an intergovernmental row, following an interview given by Dick Spring to the *Guardian* which explicitly denied the need for 'the agreement of the parties' in Northern Ireland to any settlement. The British, inevitably, were fully aware that their failure to move on this key point severely limited the likelihood of any serious reciprocal movement by the IRA leadership. They can hardly have been ignorant of the crucial point of the Hume/Adams document (which, though not then published, played such a public role in the summer of 1993 as Hume and Adams renewed their public dialogue): this lay in the proposition that the British government would use all its influence and energy to win the consent of a majority in Northern Ireland for Irish unity.[3] Consequently the British Government kept its options open. Thus, at a British-Irish Association meeting in Cambridge in September 1993, Sir Patrick Mayhew insisted on the viability of the traditional approach: the building up of consensus within the constitutional parties. 'I can report to you now my belief that the objectives of the talks process remain valid, and that their achievement remains a possibility; I can report in addition that there is rational, and not self-deluding ground, for hope that that possibility will be fulfilled in an agreed settlement.'[4]

Mayhew's Cambridge speech did not find favour with the Irish government. Increasingly, the Department of Foreign Affairs felt that intergovernmental policy had been based on the illusion that a coalition of moderates could achieve a settlement, whereas the new line insisted that it was necessary, first of all, to bring in the 'extreme' men and women of the IRA. The Irish government – well aware of the impossibility of winning British acceptance for the Hume/Adams formula – was heavily committed to the 'Peace First, Talks Later' approach. To the Irish, who were unaware at this point of the British government's secret contacts with the Provisionals, Mayhew seemed merely to be repeating a jaded and almost meaningless formula. Two months later a document leaked to Emily O'Reilly of the *Irish Press* revealed the thinking of one Department of Irish Foreign Affairs official at Iveagh House. The document apparently accepted the 'persuader' concept of the Hume/Adams proposal: the British were 'to acknowledge the full legitimacy and value of the goal of Irish unity by agreement'.[5] But this was also meant as a lure to the Republican leadership; an image of the shape of a final settlement if they called a ceasefire. There would be, for example, joint north–south bodies with executive powers. British officials were irritated by the leak, which predictably infuriated Unionists; some British officials even dismissed the leak as 'fantasy'; but, although the key 'persuader' concept was never accepted by the British, it can not be denied that the document leaked to the *Irish Press* bears a family resemblance to the language of the framework document, eventually published in February 1995.

In the aftermath of the Cambridge speech, the Irish government gradually persuaded a rather more reluctant British government of the viability of its new approach. It was a complex period when public signals did not always coincide with private initiatives. Both governments moved away from Hume/Adams in public; but the Irish government was, in private, more sympathetic to Hume's efforts. After the Brussels meeting at the end of October 1993, the two governments issued the 'Reynolds/Major' principles, or Six Points:

1 the situation in Northern Ireland should never be changed by violence or the threat of violence;

2 any political settlement must depend on consent freely given in the absence of force or intimidation;

3 there can be no talks between the two governments and those who use, threaten, or support political violence;

4 there can be no secret agreements or understandings between government and organisations supporting violence 'as a price for its cessation';

5 those claiming a serious interest in advancing peace in Ireland should renounce for good the use of or support for violence;

6 if and when a renunciation of violence has been made and sufficiently demonstrated, 'new doors could open' and both governments would wish to respond 'imaginatively' to the new situation which would then arise.

Privately, though, Reynolds told a different story to a senior aide, Sean Duignan:

> He [Albert] tells me Hume/Adams was alive and kicking after Brussels, that Major actually accepted this, insisting that he just could not publicly wear it. Albert says Major and he reasoned it out together: 'Hume/Adams was being declared dead, in order to keep it alive, in the same way as Adams carried the bomber's coffin, because otherwise he couldn't deliver the IRA'. He says Major agreed with this reasoning, Albert added: 'So it had to be done – but I hated that Brussels joint statement'.[6]

The Albert Reynolds version of events here may well simply reflect Major's willingness to accept any form of rhetoric in order to secure the public statement he was seeking; a public statement designed to fireproof him – to a degree at least – against the revelation of his government's secret contact with the Provisionals, a revelation which duly came about within weeks, but which had been predicted by senior Unionists since July of 1994. It also, of course, reflects Reynolds' determination to placate Hume; through 1993 Hume had shown a capacity to 'mobilise' grassroots opinion in Fianna Fáil and thus make it difficult for the Irish government to downplay his concerns. Even the much more sceptical British government found it difficult to disregard Hume's claim that an opportunity for peace was being spurned by inter-governmental inflexibility. John Major was tempted by the prospect of a great political prize: taking the 'gun out of Irish politics'. The result was the decision by the two governments to produce the Downing Street Declaration of December 1993.

The Declaration's key novelty was a decision by the British government to support the concept of an 'agreed Ireland' – concretely, a network of cross-border institutions – but an agreed Ireland could not, by definition, be a united Ireland except by the freely given consent of a majority in the north. Neither in public nor private does the British government ever seem to have considered embracing the most explosive tenet (the persuader for Irish unity concept) of Hume/Adams; in effect, the British and Irish governments were thus negotiating around a highly diluted version of the Hume/Adams text. The question remained: would the final product be enough to bring about a Republican cessation of violence?

During all of this, Sir James Molyneaux, the leader of the Ulster Unionists, had not been a passive spectator. His position was enhanced – though by no means decisively so – by the Major government's small parliamentary majority; he and other leading Unionists contributed ideas to the drafters of the Declaration. There were intensive discussions with the British government. From late 1993 onwards, Molyneaux was well aware of the possibility of an IRA ceasefire. On 16 October he told his party conference: 'When fellow travellers end their exploitation, intimidation and racketeering and all arms and explosive are surrendered there will be a lengthy period of quarantine before access to democratic processes can even be considered'.[7] This was in tune with Sir Patrick Mayhew's declaration on 10 October, in an RTE interview, that the IRA would have to make its guns and explosives available in order to show that its violence was over.[8] Molyneaux later argued that this delay that his 'quarantine period' – was designed in part as a protection for the Republican leadership: a rapid move towards the conference table would inevitably have led to disappointment and demoralisation.

In his discussions with John Major at this point Sir James was worried by the Irish government's proposal for a Forum in Dublin. When John Major suggested that it was a matter purely internal to the sovereign Irish jurisdiction, Molyneaux agreed but feared that such a Forum would inevitably produce a report supporting the principle of consent, which would then isolate Sinn Fein.[9]

The key concept of the Downing Street Declaration lay in paragraph 4:

> The Prime Minister, on behalf of the British government, reaffirms that they will uphold the democratic wish of a greater number of the people of Northern Ireland on the issue of whether they prefer to support the Union or a sovereign united Ireland. On this basis, he reiterates, on behalf of the British government, that they have no selfish strategic or economic interest in Northern Ireland. Their primary interest is to see peace, stability and reconciliation established by agreement among all the people who inhabit the island, and they will work together with the Irish government to achieve such an agreement which will embrace the totality of relationships. The role of the British government will be to encourage, facilitate and enable the achievement of such agreement over a period through a process of dialogue and co-operation based on full respect for the rights and identities of both traditions in Ireland. They accept that such agreement may, as of right, take the form of agreed structures for the island as a whole, including a united Ireland achieved by peaceful means on the following basis. The British government agreed that it is for the people of the island of Ireland alone, by agreement between the two parts respectively, to exercise their right of self-determination on the basis of consent, freely and concurrently given, North and South, to bring about a united Ireland, if that is their wish. They reaffirm as a binding obligation that they will, for their part, introduce the necessary legislation to give effect to this, or equally to any measure of agreement on future relationships in Ireland which the people living in Ireland may themselves freely so determine without external impediment. They believe that the people of Britain would wish, in friendship to all sides, to enable the people of Ireland to reach agreement on how they may live together in harmony and in partnership, with respect for their diverse traditions, and with full recognition of the special links and the unique relationship which exist between the peoples of Britain and Ireland.

The immediate reaction to the Declaration was rather revealing; some Nationalists took a rather rosy view of it. Sir Patrick Mayhew had certainly been forced to abandon the language of the speech he made to the Oxford Union as a young man – in which he spoke of 'two nations' in Ireland. Molyneaux, however, remained calm and insisted that it did not constitute a sell-out; the Democratic Unionist Party and the eloquent independent Unionist, Robert McCartney, disagreed. In the immediate aftermath of the Declaration, Albert Reynolds, in a major speech to the Irish Association, argued that it signalled an end to Britain's 'imperialist interest' in Ireland; but within eighteen months his cabinet colleagues and advisers, including Martin Mansergh, the probable author of the Irish Association speech, were to argue that this prospectus was too optimistic.[11] Such doubts were not to be found among constitutional Nationalist politicians in the early months of 1994; instead they urged the Republican movement to accept the Downing Street Declaration – despite the fact that the concept of Irish self-determination had been ripped from its traditional irridentist context and given a new meaning. The most spectacular indication of this was the speech given at Barberstown Castle by Albert Reynolds to the Law Society of University College, Dublin, on 20 January 1994. Directing his remarks to Republican rejectionists, the Taoiseach said:

> It has been suggested in some quarters that the Joint Declaration provides insufficient recognition of the Irish people's right to self-determination. It is also held that the so-called Unionist guarantee is in contradiction to it. It is essential to examine these assertions. It would be tragic if the peace process were to be blocked because of basic misunderstandings about how self-determination operates in international law and international politics, and because something unattainable was being sought that was not consistent with international law. Those who quote Article 1 of the United Nations Charter in support of Irish self-determination often tend to forget Article 2, which states that 'all members should settle their international disputes by peaceful means', a principle to which Ireland was already committed by Article 29 of its constitution. Unlike the colonies in Africa and elsewhere at the time of their independence, Irish self-determination involves an already sovereign Irish state, which is a member of the UN and directly bound by its charter.

Most of the public signals in the first months of 1994 suggested an IRA rejection of the Downing Street Declaration; in particular, the requirement (in para 10 of that document) of a 'permanent' renunciation of violence before Republicans could enter talks with the United Kingdom government or other parties presented a huge difficulty. A long and tedious debate about British 'clarification' – at first denied and then eventually conceded – circled again around the British government's refusal to act as a 'persuader'. But Reynolds had one card which he played with great skill; the notion that an agreement based on the framework documents might dock without the Republicans if they did not offer a cessation; as Reynolds told a senior aide on 12 August 1994:

> I've told them if they don't do this right, they can shag off; I don't want to hear anything about a six-month or six-year ceasefire; no temporary indefinite or conditional stuff; no defending or retaliating against anyone; just that it's over ... period ... full stop. Otherwise I'll walk away. I'll go off down that three strand/talks framework document road with John Major, and they can detour away for another 25 years of killing and being killed – for what? Because, at the end of that 25 years, they'll be back where they are right now, with damn all to show for it except thousands more dead, and all for nothing. So they do it now, in the name of God, and be done with it, or good-bye.[12]

The two governments claimed to have been asked to draw up an 'imaginary line of compromise' by the constitutional parties after the failure of the 1992 talks. In fact, apart from the SDLP, these parties can not have really expected the framework document to be used as bait to bring about an IRA ceasefire; but this is precisely what happened in the summer of 1994. The framework document, laden with cross-border institutions, was given a rhetorical all-Ireland 'ethos' designed to be seductive to Republicans. But the British sought in return a formal acceptance of the legitimacy of Northern Ireland; this became known as the Corfu test, following a key Reynolds/Major meeting during a European Union Conference on 24 June, 1994.[13]

In the event, the British failed decisively to achieve their full objectives in this respect, but the very fact that they had sought it has been rather written out of the nationalist accounts. A deliberate refusal to dwell on well-signalled difficulties and details became a feature of the Nationalist perception of the peace process. Perhaps such a refusal was a *sine qua non* for the IRA's declaration of a complete cessation of military operations on 31 August 1994, but it also helps to explain why the ceasefire collapsed. The new highly ideological Republican argument that an alliance of Irish America, the Irish government and northern Nationalism could sweep all before it, was bound to receive a severe test at some stage, but there was no denying that the illusions of the 'peace process' set the context for this. Certainly the ceasefire encountered a good deal of Unionist cynicism but the deputy leader of the Ulster Unionists, John Taylor, insisted: 'I have always taken the approach from the beginning of the IRA cessation to try and treat it as real and to build upon it'.[14]

Unionists had little choice but to work within the 'peace process', as Molyneaux had recognised in late 1993. His successor, as leader, David Trimble, who took over in September 1995, was no different in this respect. The British government went further: it explicitly attempted to sustain Adams with the publication of the green-tinted framework document of February 1995. The British accepted a formula on the territorial claim which did not meet the Corfu test. There was much in the text designed to annoy Unionists and thus entice Republicans; consider, for example, the proposal for cross-border bodies with executive powers. The framework text listed:

> sections including a natural or physical all Ireland framework;
> EC programmes and initiatives;
> marketing and promotion and activity abroad;
> culture and heritage.

The *Sunday Telegraph* report on the eve of the framework document's publication, added a gloss: 'this may include the management of rivers and loughs, heritage protection measures and mapping'.[15]

The 'culture and heritage' passage is a crucial index of the change in the mentality of the senior ranks of Northern Irish officialdom over the two decades. In 1974 a senior official of the Northern Irish Civil Service had concluded: 'For a government to hand over its functions in respect to arts and culture to some international authority would be to abdicate its basic responsibility'.[16] At the same time, Norman Dugdale, a senior official subsequently much admired by Chris Patten, offered a general analysis of 'cross-borderism' which was entirely in a minimalist spirit. Twenty years later, 'culture' is treated as an easily conceded sacrificial item: the absence of any sign of even token resistance reveals above all the lesson learnt by all aspirant officials after the Anglo-Irish Agreement of 1985: any sign of punctilious Unionist principle would be career death. 'Cross-borderism', once treated with pragmatic disdain, was now enthusiastically embraced. Unionists too nervously pointed out that the list of proposals for executive power were self-evidently incomplete and that there were notorious public sensitivities in areas such as health, social welfare and public administration. Remarkably, the government did little in private to discuss these matters with the Unionist leadership: this failure of communication was one of the most significant, though least commented upon, flaws in the peace process, for it inhibited the necessary development of cross-community dialogue on a realistic basis.

During the eighteenth month ceasefire, there was one area where the British government *did* move with surprising slowness: prisons policy. Despite the sensitivity of the issue, many expected the British government to allow earlier release for some terrorist prisoners. Nationalists, in particular, contrasted this with the rapid release of Private Lee Clegg who had shot a joyrider. In fact, the Northern Ireland Office put such a package to the cabinet in the summer of 1995 but it was rejected.[17] But given the concessions signalled in the framework document it has to be acknowledged that the reasons for the breakdown of the ceasefire are more deeply rooted than the prisons issue. By far the most important factor was the changing balance of forces within the Republican leadership in a more hardline direction; this expressed itself clearly in the December 1995 shooting of several drugs dealers in the aftermath of President Clinton's visit of November when he denounced punishment shootings. Already, the planning for the Canary Wharf bomb had begun. But why did Adams lose control in this way?

The key to the shift of power within the Republican leadership lies in the arms issue. Despite his many pronouncements to the opposite effect in the summer of 1995, Adams had known all along about the 'arms precondition' and had discussed it in public with his colleagues.[18] Adams had clearly gambled on the British government's fairly rapid abandonment of this precondition; the failure of this gamble inevitably reduced the credibility of any attempt to argue for a renewed ceasefire. When the Mitchell commission offered its compromise – decommissioning of arms *during* talks – it came too late, and in any event, would have been unacceptable to the IRA. Then again, Adams had entered the 'peace process' in the hope of being offered joint authority, or at a minimum, the notion of the British government as a persuader for Irish unity.[19] In the case of joint authority, he was firmly rebuffed, not only by Sir Patrick Mayhew but also Albert Reynolds and Dick Spring. In the case of the 'persuader' idea, the Department of Foreign Affairs had run with it – albeit without much hope – and the British government had rejected it.

There remained key differences between the IRA and the British. The British laid great emphasis on the need to obtain the 'agreement of the parties' within Northern Ireland, while at certain points, the Department of Foreign Affairs seemed keen to sidestep this principle. The DFA was also anxious that economic pressure be applied to induce more 'flexibility' in the Unionist position; however, these diplomats enjoyed no success in convincing the British of this proposition. The combined effort of all these developments – most of them pre-dating the fall of the Reynolds' government and his replacement by the more instinctively anti-Republican, John Bruton – was to reduce the credibility of the Adams strategy within mainstream northern Republicanism and to make a return to armed struggle all the more likely. As Mitchell McLaughlin – often seen as a Sinn Fein dove – had warned everyone on the day after the ceasefire: if Britain did not withdraw political support from Unionism then there would be a return to violence.

The return to violence excluded Sinn Fein again from the 'talks process', which was renewed again on 10 June 1995. The omens for this round of multi-party talks were not good. The Forum election of May 1995 revealed a province polarised as never before. In the aftermath of the Anglo-Irish Agreement, Austin Currie, then in the SDLP and now in the Irish government, described inter-governmental strategy in a concise phrase as the isolation of the 'two Ps': Paisleyism and the Provisional IRA. The May election demonstrated how completely that strategy had failed: one in four of the good people of Northern Ireland voted for parties with a paramilitary wing – Sinn Fein in particular, did well but so did, relatively speaking, the Paisleyite DUP.

Both in Dublin and the SDLP there were key people so wedded to the belief enunciated by the Tanaiste's most important aide, Fergus Finlay – that talks without Sinn Fein are not worth a 'penny candle' – that it was difficult to believe that they could approach these negotiations in a positive spirit. Decorum prevented Fergus Finlay's attendance at the talks but his now legendary remark haunted the proceedings.

On the other hand, the solid performance of the DUP reduced the room for manoeuvre of the Ulster Unionist leadership. Few believe at this point that the 'agreement of the parties', still less a province-wide referendum to sanctify it, is a likely outcome. Even the officials at the NIO, professional optimists in these matters, are less upbeat than they were at the time of the Brooke/Mayhew talks of 1991/2.

The talks do, however, had one advantage denied to the 1991/92 talks; despite all the frequently harsh rhetoric of the past year there was a better relationship this time between some of the Republic's ministers and some of the key Unionist leaders. Unionists should not forget that the most profound interest of the Irish state, and not alone the then Prime Minister, lies in stability in the north;[20] despite the increasingly uncomprehending and dismissive tone of much opinion in the Republic on the subject of Unionism, there is no deep-rooted urge or capacity to absorb the north.

The problem in the Unionist community is a simple one. Since the Anglo-Irish Agreement of 1985 the Unionist body politic has been consumed by a fear of British betrayal – a fear which has been both understandable and exaggerated. It is a fear which has made rational political calculation very difficult. Many Unionists can not bring themselves to consider – even as an abstract possibility – that the 'cross-borderism' of the framework document is a symbolic fig leaf which may allow northern Nationalism to accept the principle of consent within Northern Ireland. To take an example, from recent debate, the proposed changes to the Government of Ireland Act of 1920 – which were intended as part of the trade off for the dropping of the Irish Republic's territorial claim expressed in Articles 2 and 3 of the Irish Constitution – are of little significance because Northern Ireland's place within the United Kingdom is now governed by the 1973 Act. Unionists face enough genuine difficulties in these talks as it is; it is not necessary to invent them. The real problem here was not the proposed changes to the 1920 Act but the unsatisfactory state of the current Dublin offer which fell short of a definitive promise to lift the territorial claim: the key words 'the territory of Ireland is the island of Ireland' are likely to remain in the Irish constitution. The British government here decided to forego one of its principle negotiating objectives in order to prevent a bomb going off – ironically the bomb went off at Canary Wharf anyway.

The only possible deal on offer at these talks was in the words of one of the most senior Irish officials, 'Sunningdale Mark 2'. From a Nationalist point of view, Sunningdale Mark 2 is a better deal than Mark 1. This time any Council of Ireland arrangement will start with an already existing series of functions and not a blank sheet as in 1974. In 1974, Unionists in effect walked away from the Sunningdale deal; this time any attempt to do so is made much harder. There will be a continued role for some sort of Anglo-Irish Agreement – however democratised and symbolically restructured – and this too is a bonus for Nationalists. But this model is not joint authority nor does it lead to it: Albert Reynolds, Dick Spring and Sir Patrick Mayhew all ruled it out earlier in the process, long before John Bruton, the *bête noir* of northern Republicans, became Taoiseach. Nor is it the SDLP variant of joint authority proposed to the 1992 talks. The British government still refuses to be a persuader for Irish unity – the core of the Hume/Adams document – again something accepted by Albert Reynolds at the time of the Downing Street declaration.

Some of the issues are complex but, in essence, all the complexity reduces to one key point: Northern nationalists will not accept an internal settlement. But can Unionists live with a significant cross-border institutional structure designed to win acceptance through Ireland, north and south, for Northern Ireland's continued membership of the United Kingdom as long as the majority so wills it?

Unionists loathe the framework document jargon, notably the 'agreed dynamic' of the cross-border structure. There are great and legitimate sensitivities in areas such as health and public administration; social welfare may prove less problematical. Policy in areas such as industrial development is more likely to be determined by Britain's developing relationship with the EU than by Anglo-Irish negotiation. But Unionists should take comfort from the low-key, though self-evidently incomplete, nature of the functions (listed in paragraph 33 of the framework text) envisaged for the north–south body. Who is going to go to the barricades over a committee to deal with mutual recognition of teacher training qualifications, north and south? It is important not to be frightened by phrases – negotiation is bound to produce a new vocabulary anyway – and to think instead of substance and the effect on ordinary every day life. The framework reflects the shared, at times rather glib, understanding of officialdom, but the requirement for the agreement of the parties sits – however uneasily – at the heart.

Ultimately though, the odds are stacked against a settlement. A significant part of Nationalist Northern Ireland now finds it hard in principle to accept any compromise Unionists might be able to live with. But for many of the older politicians around the table, the next round of talks is probably the last chance. They can either respond with the usual sectarian imperatives, or win the enduring place in the history books reserved for those who genuinely try to end the cycle of recrimination.

NOTES

1. *Setting the Record Straight*, p28.
2. *Ibid.* The clarity is surprising because the tradition in secret contacts between the UK government and the IRA is one of 'mutual obfuscation' to use the phrase of one distinguished British participant.
3. Mallie, E., and McKittrick, D., *The Fight for Peace: The Secret Story Behind the Irish Peace Process*, London 1995, p376.
4. *Belfast Telegraph*, 14 September 1993, contains a report of this speech.
5. *Irish Press*, 19 November 1993.
6. Duignan, S., *One More Spin on the Merry Go Round*, Dublin 1995.
7. *Belfast Newsletter*, 18 October 1994.
8. *Belfast Telegraph*, 11 October 1995.
9. Sir James Molyneaux's reflections were offered to a meeting of the Irish Association in Belfast, June 1994.
10. See Bew, P., and Gillespie, G., *The Northern Ireland Peace Process*, London 1996, for this speech.
11. Martin Mansergh, the most important adviser to Albert Reynolds, later said: 'The British government wish to promote enough agreement to prevent the two communities from fighting each other and harming British interests ... They had made it clear that they will not be persuaders for a united Ireland nor do they wish to see it come about. He spoke of Britain still having a "divide and rule" mentality'. Mansergh is the likely author of the Irish Association speech, *Irish Times*, 3 July 1995.
12. Duignan, *op cit*, p147. Entry for 12 August 1994.
13. Three weeks later Sir Patrick Mayhew insisted that the Irish government had to offer an unambiguous formula on the territorial claim. Corfu is not analysed in any of the nationalist accounts – Mallie and McKitterick's *The Fight for Peace*; Duignan's *One More Spin*; or Coogan's book *The Troubles*.
14. *Sunday Business Post*, 3 March 1996.
15. *Sunday Telegraph*, 19 February 1995.
16. Bew and Patterson, *The British State and the Ulster Crisis*, London 1985.
17. Mallie and McKitterick, *op cit*, p358.
18. Bew and Gillespie, *The Northern Ireland Peace Process 1993–1996*, London 1996, p41.
19. *Ibid*, p12.
20. Even the Department of Foreign Affairs operates within this framework, despite a penchant for self-defeating tactical opportunism. The best proof of its underlying conviction may be seen in the production of the 'Spring principles' in the autumn of 1993, when the Unionist body politic was being destabilised by wild talk of a simplistic mode of Irish self-determination as promoted in the Hume/Adams initiative.

APPENDIX

Since this book was written, there have been elections both in Britain and the Republic of Ireland. The following (edited) speeches, by Tony Blair in May 1997, and by Bertie Ahern in February 1995, give a clear picture of the perspectives of the two prime ministers who now take responsibility for the affairs of Ireland North and South.

TONY BLAIR, 16 MAY 1997

It is no accident that this is my first official visit outside London. I said before the election that Northern Ireland was every bit as important for me as for my predecessor. I will honour that pledge in full.

We know the situation here is fragile and fraught. There may be only one chance given to a new government to offer a way forward. Our very newness gives possibilities. But governments are not new forever. There are times when to calculate the risks too greatly is to do nothing; there are times too when a political leader must follow his instinct about what is right and fair.

Our destination is clear: to see in place a fair political settlement in Northern Ireland – one that lasts, because it is based on the will and the consent of the people here.

It is a long march; and every footstep has its pitfalls. But when there is not movement, hope falters and we are left surrounded by the ancient grievances returning to destroy us.

I am convinced that the time is right finally to put the past behind us and meet the deep thirst of the people of Northern Ireland for peace, normality and prosperity.

My message is simple. I am committed to Northern Ireland. I am committed to the principle of consent. My agenda is not a united Ireland – and I wonder just how many see it as a realistic possibility in the foreseeable future. Northern Ireland will remain part of the United Kingdom as long as a majority here wish.

What I want to see is a settlement which can command the support of nationalists and unionists. That is what the people of Northern Ireland rightly demand of me and of their political leaders.

We should not forget there *has* been progress. Fair employment legislation and equality of opportunity have improved the lives of ordinary people. More change must come. But Northern Ireland in 1997 is not the same place as it was in 1969.

The benefits of economic growth and investment have also begun to make themselves felt. During the last ten years, unemployment in Northern Ireland has fallen significantly. Though Northern Ireland still lags behind the rest of the UK in many ways, again the situation is better than for years.

The *quality* of life has also improved immeasurably since the 1970s, particularly in the period after the IRA ceasefire of August 1994. The opening of the Waterfront Hall earlier this year symbolised a new determination to get on with living life as it should be.

The prospects for Northern Ireland are excellent if we can get the politics right. If. I concede it is a big if.

But confidence about the future is heavily masked by continuing divisions, and by feelings of great insecurity in both communities. People on each side fear for their identity. They still react instinctively, and retreat into the comforting certainties of tradition. We saw this in full measure after the dreadful and depressing events of Drumcree last year.

Many have been tempted to conclude that the gulfs cannot be bridged, that one side or the other does not really want a settlement, or at least is not ready to make the compromises necessary to achieve one.

It is a counsel of despair and I am not prepared to accept it. I believe the forces pushing us all towards a settlement are stronger than those that stand in our way. I aim to harness those forces more effectively than in the past. And I want to assure both communities that they have nothing to fear from a settlement and everything to gain.

The Union

Northern Ireland is part of the United Kingdom, alongside England, Scotland and Wales.

The Union binds the four parts of the United Kingdom together. I believe in the United Kingdom. I value the Union.

I want to see a Union which reflects and accommodates diversity. I am against a rigid, centralised approach. That is the surest way to weaken the Union. The proposals this government are making for Scotland and Wales, and for the English regions, are designed to bring the Government closer to the people. That will renew and strengthen the Union.

I support this approach for Northern Ireland too, with some form of devolution and cross-border arrangements which acknowledge the importance of relationships in the island of Ireland. This is what the negotiations are about.

We must of course devise arrangements which match the particular circumstances of Northern Ireland. Domination by one tradition or another is unacceptable.

But let me make one things absolutely clear. Northern Ireland is part of the United Kingdom because that is the wish of a majority of the people who live here. It will remain part of the United Kingdom for as long as that remains the case. This principle of consent is and will be at the heart of my Government's policies on Northern Ireland. It is the key principle.

It means that there can be no possibility of a change in the status of Northern Ireland as a part of the United Kingdom without the clear and formal consent of a majority of the people of Northern Ireland. Any settlement must be negotiated not imposed; it must be endorsed by the people of Northern Ireland in a referendum; and it must be endorsed by the British Parliament.

Of course, those who wish to see a united Ireland without coercion can argue for it, not least in the talks. If they succeeded, we would certainly respect that. But none of us in this hall today, even the youngest, is likely to see Northern Ireland as anything but a part of the United Kingdom. That is the reality, because the consent principle is now almost universally accepted.

All the constitutional parties, including the SDLP, are committed to it, which means a majority of the nationalist community in Northern Ireland is committed to it. The parties in the Irish Republic are committed to it. The one glaring exception is Sinn Fein and the republican movement. They too, I hope, will soon come to accept that vital principle.

So fears of betrayal are simply misplaced. Unionists have nothing to fear from a new Labour government. A political settlement is not a slippery slope to a united Ireland. The government will not be persuaders for unity. The wagons do not need to be drawn up in a circle. Instead we offer reassurance and new hope that a settlement satisfactory to all can be reached.

A Political Settlement

This government is fully committed to the approach set out in the Downing Street Declaration. I believe the Joint Framework Document sets out a reasonable basis for future negotiation. We must create, through open discussion, new institutions which fairly represent the interests and aspirations of both communities.

The challenge, simply put, is to arrive at an agreement with which all the people of Northern Ireland can feel comfortable, and to which they can all give lasting allegiance; one which reflects and celebrates diversity and the traditions and cultures of both communities; which can provide the opportunity for local politicians of both sides to take local decisions as they should.

This is achievable. I know it is. And it can be combined with sensible arrangements for cooperation with the Republic of Ireland, practical and institutional, which will be significant not only on the ground, but also politically for the nationalist community.

If such arrangements were really threatening to Unionists, we would not negotiate them. Any fears would of course be much reduced if the Irish Constitution were changed to reflect their Government's strong support for the consent principle. That must be part of a settlement, and would be a helpful confidence-building step in advance of it.

Nor should nationalists fear for their future. Agreement to any settlement must be clear on both sides. There can be no question of their views being ridden over rough-shod. Their involvement must be complete and full-hearted.

The British and Irish Governments have worked together in the past to make progress. This is a key relationship. I have every confidence we can work together closely in the future, whatever the result of the Irish elections.

Democracy and Violence

These political issues should be addressed in the talks which are due to resume in just over two weeks. Many will share my deep frustration that they have not already been addressed. Discussion has not progressed beyond questions of procedure and participation. The parties have been unable to agree on a way of dealing with decommissioning. We continue to support the parallel approach proposed by George Mitchell. But why has decommissioning been so difficult to tackle successfully?

The truth is there is no confidence on either side about the motives and intentions of the other. The procedural problems are a product of this deep distrust. Each party often seems utterly convinced of the duplicity of all the others.

What gives these suspicions their uniquely corrosive character, on both sides, is the current prominence of violence in the equation.

Violence has no place in a democratic society, whatever the motivation of those practising it. Terrorism, republican or so-called loyalist, is contemptible and unacceptable.

The people here have stood up to terrorist violence for 25 years. They have not been destroyed by it. But the legacy of bitterness has made normal political give and take difficult, at times virtually impossible.

What today is the aim of IRA violence?

- Is it a united Ireland? Violence will not bring a united Ireland closer, because now all the parties in Northern Ireland, save Sinn Fein, and the parties in the Republic of Ireland agree consent is the basic principle.
- Is it to defend the nationalist community? It is hard to see, to put it no higher, how killing people and damaging the Province's economy and local services helps the nationalist community from any point of view.
- Is it to force a way into talks? This is manifestly absurd, since the only obstacle to Sinn Fein joining the talks is the absence of a credible and lasting halt to the violence.
- Do they hope a loyalist backlash or a security crackdown would justify their violence and lead to communal trouble where republican aims might have more chance of flourishing? Such an approach would be the height of cynicism. I hope the Loyalists will not fall for it. The Government certainly won't.

Any shred of justification terrorists might have claimed for violence has long since disappeared.

Not only does this violence achieve nothing. There is nothing it *can* achieve, save death, destruction and the corruption of more young lives. Progress can only be made through genuine negotiation and agreement. Violence makes both more difficult and more distant.

Since last June we have had multi-party talks in being – talks which Sinn Fein above all others pressed for, where all parties are treated equally, with a comprehensive agenda, and no predetermined outcome. But the IRA broke their ceasefire just at the point when the conditions for getting everyone round a table were coming together. That violence automatically excluded Sinn Fein from the talks.

They could still have joined on 10 June by declaring a ceasefire. They did not do so. They have continued to miss every opportunity since then.

I want the talks process to include Sinn Fein. The opportunity is still there to be taken, if there is an unequivocal IRA ceasefire. Words and deeds must match, and there must be no doubt of commitment to peaceful methods and the democratic process.

I want the talks to take place in a climate of peace. If there is an opportunity to bring this about, I am ready to seize it. This Government will respond quickly to genuine moves to achieve peace.

But we will be correspondingly tough on those who will not make this move. The IRA and Sinn Fein face a choice between negotiations and violence. Violence is the failed path of the past. I urge them to choose negotiations, once and for all.

If they do not, the talks cannot wait for them but must and will move on. And meanwhile the police and armed forces will continue to bring their full weight to bear on the men of violence.

I am ready to make one further effort to proceed with the inclusive talks process. My message to Sinn Fein is clear. The settlement train is leaving. I want you on that train. But it is leaving anyway, and I will not allow it to wait for you. You cannot hold the process to ransom any longer. So end the violence. Now.

I want to hear Sinn Fein's answer. And to make sure there is no danger of misunderstanding, I am prepared to allow officials to meet Sinn Fein, provided events on the ground, here and elsewhere, do not make that impossible. This is not about negotiating terms of a ceasefire. We simply want to explain our position and to assess whether the republican movement genuinely is ready to give up violence and commit itself to politics alone. If they are, I will not be slow in my response. If they are not, they can expect no sympathy or understanding. I will be implacable in pursuit of terrorism.

Loyalist terrorism is equally contemptible, equally unacceptable, just as futile and counter-productive. The Loyalist paramilitaries have so far maintained their ceasefire in formal terms. I welcome that signal of restraint, as far as it goes, and urge them and those with influence on them to hold fast to it. The Loyalist parties' participation in the talks has been welcome and constructive.

But let us have no illusions. Commitment to democracy means no violence or threat of violence. There can be and will be no double standards.

The last few weeks have seen an appalling rush of killings, beatings, arson and intimidation. The vast majority are horrified by these dreadful acts. But they continue in your midst. They are crimes against humanity, which must be stamped out. The police have my full support in taking the firmest possible action against those responsible. And I appeal to the people of Northern Ireland to give their full-hearted support too.

Parades

Lurking behind these terrible deeds is the shadow of this summer's marching season. This is where the clash of identity and allegiance can so easily emerge most directly and most brutally; where the conflict of rights is hardest to resolve: the right to march and the right to live free of disruption and apparent intimidation; where the rule of law is most difficult to uphold, as it must be.

Local agreements solve the vast majority of problems over marches. With minimal goodwill and flexibility, they could solve the rest too – as long as neither side insists on using a particular parade to make a broader political point. That is a dangerous game to play, as last summer showed only too clearly.

The North Report recommended changes to the way marches are handled. We will implement those recommendations quickly, although the new arrangements cannot be in place this summer. The legislation will be able to take account of any lessons from this summer. But the key remains in the hands of the local people on both sides. No one with any sense wants more Drumcrees. I call on all with any influence on the process to use it for reconciliation, not confrontation.

The Future

I have said Northern Ireland has a bright future if only we get the politics right and the gun out of the picture. You all know that to be true.

Look at the advantages you have:

- dynamic and enterprising businesses and businessmen
- a record of success on inward investment, despite the violence
- a workforce ready to take every opportunity
- a potential quality of life second to none in the United Kingdom
- huge tourist potential

This Government will be building on that potential. The raising of education and training standards, and measures to put the unemployed back to work, will be particularly relevent here. We will be introducing further measures to promote equality of opportunity in the labour market.

We are also determined to build trust and confidence in public institutions. Incorporation of the European Convention on Human Rights into United Kingdom law will help protect basic human rights. We want to increase public confidence on poilicing through measured reform based on the Hayes Report on the complaints system and last year's consultation paper on structural change.

All this will help to make Northern Ireland a more prosperous, more democratic part of Britain, where opportunities really are equal for all. Yet governments cannot deliver without the help of the people themselves.

Overcoming violence and prejudice, and learning to compromise and live together, is *your* responsibility as much as it is ours. The politicians of Northern Ireland, who show great courage in accepting positions of prominence, will have to show leadership and vision. They need and deserve your support. The business community of Northern Ireland has a vital role to play. Some are already doing so. But too many hang back and blame the politicians rather than helping them find a way forward. It is no good just hoping peace will come. Everyone in a position of authority or influence will need to use that authority and influence in the direction of reconciliation and cooperation.

SPEECH BY BERTIE AHERN TO THE IRISH ASSOCIATION, 2 FEBRUARY 1995

I am aware of the history of this Association, that it was founded by some liberal Unionists in the 1930s, who wanted to keep alive the Irish dimension, which, to put it mildly, not all their colleagues wished to acknowledge. It serves to underline an important point, that the Irish identity, while greatly valued by Northern Nationalists, is not exclusive to one community or tradition. Some thought has also to be given to the wider Irish identity or dimension, which Unionists too might also be able to acknowledge and feel part of.

I and my party have always believed that in many ways it is easier to reach out successfully across the divide, from the strength of one's own tradition.

My late father was active in the struggle for independence, and would certainly have been on the more Republican wing of Fianna Fail. But attitudes evolve. For me, Fianna Fail has always been a democratic party, that is both Nationalist and Republican. In the state, we are the principal repository and expression of the historic ideals of the Irish nation. We place a high value on national independence and sovereignty and the goal of unity, recognising that each of these have a political, economic and cultural dimension. They also have to be set today in the changed context of closer European Union. As is shown in our positive commitment to Europe, we have a healthy nationalism that has no need to be chauvinistic.

Our role cannot be a passive one, clinging to the certainties and the orthodoxies of the past. We must be active in giving our ideals modern expression, in adapting them to new circumstances and to a new depth of understanding of the complexities of the problem. We must tread where no one has gone before in order to address the major unresolved problems left over from the past.

My party has played an historic role in the development of the peace process. We were able through shared ideological roots to understand Republican thinking in the North, and also to make Northern Republicans aware that there was at least one major political force in the South that had an understanding, however imperfect, of the way that they perceived their experience.

Above all, we were prepared to become actively engaged in the search for peace, without being inhibited by the heavy political risks accompanying any form of contact, while violence was going on. After the ceasefire, we took immediate steps to bring Sinn Fein fully into the democratic life of this country, and we quickly established the Forum for Peace and Reconciliation in which they play a full and equal part. Our role in Opposition will in many ways be a continuation of our role in Government, trying to push the peace process forward by tackling the many issues, some difficult, some not, that need to be addressed, if vital momentum is to be maintained. We must never forget, particularly in the furore of the last 24 hours, the basic equation, peace equals lives saved.

The peace was built on skilful contact work right across the Northern communities. A channel was developed into virtually every strand of political opinion. In addition to the excellent relations my party always had with the SDLP, we have built up a good relationship with both Sinn Fein and the Alliance Party. Earlier this week, I was the first Fianna Fail leader to set foot in West Belfast since Eamon de Valera was arrested there in 1929. I was also the first Fianna Fail leader to step inside the headquarters in Glengall Street of the Ulster Unionist Party, and to be received by the Lord Mayor of Belfast. We were glad to have one of the leading members of the PUP David Ervine address a Fianna Fail Comhairle meeting in Dun Laoghaire last October. We must break down the barriers, and engage in political dialogue with all strands of opinion, even where immediate results cannot be expected.

From a policy point of view, we will continue the approach that we adopted in Government. We will stand over the positions and the compromises we were prepared to make in Government, even if it is more difficult to do that in Opposition. The Joint Declaration, above all, was our initiative, and we are pleased that it has now become the cornerstone of democratic politics in the North, and is owned by virtually all parties both North and South and by both Governments. We all have a common interest in the success of the peace process, and we will support the Government's efforts to consolidate it and move it forward for the duration of their term of office.

The maintenance of peace, the vindication of the democratic method of resolving deep political differences, is the overriding priority of all of us, ahead of any other political aim. Peace is the only absolute imperative, to which we must all subscribe. The last 25 years showed conclusively that political violence, in relation to solving the problems of the North, was indeed the cul de sac that the independence generation in the 1920s rightly suspected it to be.

The Joint Declaration enshrines not just the principle of consent, but also the principle of self-determination, and in that respect goes beyond the Anglo-Irish Agreement. The two principles are in many ways different sides of the same coin.

The central aim of new negotiations is to reach a new agreement on how the people of Ireland will share the island. The focus is not an internal settlement, which on its own will not work, or devolved Government on a responsibility-sharing basis though that should be part of the solution. The aim is to achieve an agreed Ireland, which will allow everyone in this island to live in peace and reconciliation, with a sense that justice has been vindicated. Equality of treatment must replace second-class citizenship. North-South institutions are firmly written into the Downing Street Declaration, and are part of the foundation of peace, as they were meant to be back in 1920.

North-South institutions with executive powers are a fundamentally different concept from joint authority. Joint authority, which Fianna Fail have never advocated or regarded as a realistic possibility, is essentially joint rule over Northern Ireland by the Irish and British Governments. North-South institutions relate not just to the North, but to North and South equally. They mean North and South working together freely in their common interest, on the basis of a democratic mandate. Even if Government institutions in the North were to break down, there is no question of resorting to joint authority, but equally it does not necessarily mean that all functioning North-South cooperation would break down. The Lough Foyle Fisheries Commission continued in existence after Stormont was abolished, and no one has seriously suggested that that is a manifestation of joint authority.

We are all aware of developments in the South over the last 25 years. In terms of the two traditions, we have been moving away from majority rule tempered by the fair individual treatment of the minority, which characterised Ireland from the 1920s to the 1960s, towards a pluralist society, which recognises many different traditions and minorities.

The North in a different way is also becoming a more pluralist society, although the degree of segregation between the two communities has been reinforced in many places by the Troubles. There too, while a majority has its constitutional rights recognised, if it wants any kind of agreement it can no longer determine alone the entire character of the laws, institutions and political life within Northern Ireland, or unilaterally lay down that there will be no formal relations or structures shared with the rest of the island, even where they do not impinge on its constitutional status, regardless of the desires of the other community. None of us are asking for Unionists to give an inch on their rights, on their birthright, on their traditions, on their right to safeguard their future in any new dispensation. What we are asking is that they accord the same rights to Nationalists, recognising that they too value their birthright, their traditions, and the promise of a future that is better than the past.

Northern Ireland will only work as a political entity, if there is a spirit of give and take, if there is genuine partnership. It cannot operate as a one-party or one-tradition hegemony. Consent is a two-way process. The Nationalist community were incorporated into Northern Ireland against their will and have been subjected in the past to both discrimination and coercion; that still lingers on, as one can see graphically in West Belfast. Unionists now have to ask themselves, do they want to win the consent of Nationalists for the political and constitutional arrangements that they wish to preserve in Northern Ireland, or do they believe deep down that even reasonable Nationalist wishes are profoundly subversive, and can or should simply be ignored, as they were for 50 years under Stormont?

Irish Nationalism has changed. Irredentism is dead. I know of almost no one who believes it is feasible or desirable to attempt to incorporate Northern Ireland into the Republic or into a united Ireland against the will of a majority there, either by force or coercion. Ireland is, in the view of the vast majority of us, one nation, which is divided, because its two traditions have by and large chosen up till now to live under two different jurisdictions. In my view, we have to leave behind us the territorial claims, if that is the correct description, of the Irish and British States, and vest the future of Ireland exclusively in the hands of its people, North and South, in keeping with the principles set out in the Joint Declaration. In keeping with our principles, it is the people of Ireland who are sovereign, not the State, be it British or Irish.

But equally the legitimacy of any new dispensation, of new agreed political arrangements for Northern Ireland and Ireland as a whole must be capable of winning the consent of the Nationalist community. That is the challenge facing us all in the talks that will follow publication of the Framework Document. Our position of principle is clear. The Framework Document is intended to provide a basis for discussion and negotiation. We must wait for its completion, before engaging in full scale debate on the issues involved.

No one should condemn the document in advance without having seen it in full. No one, who cherishes peace, should refuse to face up to the real issues. As Paul Bew writes in today's *Times*, there is no future for simplistic vetoes. A new accommodation has to be achieved, with a readiness to engage in all reasonable forms of cooperation.

If negotiations are to be successful, then all parties must be included. It is not only a question of full Sinn Fein participation. Ways must be found of allowing the small Loyalist parties to take part at the Conference table.

In our view, it would be premature to attempt to insist at this stage on the decommissioning of weapons being dealt with first, even though it is a very important issue. Confidence in peace and mutual trust requires to be further built up through negotiation, before a permanent disposal of weapons becomes a real possibility, either for Loyalists or Republicans.

Apart from political negotiations, there is progress to be made on many other fronts.

I welcome the fact that the Government here have carried forward our programme of releasing prisoners. I accept the point put to us by Unionists in Belfast earlier this week that all releases should take place within the framework of law, rather than outside it. Respected authorities on the situation, who are implacable enemies of paramilitary organisations, such as Father Denis Faul, have long seen prisoners as a key factor in the situation. We know that both Republican and Loyalist prisoners mostly exercised a positive and constructive influence on the ceasefire decisions. It would be ironic, if the British Government were to adopt a harder line on prisoners, following the ceasefire, than they did before it.

I do not think any of us, Governments, States, Political Parties, or opinion-formers are entitled to comfortable feelings of moral superiority. The responsibility for the tragedy in Northern Ireland and the fact that it lasted 25 years and cost over 3000 lives is widely shared. Church leaders in England and Ireland have frankly acknowledged this. If we want peace, there has to be an acknowledgement of wrong, forgiveness, and the will to reconciliation on all sides. There must be an active determination to clear up the legacy of the past informed by a moral purpose. Once we are certain that no more terrible deeds will be committed and that there is no risk of the conflict resuming, then I would be for the phased release, in accordance with law, of the vast majority of prisoners on all sides who were caught up in the conflict.

That, I believe, is the morally and politically correct thing to do.

At the Forum recently, we heard the genuine feelings and concerns of the families of the victims of violence. They should not be forgotten, and policies and support frameworks need to be developed, to make it clear that the memory of their loved ones is cherished by society.

There are many other issues, which should now be pursued. All emergency legislation should be reviewed with regard to its continued relevance. The last Government had intended before Christmas to lift the State of Emergency, and ratify the European Convention on the Transfer of Prisoners.

Economic regeneration and jobs were an issue that we encountered all over West Belfast. Where there is an unemployment black spot down here, the IDA are encouraged and treated as a priority. The North's Industrial Promotion Bodies should likewise be encouraged to focus on areas on high unemployment in the North. We also see great potential in North-South economic cooperation, both all along the border, and down the East Coast corridor. We are developing some new policy proposals in this area.

There are two other issues, which I wish to refer to, arising from my visit to Belfast.

State funding has so far been refused to Mean Scoil Feirste, the only Irish speaking secondary school in the North, which I visited on Monday. Yet, State funding is given both North and South to smaller Church of Ireland schools in rural areas. This issue of the Mean Scoil is a basic test of pluralism in the North. Mr Chris McGimpsey of the UUP has supported funding for the Mean Scoil. I would urge Sir Patrick Mayhew to find his way through the bureaucratic obstacles.

I also visited the Conway Mill, a large community centre with small enterprises, which for political reasons has been persistently refused State funding. Political vetting must be replaced by proper systems of financial accountability for public funds. Official discrimination against communities because they are Loyalist or Republican minded must stop forthwith, if we want the people of those communities to believe that peace will make a real difference.

There is a price to be paid by everyone for peace. For us, that price is that we, the people of this State, must remain involved and engaged in helping to address the concerns and the problems of the people of the North, and that we do not again abandon them, as many Nationalists believed that we did over a long period. But we have the chance, not simply to be champions of the rights of Nationalists, but to develop through greater exchanges and the building up of trust a sense of partnership with Unionists and with the people of Northern Ireland as a whole. Unity and division are opposite ends of a spectrum, with a continuum in between. We do not have to be at one end or the other in order to create a better life for us all. It is the ground in between that will be most profitable to cultivate in the time ahead.